MW00834894

A SOCIAL HISTORY OF IRANIAN CINEMA

PRAISE FOR *A Social History of Iranian Cinema*

"Hamid Naficy is already established as the doyen of historians and critics of Iranian cinema. Based on his deep understanding of modern Iranian political and social history, this detailed critical history of Iran's cinema since its founding is his crowning achievement. To say that it is a must-read for virtually all concerned with modern Iranian history, and not just cinema and the arts, is to state the obvious."
—HOMA KATOUZIAN, author of
The Persians: Ancient, Mediaeval and Modern Iran

"This magisterial four-volume study of Iranian cinema will be the defining work on the topic for a long time to come. Situating film within its sociopolitical context, Hamid Naficy covers the period leading up to the Constitutional Revolution and continues after the Islamic Revolution, examining questions about modernity, globalization, Islam, and feminism along the way. *A Social History of Iranian Cinema* is a guide for our thinking about cinema and society and the ways that the creative expression of film should be examined as part of a wider engagement with social issues."
—ANNABELLE SREBERNY, co-author of
Blogistan: The Internet and Politics in Iran

"*A Social History of Iranian Cinema* is an extraordinary achievement, a scholarly, detailed work in which a massive amount of material is handled with the lightest touch. Yet it is Hamid Naficy's personal experience and investment that give this project a particular distinction. Only a skilled historian, one who is on the inside of his story, could convey so vividly the symbolic significance of cinema for twentieth-century Iran and its deep intertwining with national culture and politics."
—LAURA MULVEY, author of
Death 24x a Second: Stillness and the Moving Image

"Hamid Naficy seamlessly brings together a century of Iran's cinematic history, marking its technological advancements and varying genres and storytelling techniques, and perceptively addressing its sociopolitical impact on the formation of Iran's national identity. *A Social History of Iranian Cinema* is essential reading not only for the cinephile interested in Iran's unique and rich cinematic history but also for anyone wanting a deeper understanding of the cataclysmic events and metamorphoses that have shaped Iran, from the pivotal Constitutional Revolution that ushered in the twentieth century through the Islamic Revolution, and into the twenty-first century."
—SHIRIN NESHAT, visual artist, filmmaker, and
director of the film *Women Without Men*

A Social History of Iranian Cinema

VOLUME 3

Hamid Naficy

A SOCIAL HISTORY

OF IRANIAN CINEMA

Volume 3

The Islamicate Period, 1978–1984

Duke University Press   Durham and London   2012

Printed in the United States of America on acid-free paper ∞

Designed by Julie Allred

Typeset in Scala by BW&A Books, Inc.

Library of Congress Cataloging-in-Publication Data appear on
the last printed page of this book.

Duke University Press gratefully acknowledges the support of
the School of Communication at Northwestern University,
Northwestern University in Qatar, and the School of Humanities
at Rice University, which provided funds toward the production
of this book.

To my parents,
Batul Okhovat and Abutorab Naficy,
who instilled in me the love and
pleasure of knowledge and arts

To my country of birth, Iran,
and its extraordinary culture and history

To my adopted country, the United States,
and its cherished democratic ideals

CONTENTS

ILLUSTRATIONS

ACKNOWLEDGMENTS

During the three decades spent researching and writing this book, I accrued debts to many people who helped me in various ways big and small, which are briefly acknowledged here. First of all I thank all the film directors, producers, camerapersons, actors, critics, and television producers who supplied me with copies of their films, videos, and biographies, and sometimes with stills of their films. Many of them also granted me interviews, in person or by telephone, mail, e-mail, and even tape recording. Underscoring the globalization and diasporization of Iranians—including mediamakers—these interviews spanned the globe, from Iran to various European countries, and from New Zealand to the United States. And underscoring the duration of the project, they extended in time from the mid-1970s to the late 2000s. The interviewees and filmmakers were Abbas (Abbas Attar), Nader Afshar Naderi, Jamsheed Akrami, Mohammad Reza Allamehzadeh, Farshad Aminian, Amir Amirani, Taghi Amirani, Jahanshah Ardalan, Shoja Azari, Fuad Badie, Ramin Bahrani, Bahram Baizai, Rakhshan Banietemad, Manuchehr Bibian, Arlene Dallalfar, Mahmud Dorudian, Ghasem Ebrahimian, Esmail Emami, Tanaz Eshaghian, Shirin Etessam, Anna Fahr, Golshifteh Farahani, Shahriar Farahvashi, Simin Farkhondeh, Bahman Farmanara, Aryana Farshad, Jalal Fatemi, Tina Gharavi, Ali Ghelichi, Ebrahim Golestan, Shahla Haeri, Mohammad Reza Haeri, Khosrow Haritash, Melissa Hibbard, Mohammad Ali Issari, Erica Jordan, Pirooz Kalantari, Shahram Karimi, Maryam Kashani, Mehrdad Kashani, Maryam Keshavarz, Laleh Khadivi, Hossein Khandan, Fakhri Khorvash, Abbas Kiarostami, Bahman Kiarostami, Masud Kimiai, Parviz Kimiavi, Kim Longinotto, Bahman Maghsoudlou, Moslem Mansouri, Dariush Mehrjui, Ziba Mir-Hosseini, Mojtaba Mirtahmasb, Behnaz A. Mirzai, Bahman Mofid, Ebrahim Mokhtari, Ali Mortazavi, Manuchehr Moshiri, Fatemeh Motamed Aria, Marva Nabili, Amir Naderi, Shirin Neshat, Asadollah Niknejad, Sara Nodjumi, Annette Mari Olsen, Mehrdad Oskoui, Soudabeh Oskui-Babcock, Faramarz Otan, Katia Forbert Petersen, Rafigh Pooya, Ghazel Radpay, Hamid Rahmanian, Hosain Rajaiyan, Neda Razavipour, Persheng Sadegh-Vaziri, Robert Safarian, Fereydoun Safizadeh, Mehrnaz Saeed-Vafa, Marjan Safinia, Bigan Saliani, Mohammad Shahba, Sohrab Shahid Saless, Mahvash Sheikholeslami, Amir Shervan, Kamran Shirdel, Khosrow Sinai, Manuchehr Tabari, Nasrin Tabatabai, Mitra Tabrizian, Parisa Taghizadeh, Mohammad Tahaminejad, Barbod Taheri, Hosain Taheridoust, Mohammad Tehrani, Susumo Tokomo, Shahin Yazdani, Abbas Yousefpour, and Caveh Zahedi. Each volume's bibliography provides details of the interviews.

I interviewed several cinema and television administrators in Iran during the Pahlavi and Islamic Republic periods to gain insight into official procedures and perspectives. Those interviewed included Gholamhosain Alaqehband, Mohammad Beheshti, Mohammad Hasan Khoshnevis, Kambiz Mahmoudi, and Alireza Shojanoori. To gain insight into the movies' sociohistorical contexts of production and reception I interviewed spectators, witnesses, relatives, and scholars. These included Mehrdad Amanat, Zia Ashraf Nasr, Hamid Khan Bakhtiari, Cosroe Chaqueri, Mohammad Ali Djamalzadeh, Houshang Golmakani, Faezeh Golshan, Jalal Golshan, Shusha Guppy, Ahmet Gurata, Latifeh Haghighi, Jafar Hakimzadeh, Amir Hassanpour, Badi'eh Misaqiyeh (Eshraghian), Reza Nafisi (my uncle), Parviz Navi, Alaviyeh Okhovat (my grandmother), Batul Okhovat (my mother), Amir Bahman Samsam, Emmanuel Sevrugian, and Ali Shakeri.

The Foundation for Iranian Studies in Washington, D.C., kindly supplied me with transcripts of interviews with major cinema, television, and culture industry leaders of the Pahlavi era, including transcripts of lengthy interviews with Farrokh Gaffary, Shahrokh Golestan, Kambiz Mahmoudi, Mohammad Naficy, Arby Ovanessian, and Mehrdad Pahlbod. Likewise, the Boroumand Foundation in Washington, D.C., which documents human rights violations in Iran, provided me with newspaper clippings on the Rex Cinema fire in Abadan and political persecutions in Iran.

Poori Soltani, a senior research librarian at the National Library of Iran, graciously supplied me with data on film periodicals. Hosain Tousi, the director general of MCIG's Research and Cinematic Relations immediately after the revolution, provided me with the early, unpublished regulations and guidelines governing film review and censorship under the Islamic Republic.

Hasan Khoshnevis, director of the National Film Archive of Iran, facilitated my research and film viewing at the archive in Tehran and sat for interviews with me. I also benefited from discussions with other colleagues at the national film archive, namely Gholam Haidari, Fereydoun Khameneipour, and Ladan Taheri.

To examine nonfiction films about Iran, I visited the United States National Archives and Records Services and the Library of Congress's Motion Picture, Broadcasting, and Recorded Sound Division, both in Washington, D.C., to examine records of USIA/USIS films and other documentaries. A visit to the Defense Audiovisual Agency at Norton Air Force Base, San Bernardino, California, produced information on military newsreels and raw footage shot by U.S. military units inside Iran after the Second World War. The UCLA Film and Television Archive helped me with information on *Hearst News* and *Hearst Metrotone News* newsreels. A visit to the University of South Carolina helped with materials on the following newsreels about Iran: *Fox News, Fox Movietone, Paramount News, Pathé News, Universal Newsreel, UPITN, Visnews,* and *Pathé Sound News.* The British National Film Archives and the British Film Institute in London were helpful on various newsreels and documentaries on Iran. I also visited the British Public Records Office in London to examine the files of the British Council's cultural activities in Iran. In the United States I obtained the Confidential United States Central Files on Iran's Internal Affairs and the Foreign Affairs Records of the Department of State Relating to Internal Affairs of Iran for the Second World War and the Cold War through microfilm and Internet research. These British and American diplomatic files are rich in documents relating to Iran's sociopolitical and cultural conditions, if one persists long enough in sifting through thousands of pages of unrelated materials. They proved invaluable in my charting the rivalry among the former allies after the Second World War to influence the hearts and minds of Iranians through cinema.

At the Danish Film Institute in Copenhagen, the archivist Mikael Braae helped me with screening and translating the railway film *Iran, the New Persia.* Another archivist, Palle Bøgelund Petterson, supplied additional printed information and films. Professor I. B. Bondebjerg, head of the University of Copenhagen's Department of Media, Cognition, and Communication, facilitated my visit and research in the Danish capital. In Washington, D.C., I was able to examine the collection of Antoin Sevruguin's photographs at the Arthur M. Sackler Gallery thanks to Massumeh Farhad, the chief curator and the curator of Islamic art. In Heidelberg I interviewed Sevruguin's grandson, Emmanuel Sevrugian, for further insight into his photographic and filmic career. At the University of Wisconsin, Milwaukee, I examined the M. Eleanor Fitzgerald Papers for materials on Nilla Cram Cook, with assistance from the archivist Christel Maass. Finally, I visited the Brigham Young University Archives to examine Merian C. Cooper's papers on *Grass* and *King Kong*, and I visited the Museum of Modern Art in New York to view the original black-and-white and tinted versions of *Grass*, as well as footage shot for its remake.

I gained further information about films on Iran by corresponding with the Imperial War Museum in London (for wartime newsreels), the Scottish Film Archive and the British Petroleum Company Limited (for oil films), the United Nations Visual Material Library (for UN films on Iran), the Sherman Grinberg Film Library (for various newsreels), the John E. Allen Inc. Film Library (for *Kinogram* and *Telenews* newsreels), and the Abraham F. Rad Contemporary Jewish Film Archive in Jerusalem. For television newscasts and documentaries on Iran, I visited and corresponded with various television archives, including the ABC News Television Archive, the CBS News Film/Tape Documentary Archive, the NBC News Television Archive, the PBS News Tape Archive, the BBC News Television Archive, the Canadian Broadcasting Corporation, the CTV Television Network (Canada), and the Vanderbilt Television News Archive in Nashville.

Abazar Sepehri, head Middle Eastern librarian at the University of Texas, Austin, helped me many times to track down Persian-language sources and articles. Likewise, Jet Prendeville, the art and architecture librarian at Rice University, assisted me in tracking down English and foreign-language film sources.

Academic colleagues in various disciplines in the United States were very helpful. Paula Amad and Peter Bloom provided me with copies of the film *Yellow Cruise* and with relevant materials on it; Jennifer Fey commented on my paper on Rakhshan Banietemad, as did Janet Afary on the chapters on Reza Shah and the preface, Marianne Hopmann on my discussion of the oral tradition, and Majid Naficy on parts of chapter 6 (vol. 2) and the preface (vol. 1). George Marcus, Chuck Kleinhans, Mehdy Naficy, Nahal Naficy, Azar Nafisi, and Mohammad Nafissi commented on the preface. Philip Lutgendorf shared with me his unpublished paper on Indian cinema, and Natasa Durovicova shared her articles on sound and dubbing. Camron Michael Amin provided information on U.S. government files on Iran, and Amir Hassanpour provided information on Kurdish cinema and satellite television. Jalil Doostkhah helped with the names of the Isfahan circle of intellectuals. Mehrnaz Saeed-Vafa was extremely helpful throughout my research, supplying me with films and assisting me in tracking down information on Iranian cinema and filmmakers. Colleagues in Iran were also very helpful. Houshang Golmakani, editor in chief of *Mahnameh-ye Sinemai-ye Film*, made sure that I received issues of the journal, sent me stills that I requested, and assisted with other inquiries. Mohammad Atebbai of Iranian Independents put several documentaries at my disposal. The documentarian Pirooz Kalantari was conscientious and generous in supplying me with documents, books, films, photographs, and other research materials from Iran, far beyond his own works. Shahin Kharazmi of Tehran's Industrial Management Institute supplied me with data on media uses and audience demography in Iran. Esmail Emami facilitated my meeting with members of the Iranian Society of Documentary Filmmakers in Tehran. Mohammad Tahaminejad and Homayun Emami also helped with information on documentary cinema. Elsewhere, the art curator Rose Issa in London shared with me videos and posters of Iranian movies. The journalist Homa Sarshar and the Center for Iranian Jewish Oral History in Los Angeles kindly supplied me with a copy of the film *A Mother for Shamsi*. Mehdi Zamani facilitated my interview in Los Angeles with the actor Bahman Mofid, while Mohammad Ali Yazdi did the same for my interview with Sohrab Shahid Saless. The photographer and artist Soody Sharifi kindly put at my disposal her photograph of the "movie set." Sima Shakhsari of the University of California, Berkeley, helped to identify Iranian blogs and movie blogs. Debra Zimmerman of Women Make Movies made Iranian films available for my viewing, as did Barbara Scharess, the director of programming at Chicago's Gene Siskel Film Center.

I helped launch two long-lasting annual film festivals at universities in the United States. I worked with Geoffrey Gilmore in 1990, then of the UCLA Film and Television Archive, to curate one of the first and longest-running festivals of Iranian cinema in the United States. In Houston I worked with Marian Luntz, the film curator of the Museum of Fine Art, and Charles Dove, cinema director at Rice University, to organize an annual festival of Iranian films there. Programming and curating these festivals, which still continue, provided me with important venues and opportunities for further research, film viewing, interviews with filmmakers, and the promotion of Iranian cinema.

At Rice University my research assistant Danny Stuyck and the visual resource assistant Kathleen Hamilton scanned still images for the book. Michael Dyrby Jensen translated a Danish text for me. The anthropology doctoral student Nahal Naficy was a valuable, resourceful, and cheerful help as my primary bilingual research assistant. She wrote the draft of the caption on Sharifi's "movie set" artwork (chapter 4, vol. 2). At Northwestern University my research assistants Neha Kamdar, Daniel Bashara, John Nicolau, Jason Roberts, and Racquel Gates helped with the book's images and bibliography.

The research phases of the book were funded in large part by summer research grants that I received from the deans of humanities at Rice University, Gayle Stokes and Gary Wihl, which allowed me to take research trips and to visit archives in various countries, as well as to write. The Art History Department's Segal Fund at Rice University paid for my research assistants and equipment. A travel-to-collection grant from UCLA's Von Gruenbaum Center for Middle East Studies made possible my research visit to the Museum of Modern Art in New York.

The writing phase of the book was primarily funded by major national grants from the National Endowment for Humanities Fellowship (NEH-05020401) and the American Council of Learned Societies, the Social Science Research Council, and the National Endowment for Humanities International and Area Studies Fellowship (RI4820–363000, NEH FA-51979, OSR 05020401), which Rice University matched, thus allowing me to spend the academic year 2004–5 entirely on writing the bulk of the manuscript. Gary Wihl also kindly provided subvention funds for the publication of this multivolume book, as did Barbara O'Keefe, Northwestern University's dean of the School of Communication. Northwestern University in Qatar also contributed. I thank all these institutions and individuals for their generous assistance.

My editor Ann Klefstad went through the manuscript as usual with a fine-toothed comb, helping to sculpt the text. Ken Wissoker, editorial director at Duke University Press, was a delight to work with; he guided the project with openness, patience, wisdom, and élan.

A project as extensive as this naturally involves not only professional colleagues but also family and friends in various witting and unwitting capacities. My siblings—Naficeh, Nahid, Nasrin, Nooshin, Mehdy, and Majid—all helped in one way or another with research, information gathering, and the mailing of films and other materials for the book. I interviewed my mother and my paternal grandmother about their social lives and experiences with cinema. I learned to appreciate Iranian popular culture, perhaps initially from the joyful and lilting manner in which my mother sang the popular songs of her youth, songs that her strict Muslim parents had forbidden to her. My father's research-mindedness and intellectual curiosity, which turned our childhood outings into lessons in local botany and medical anthropology, became a model for my commitment to academic research and education. During my research travels many family members and friends in various places provided me with a home away from home: Mehdy Naficy and Fariba Jafar-Shaghaghi in Heidelberg; Mohammad Nafissi and Georgiana Parry-Crooke in London; Fatemeh Ebtehaj and Hamid Hakimzadeh in London; Azar Nafisi and Bijan Naderi in Washington, D.C.; Nastaran and Vahid Naficy in Tehran; and Paul and Helen Edwards in Helena, Montana. Montana's majestic and enduring natural world offered an implacable contrast against which human history, particularly one as recent and as marred with moral and political ambiguities as that of the cinema and entertainment fields, found its proper perspective.

This book has been with me for so long that it feels like a third child, older than my two biological children, Cameron and Shayda, both of whom are now thriving, idealistic young people close to the age at which I unknowingly began this project. My life partner Carol (Kelly) Edwards has been with me every step of the way, through thick and thin, in Iran, in the United States, and in many other places in between. All three have been unconditionally supportive of my life choices, my career and its demands, including this book project. I hope that I have, in the end, been deserving of their respect, love, and trust.

ORGANIZATION OF THE VOLUMES

The book is divided into four volumes, covering the social history of over a century of Iranian cinema, from around 1897 to about 2010. The history of Iranian society and the cinema it produced in this period is bookended by two revolutions: the 1905–11 Constitutional Revolution, which brought in a constitutional monarchy, and the 1978–79 Islamic Revolution, which installed a republican theocratic state. While the impact of the first revolution on cinema and film culture was apparently limited and inchoate, the latter revolution profoundly affected them, resulting in their unprecedented efflorescence.

As a work of social history and theory, these volumes deal not only with such chronological developments in society and in the film industry but also with the synchronic contexts, formations, dispositions, and maneuvers that overdetermined modernity in Iran and a dynamically evolving film industry and its unique products. I locate the film industry and its mode of production, narratives, aesthetics, and generic forms in the interplay of deeply rooted Iranian performative and visual arts and what was imported, adopted, adapted, translated, mistranslated, and hybridized from the West. The interplay between Iranian and Islamic philosophies and aesthetics complicated and channeled cinema, particularly that involving women, in ways unique to Iran, which are discussed throughout the volumes. Likewise, the contribution of Iranian ethnoreligious minorities, both widespread and profound, gave Iranian cinema additional specificity.

The volumes also situate Iranian cinema at the intersection of state-driven authoritarian modernization, nationalist and Islamist politics, and geopolitics during its tumultuous century, charting the manner in which local, national, regional, and international powers competed for ascendancy in Iran, affecting what Iranians saw on screens, what they produced, and the technologies they adopted.

The logic of dividing the work into four volumes is driven by both sociopolitical developments and the evolution of the film industry. While these volumes are autonomous, each contributes to the understanding and appreciation of the others, as certain theoretical, stylistic, industrial, commercial, cultural, religious, sociopolitical, biographical, authorial, and governmental elements form lines of inquiry pursued throughout, gathering momentum and weight. Each volume has a table of contents, a bibliography, an index, and when needed appendices.

Volume 1: The Artisanal Era, 1897–1941

This volume offers a theory linking Iranian modernity and national identity with the emergence of an inchoate artisanal cinema and with an othered cinematic subjectivity. Qajar-era cinema consisted of the exhibition of foreign actualities and narratives and the production of a limited number of domestic actualities and comic skits by pioneer exhibitors and producers, all of whom are featured. The image of women on the screens and the presence of women as spectators in movie houses proved controversial, resulting in the first act of film censorship. Borrowing from the curtain reciting tradition, live movie translators (*dilmaj*) helped increase narrative comprehension and the enjoyment of Western movies.

Reza Shah Pahlavi dissolved the Qajar dynasty in 1925 and ruled until 1941. During his rule, the first Pahlavi period, the state implemented an authoritarian syncretic Westernization program that attempted to modernize and secularize the multicultural, multilingual, and multiethnic Iranians into a homogeneous modern nation. Cinematic representations of a fast modernizing Iran in documentaries and fiction movies were encouraged, photography and movie production were tightly controlled, movie houses were regulated, and perceived affronts to Iran in Western documentaries were taken seriously. The veil was outlawed and dandies flourished. All these developments receive extensive coverage in this volume. Despite efforts to centralize and control cinema, film production proved marginal to state formation and remained artisanal. Only one silent feature film was produced domestically, while all sound features were produced by an Iranian expatriate in India. This latter fact and others discussed in the volume show Iranian cinema's transnational nature from the start.

Volume 2: The Industrializing Years, 1941–1978

During the second Pahlavi period (Mohammad Reza Shah, 1941–79), cinema flourished and became industrialized, producing at its height over ninety films a year. The state was instrumental in building the infrastructures of the cinema and television industries, and it instituted a vast apparatus of censorship and patronage. During the Second World War and its aftermath, the three major Allied powers—the United Kingdom, the United States, and the USSR—competed with each other to control what Iranians saw on movie screens. One chapter examines this fascinating history.

In the subsequent decades, two major parallel cinemas emerged: the commercial filmfarsi movies, popular with average spectators, forming the bulk of the output, and a smaller but influential cinema of dissent, the new-wave cinema. The commercial filmfarsi movies, exemplified by the stewpot and tough-guy genres discussed extensively in two chapters, were for entertainment purposes and drew their power and charm from their stars and their rootedness in Iranian traditions, which were juxtaposed favorably and often comically or melodramatically with modern Western traditions. A dynamic nonfiction cinema evolved, which receives a chapter. Ironically, the state both funded and censored much of the new-wave cinema, which grew bolder in its criticism and impact as Pahlavi authoritarianism consolidated. The new-wave films, produced by the collaboration of Westernized filmmakers with modernist dissident writers, did well in international film festivals, starting the globalization of Iranian cinema. The impending revolution could retrospectively be read in the fear-driven narratives of the new-wave films and in the various cultural struggles around official culture and arts festivals, the censorship of films, religious sermons on audiocassettes, poetry reading nights, television trials and confessions, and underground filming, all of which I discuss at length.

Volume 3: The Islamicate Period, 1978–1984

Identified toward the end of the Shah's rule as one of the agents of moral corruption in the country, movies and movie houses became targets of a rising anti-Shah movement, resulting in the destruction of a third of all movie houses nationwide. This volume charts both such revolutionary destruction and the subsequent rebuilding and evolution of the film and media industries. Many above-the-line personnel in these industries found themselves sidelined, banned, arrested, deprived of property, or exiled. The star system, a major attraction of filmfarsi cinema, was thus dismantled. Movies were banned, cut, redubbed, and painted over to remove offending features.

After such iconoclastic destructions and purification the new Islamic regime undertook a wide-ranging effort to institutionalize a new film industry whose values would be commensurate with the newly formulated Islamicate values. The first rules and regulations governing film production and exhibition were adopted in 1982. Like the second Pahlavi regime, the ayatollahs' regime put into place a strong, centralized, and draconian system of state regulation and patronage to encourage politically correct movies. The import of foreign movies oscillated but was eventually banned, leaving the field open for a new domestic cinema. The long war with Iraq, the gendered segregation of space, and the imposition of the veil on women encouraged certain ideological and aesthetic trends. Foremost was the reconceptualization of cinema from a despised agent of corruption and othering to an agent of nation building and selfing. However, the resulting Islamicate cinema and culture were neither homogeneous nor static. They evolved with considerable personal, institutional, and ideological struggles.

Volume 4: The Globalizing Era, 1984–2010

The revolutionary experience, the bloody eight-year war with Iraq, and the perceived Western cultural invasion of Iran all encouraged soul searching, national epistemophilia, and a desire for self-representation, resulting in an array of documentary films and film forms about the revolution, war, and the various social ills and inequalities that accumulated under the Islamist regime. The state-run television and fiction film industries, too, funded and supported filmmakers committed to Islam who made powerful "imposed war" movies in which sacred subjectivity replaced modernist subjectivity. Women's presence both on camera and behind the camera increased significantly in all genres and types of films, in both the television and movie industries, leading to a veritable "women's cinema." The veil evolved from a repressive social institution to a dynamic social practice and critical aesthetics.

A deepening sociopolitical and cultural struggle over cinema, media, and culture, and ultimately the legitimacy of the Islamic Republic, emerged in the country. This was reflected in, and shaped by, a new form of public diplomacy, chiefly between Iran and the United States, during Mohammad Khatami's presidency, which intensified under his successor, Mahmoud Ahmadinejad. In a new "cultural turn" the antagonistic governments began to recruit all sorts of mutual domestic, diasporic, and international film, television, radio, and Internet media and formations to serve this diplomacy, sometimes with dire consequences for the participants. Foreign and exile videos and satellite televisions were officially banned, but enforcement was chaotic, encouraging a thriving culture of resistance that continues to date. With the rise of opposition to the Islamic Republic regime a dissident Internet cinema emerged.

The postrevolution era bred its own dissident art-house parallel cinema, involving some of the best Pahlavi-era new-wave directors and a new crop of innovative postrevolution directors, placing Iranian cinema on the map of the vital world cinemas. They brought self-respect and prestige for Iranians at home and abroad. The displacement, dispersion, and exile of a massive number of Iranians, many in the visual and performing arts and cinema and television, resulted in new formations in Iran's social history and cinematic history—a diasporic formation of people with a complex subjectivity and an "accented cinema," made by first-generation émigrés and their second- and third-generation descendants. Both the wide circulation of Iran-made films and those Iranians made in the diaspora, as well as the vast diasporic dispersion of Iranians helped globalize Iranian cinema. One chapter deals with each of these developments.

A WORD ABOUT ILLUSTRATIONS

I have used several types of illustration here, each providing supplementary or complementary material to the text. Production stills show something of the behind-the-scenes process. Frame enlargements, taken directly from films or videos, offer visuals for textual analyses of the films' aesthetic and generic systems. Posters offer not only an encapsulated rendition of the film by artists other than filmmakers but also showcase the art of poster design and production, which form important components of the movies' publicity, exhibition, and reception. Like the movies themselves, this art also evolved over time, an evolution discernible in the posters included in the present volumes. Cartoons and other material objects about cinema demonstrate the wider circulation of things filmic among Iranians. The flyers announcing film screenings and cultural and political events featuring screenings served as important vehicles in exile for advertising, political agitprop, and film exhibition immediately after the 1978–79 revolution. They provide a good sense of the films, of the political culture of the time, and of the sponsoring groups. Finally, the many tables in the book offer other forms of data for the analysis of the films' cultural contexts, such as audience demography, production output, film export and import, organizations involved in production, and the regulations concerning censorship and banning of movies. Because of the diversity of sources and the deterioration of some films and videos, the quality of the pictorial illustrations varies.

ABBREVIATIONS

ABF Abdorrahman Boroumand Foundation for the Promotion of Human Rights and Democracy in Iran
AFRT American Forces Radio and Television
AIDFP Association of Iranian Documentary Film Producers (Anjoman-e Tahiyeh Konandegan-e Sinema-ye Mostanad-e Iran)
AIOC Anglo-Iranian Oil Company
API Anglo-Persian Institute
BBC British Broadcasting Corporation
BC British Council
BMF Basij Militia Force
CIA Central Intelligence Agency, United States
CIDCYA Center for the Intellectual Development of Children and Young Adults
CUSCF–Iran, 1945–49: *Confidential United States Central Files on Iran's Internal Affairs and Foreign Affairs, 1945–1949.* Washington: National Archives Microfilm Publication, 1981.
CUSCF–Iran, 1950–54: *Confidential United States Central Files on Iran's Internal Affairs and Foreign Affairs, 1950–1954.* Washington: University Publication of America. Frederick, Md., microfilm, 1958.
DEFC Documentary and Experimental Film Center
EMB Empire Marketing Board (Britain)
FAA Fine Arts Administration
FCF Farabi Cinema Foundation
FF Filmfarsi (Farsi-language films)
FHI Film House of Iran
FIDCI Film Industry Development Corporation of Iran
FOD Foundation of the Dispossessed (Boniad-e Mostazafan)
GFW Golestan Film Workshop
GPO General Post Office (Britain)

HOC House of Cinema (Khaneh-ye Sinema)
IATC Islamic Art and Thought Center (Howzeh-ye Andisheh va Honar-e Eslami), a division of the Islamic Propaganda Organization
IAUSA Iranian Student Association in the United States
IDHEC Institut des Hautes-Études Cinématographiques, Paris, France
IFVC International Film and Video Center
IRGC Islamic Revolutionary Guard Corps (Sepah-e Pasdaran Eslami)
IRI Islamic Republic of Iran
IRIB Islamic Republic of Iran Broadcasting (a.k.a. VVIR)
ISDF Iranian Society of Documentary Filmmakers (Anjoman Mostanadsazan-e Sinema-ye Iran)
IYPCS Iranian Young People's Cinema Society
MCA Ministry of Culture and Art
MCHE Ministry of Culture and Higher Education
MCIG Ministry of Culture and Islamic Guidance
MFH Makhmalbaf Film House
MFS Misaqiyeh Film Studio
MOS Mithout (without) sound, filming without sound
MPAA Motion Picture Export Association of America
MRC Ministry of Reconstruction Crusade (Jehad-e Sazandegi)
MSF *Mahnameh-ye Sinemai-ye Film* (a monthly periodical)
NEFC National Educational Film Circuit
NFAI National Film Archive of Iran
NGO Nongovernmental organization
NIOC National Iranian Oil Company
NIRT National Iranian Radio and Television
OPEC Organization for Petroleum Exporting Countries
PFC Progressive Filmmakers' Cooperative (Kanun-e Sinemagaran-e Pishro)
PFOI People's Fadaiyan Organization of Iran
PMOI People's Mojahedin Organization of Iran
POGO Public Opinion Guidance Organization (Sazman-e Parvaresh-e Afkar)
POV Point of view
RDS–*Iran, 1930–39: Records of the Department of States Relating to Internal Affairs of Iran, 1930–1939.* Washington: National Archives Microfilm Publication, 1981.
SAVAK Sazman-e Amniat va Ettela'at-e Keshvar, Homeland Information and Security Organization
SNH Society for National Heritage (Anjoman-e Asar-e Melli)
USIA United States Information Agency
USIS United States Information Service
VOA Voice of America
VOKS All-Union Society for Cultural Relations (Soviet Union)
VVIR Voice and Vision of the Islamic Republic (a.k.a. IRIB)

TRANSITION FROM

"CINEMA OF IDOLATRY" TO

AN "ISLAMICATE CINEMA"

The transition from the Pahlavi-era cinema to the Islamic Republic–era cinema was slow but tumultuous, fiery, and destructive, and it offered an indelible contemporary example of the classic violence waged in all religions between idolaters and iconoclasts. While the torching of the movie houses had occurred before, what happened in the Abadan's Rex Cinema on a hot summer night elevated it into a whole new revolutionary—and criminal—tactic.

Rex Cinema Inferno

On 19 August 1978, Hosain Takabalizadeh and three friends, Farajollah Bazrkar, Yadollah, and Fallah, walked into Rex Cinema, a second-tier movie house in a poor part of the city of Abadan, the site of one of the world's largest oil refineries. Each carried a brown bag that looked like the bags of mixed nuts and roasted seeds (*ajil*) that moviegoers customarily took into the cinemas—except that theirs each contained a bottle of high-octane airplane fuel. The men joined the spectators who were engrossed in Masud Kimiai's controversial movie, *The Deer*, about a down-on-his-luck smuggler and a heroin addict, characters widely interpreted as symbolizing anti-Shah revolutionaries. Halfway through the film, Hosain and Farajollah left the screening hall on the pretext of going to the bathroom; instead they doused the theater's wooden doors, the corridor walls, and the concession stand with gasoline. Apparently, all the arsonists returned to their seats so as to avoid being associated with setting the fire, except Takabalizadeh, who stayed behind to ignite the fire, which frightened him because of its speedy progress through the building. Ironically and tragically, the cinema's only emergency exit door had been locked from the outside to prevent terrorist arson. The fire quickly spread, engulfing the entire building.[1] The mainstream press reported that of the approximately 700 spectators, 377 burned to death (Abkashak 1985:14–15); others claimed 600 deaths (Nabavi 1999). The fire, which began at about 10 P.M., "burned throughout most of the night, and the victims' cries could be heard by hundreds helplessly watching from outside the theater. . . . The screams stopped after the first few hours."[2] Grief, mourning, and anger gripped the entire city. Some families bore an undue share of the calamity, having lost multiple members, among them Jafar Sazesh, who lost five of his children, and Yusef Radmehr, who lost ten children (fig. 1).

Although the Pahlavi government placed the blame on the religious zealots involved in the widening protest movement, the overwhelming public consensus held the by then discredited government responsible for engineering the fire and for the inept responses to it. In fact, the Shah's own words, broadcast before the fire, were interpreted as his foreknowledge and complicity in the upcoming disaster. Apparently referring to the burning of cinemas, which had already taken place across the country, he had stated, "While we promise you the Great Civilization, others are promising you the Great Terror." The leading cleric, Ayatollah Ruhollah Khomeini, in exile in Najaf, Iraq, was quick to refer in a message to that broadcast as proof of the government's complicity in the terror, calling the event "One of the Shah's masterpieces" of public deception, intended to make the world think that "the Justice-seeking Iranian nation is not bound by any human and Islamic values."[3] Likewise, a prominent secular opposition politician, Karim Sanjabi, of the National Front, called it a "Reichstag fire," designed to turn public sentiments against the anti-Shah forces (Green 1982:96).

However, the leaflets and samizdats that the opposition groups issued either clearly urged the destruction of cinemas, banks, liquor stores, discos, and Westernized restaurants as representatives of the "corrupt" and "decadent" (taquti) Pahlavi cultural and economic system, or they reported such actions in glowing and approving terms.[4] Testimonies and documents compiled after the fall of the Shah also established a clear link between the arsonists and the anti-Shah clerical leaders (Nateq 1987:17–19; Sreberny-Mohammadi and

1 Exterior of Rex Cinema in Abadan after the fire. The large billboard advertised Masud Kimiai's movie, *The Deer*, which was screening when the cinema was set afire. Courtesy of Majid Jafari Lahijani.

Mohammadi 1994:145–46; Nabavi 1999).[5] An Islamist functionary, Hosain Boroujerdi, who had been intimately involved in various revolutionary acts of terrorism that had helped bring the Islamic Republic to power, made a more serious charge.[6] Disillusioned with the revolutionary outcome, he later turned against the regime and in a massive book-length confession claimed that the cleric who presided as judge over the Rex Cinema criminal trial, Hojjatoleslam Musavi Tabrizi, was himself one of the architects of the Rex Cinema fire and had personally directed the arsonists (Boroujerdi 2002:91–94).

Abadan and the nation were both transfixed and transformed by the Rex Cinema tragedy. The event immediately became a potent rallying cry for the anti-Shah forces and for Abadan, with its large force of skilled oil workers, which was galvanized into action and joined the protest movement.[7] Revolutionary slogans reverberated throughout the city during the funerals and memorials, which were attended by hundreds of thousands: "The killer of our dear ones must be executed"; "No to misery, no to contempt, only freedom, freedom"; "Canons, rifles, and machine guns are powerless against us."[8] Other movie houses had been destroyed in Tehran and Tabriz, but without casualties; it was the massive scale of the Rex Cinema crime along with the tragedy and surrounding ambiguity that transformed the destruction of cin-

2 The protagonist of Khosrow Sinai's fiction movie, *In the Alleys of Love,* visits the actual ruins of the Rex Cinema during his nostalgic tour of the city. Courtesy of Masud Mehrabi and *Film International.*

emas into a key symbolic act against the Shah, during whose reign, as Ayatollah Khomeini claimed, Western sex and violence had turned the movies into an imperialist technology to "spray poison," corrupting people's minds and values (1981b:188).

Some postrevolution fiction films featured Rex Cinema in their narratives, notably Khosrow Sinai's city film, *In the Alleys of Love* (*Dar Kuchehha-ye Eshq,* 1990), in which a young man returns to his hometown of Abadan after the war, but is undecided about whether to resettle there (fig. 2). Several documentaries dealt with this pivotal event. Alireza Davudnezhad's *A Report on Abadan's Rex Cinema* (*Gozareshi az Sinema Rex-e Abadan,* 1978–79), is an eighty-minute film which contains interviews with survivors and footage of the charred cinema auditorium and projection booth. Masud Navai's film *Abadan's Rex Cinema* (*Sinema Rex-e Abadan,* 1979–80) contains an important interview with Takabalizadeh, an interview that was used as evidence in the trial against him, as were scenes of Davudnezhad's film. Both films were shown by television networks.

This volume deals with cinema and film industry during the *transition* from the Pahlavi state and cinema to an Islamicate state and cinema (chap. 1), the filmic *documentation* of the revolution and its immediate aftermath (chap. 2), and the *consolidation* of the Islamic Republic regime and the film industry structures, censorship regulations, and narrative regimes (chap. 3).

Islamicate values, whose hold on the population deepened with each revolutionary act, played a significant part both in the material destruction and symbolic violence against the movie houses and film industry of the Pahlavi era as well as in the constructive and contestatory attempts to create a new cinema and film industry from their ashes.[9]

Islamicate Values and Cinema

Anti-cinema feelings ran deep, particularly among religious strata. The clerical elite subscribed to what might be called a "hypodermic theory" of ideology and cinematic effect, whereby, similar to Althusser's formulation (1971), the exposure to dominant ideology and cinema would cause interpellation, transforming autonomous and ethical "individuals" into dependent, corrupt "subjects" of that ideology and cinema. Four samples of such a formulation of cinematic othering, from the beginning, the middle, and end of the twentieth century and covering the span of this book, suffice. Shaikh Fazlollah Nuri is said to have condemned Tehrani's Cheraq Gaz Street Cinema in December 1904 because it showed images of unveiled foreign women in public and because he allegedly considered film to be the satanic work of "polluted foreigners." These reported objections to cinema were in line with Nuri's general critique of modernity as a "contagion" in his published pronouncements. Mojtaba Navvab Safavi, a leader of the fundamentalist Islamist group Fadai-yan-e Eslam in the 1950s, called cinema, along with other Western imports (such as romantic novels and music), a "smelting furnace," which melts away all the wholesome values and virtues of a Muslim society (1978:4). Ayatollah Khomeini linked cinema directly to the onset of corruption, licentiousness, prostitution, moral cowardice, and political dependence. According to him, cinema and other manifestations of Westernization (theater, dancing, and mixed-sex swimming) "rape the youth of our country and stifle in them the spirit of virtue and bravery" (n.d.a.:194). If Nuri's metaphor for cinema was medical (contagion) and Navvab Safavi's industrial (smelting furnace), Khomeini's, in his book *Kashf-ol Asrar*, was sexual (rape). Indeed, Khomeini was a proponent of the hypodermic theory, using the term "injection" (*tazriq*) to describe the dire and direct effects of Westernization.[10] Updating his predecessor Khomeini, Ayatollah Ali Khamenei claimed in the 1990s that the

West "injected" its corrupting culture into Iran, "not with a hypodermic needle, but with radio and television, fashion magazines, advertising, and ballyhoo" (1994:17). Injection theory would soon become part of the new regime's counteroffensive against Western cultural invasion and imperialism.

Despite this hypodermic formulation of the effects of motion pictures, these leaders did not consider cinema's ideological "work" alone; rather, they rightly viewed it in the context of the overdetermination of Westernization and modernity in Iran, and as a component of mediawork. This view considered, however crudely and instrumentally, the intertextuality and cross-fertilization of society's signifying institutions. The chief drawbacks to these religious formulations were their hypodermic conceptions of Western mediawork in general and of cinema in particular. Foreseeing as the only possible outcomes of contact with Western mediawork and cinema identification with the West and alienation from the self, they elided the possibility of resistance by modern, individualized Iranians—secular or religious—capable of independent subjectivity as well as of other mitigating local social conditions, frames of knowledge, and practices. In addition, they disregarded the competitions among cinema and the other media and the specificity of each medium's unique ideological and technological work. As a result, they posited a homogeneous and hegemonic mediawork and culture resulting from the introduction of Western media and modernity, which Khomeini called the "culture of idolatry" (*farhang-e taqut*), which was said to be imposed on, or injected, from above and from without—primarily from the West—onto the helpless and hapless autochthonous Iranians.[11] However, as I have amply demonstrated in volumes 1 and 2, the cultures of spectacle of both Pahlavi periods were neither homogeneous nor monolithic. They were subject to the play of various contesting formations, to whose emergence the state contributed. As will be seen in volumes 3 and 4, the Islamic culture of spectacle that the ayatollahs tried to foster, likewise, turned out to be full of contingencies, contradictions, and countercurrents.

Throughout the history of the Islamic Republic, its leaders praised Iranians for being a "performative nation" that readily and publicly displayed its support for the regime and the culture it imposed and inculcated.[12] However, a performative nation, even one that is ideologically committed, requires a masterful stage manager and cheerleader. The Islamist regime proved to be one such masterful manipulator, exhorting the nation to support its causes and facilitating its emergence onto the stage of history. It is in this context that the characterization of the Islamic Republic regime by the dissident exile, writer, and psychiatrist Gholamhosain Saedi as "the government of show" makes good sense (1984b). More astute and more adept than the Shah's regime at organizing public spectacles in which the populace had a stake through grievance and injustice and by which it had venues of expression and participation through Shiite religious doctrines, myths, narratives, iconography, rituals, and performance tradition, the Islamic Republic was able to turn Iranian life and history into powerful, self-serving theatrical spectacles: *taziyeh* passion plays, chest-beating, self-flagellation, head-cutting, religious chanting and music, Friday prayers and sermons, and massive street demonstrations and marches in which participants wore Islamic headbands and white shrouds of martyrdom. In the process, and assisted by the state coercive apparatuses, the regime masterminded and certain segments of population participated in a vast orchestration of emotions, irrationality, cult of leader worship, sadomasochism, collectivism, monumentalism, preference for perfection and idealism over realism, and transformation of sexual energy into spiritual and political force—what Susan Sontag in discussing Leni Riefenstahl's spectacular films for National Socialism, *The Olympiad* (*Olympia*, 1938), and *Triumph of the Will* (*Triumph des Willens*, 1935), called "Fascinating Fascism" (1980). However, as in the Pahlavi era, beneath the surface show of unity and spectacle, stage-managed by the Islamist regime and its ideological and coercive apparatuses, lurked dark waves of division and discontent, awaiting suitable conditions to surface.

It is also significant that both Navvab Safavi and Khomeini entertained the idea of adopting cinema provided it was done "properly" and "ethically." In rare passages they both spoke about this. Navvab Safavi said,

> Movie houses, theatres, novels, and popular songs must be completely removed and their middlemen punished according to the holy Islamic law. And if the use of motion picture industry is deemed necessary for society, [then] the history of Islam and Iran and useful material such as medical, agricultural, and industrial lessons should be produced under the supervision of chaste professors and Islamic scholars observing the principles and criteria of the holy religion of Islam and then shown for education, reform, and socially wholesome entertainment. (1978: 11)

Khomeini spelled out a similar theme, years later, on his triumphant return to Iran after the fall of the Shah, in February 1979. In Tehran's giant Beheshte Zahra Cemetery, in his first post-exile speech, he announced: "We are not opposed to cinema, to radio, or to television. . . . The cinema is a modern invention that ought to be used for the sake of educating the people, but as you know, it was used instead to corrupt our youth. It is the misuse of cinema that we are opposed to, a misuse caused by the treacherous policies of our rulers" (1981a:258). These passages do not speak of proscription or destruction of cinema—or of modernity, for that matter. Rather, they advocate the adoption of cinema to combat the Pahlavi culture and to usher in an Islamic culture, consisting of what they repeatedly called "Islamic values." In fact, soon after Khomeini's speech, in many cities, including Shiraz, exhibitors hung large banners outside their movie houses and below pictures of the ayatollah, carrying some of these words like a fatwa reauthorizing cinema and moviegoing.

However, the culture the state has promulgated is not strictly "Islamic," emanating directly from the core precepts of Islam. Instead, it is based on the specific traditions of Persia, associated not only with Islam, but also with other ethnoreligious peoples on the Iranian plateau. I speak of it as "Islamicate culture." This is not to belittle Islam's enormous historical contribution to Iranian culture, but to recognize the mutual contributions of Iranian culture and Islam to each other. As Marshall Hodgson formulated it, "Islamicate" refers not directly to Islam as religion, but to the "social and cultural complex historically associated with Islam and the Muslims, both among Muslims themselves and even when found among non-Muslims" (1974:59). Thus, the difference between "Islamic cinema" and "Islamicate cinema" would be that between a cinema that is about the religion of Islam and its tenets, characters, and stories, and a cinema that is made in a predominantly Muslim country, such as Iran.

The major concepts frequently pronounced by Islamic Republic authorities when speaking of "Islamic values" are called here Islamicate values, and the resulting culture, Islamicate culture. These consist of the following, which at once reveal the old tensions over national identity in Iran between tradition and modernity, between what is pre-Islamic and Iranian and what is Islamic and Iranian, between what is Iranian and what is foreign, Arab, and Western, and between what is collective and inherited and what is individual and invented. The concept of "monotheism," inscribed in the Islamic Republic constitution, refers to one of the principles of Islam (towhid). "Theocracy," a concept that integrated religion and the state and, most dramatically, the "guardianship of the supreme religious jurist" as the head of government (velayat-e faqih), is an innovation introduced by Ayatollah Khomeini, who in later years further upgraded the concept to the "absolute guardianship of religious jurist" (velayat-e motlaqeh-ye faqih). "Anti-idolatry" refers to opposition to the Pahlavi-era culture, which was dubbed the culture of idolatry (farhang-e taquti). "Ethicalism and moralism" mean leading a life of spirituality and concern for fellow human beings, during which individuals must engage in jihad both with their own internal temptations (*nafs-e ammareh*) and with external social temptations and corruptions (*amr-e beh maruf va nah-ye az monkar*). If in pursuit of this jihad one were to be killed, one would be honored on earth as a "martyr" (*shahid*), and would be further rewarded by going to heaven. The symbol of martyrdom is a red tulip, an icon that was widely used on stamps, in schoolbooks, on the Islamic Republic's logo, on the national flag, and on the poster of the first Milad film festival, in 1981.

The premodern Iranian dualities—perhaps Zoroastrian and Manichean in origin—of good (*nik*) vs. evil (*sharr*), interior (*baten*) vs. exterior (*zaher*), insider (*khodi*) vs. outsider (*gharibeh*) were applied to filmmakers and artists to differentiate supporters and critics of the regime. In addition, these dualities were overlaid strongly with Islamic dualities of related (*mahram*) vs. unrelated (*namahram*) and permissible (*halal*) vs. impermissible (*haram*), stifling individuality, equality, and freedom of expression and conduct. These concepts were mobilized into all-encompassing panoptic systems of surveillance, modesty, and gender segregation and regulation that affected architecture, professional fields of study, human relations, dress, gaze, voice, body language, and gender relations, with particularly serious consequences for the social presence and cinematic representation of women. To promulgate the modesty system, called *hejab*, vast bureaucracies were set up in the legislative, judicial, and executive systems, including the morality police and the Ministry of Culture and Islamic Guidance (MCIG), which oversaw cinema.

Political and economic "independence" (*esteqlal*) means combating both communist and capitalist world orders, condensed in the slogan "Neither East nor West." With the dissolution of the Soviet Union, independence was transformed into battle against the sole remaining superpower, the USA. This conceptual transformation is evident in the ideological label that Islamist leaders bestowed on their archenemy. In the 1980s, Ayatollah Khomeini memorably called the United States the Great Satan (*shaitan-e bozorg*) (Beeman 1983). This moniker not only referred to the global military and political prowess that allowed the United States to perpetrate mischief against others, including the Iranian regime, but also to the financial and cultural power that allowed the United States to seduce the Iranian nation against its government. The Great Satan was, therefore, more properly the Great Seducer. By the mid-2000s, the emphasis had shifted to critiquing American unilateralism and triumphalism, as President Ahmadinejad and Iranian official media began to routinely refer to the United States as the Global Arrogance (*estekbar-e jahani*).

"Purification" (*paksazi*) means cleansing the society and culture politically and morally from the vestiges of unwanted Pahlavi and Western cultures, ideologies, and corruptions, and replacing them with appropriate, "pure," and "true" Islamic ideologies. The terms "true Islam" (*eslam-e rastin*) and "pure Mohammadan Islam" (*eslam-e nab-e mohammadi*) were invoked frequently, both to acknowledge the existence of different forms of Islam and to claim that the Twelver Shiite Islam practiced in the Islamic Republic is the true and pure one. By the same token, impurity, admixture, and hybridity, and any attempt at modernity through syncretic adoption of things Western, were condemned as heretical. Thus, the postcolonial identity strategies of syncretism and hybridity acquired the negative religious connotations of syncretism (*elteqat*) and hypocrisy (*monafeq budan*), labels the government used lethally against its political enemies, particularly PMOI. "Nationalism" is redefined from a secular nation (*mellat*) to a religious one (*ummat*), a concept that subjugates minority religions and transcends national borders. The latter fed into the early Khomeini speeches advocating the "export of the Islamic revolution" to other countries, a kind of Islamic supranationalism. The ideology of "authenticity," a response to the failures of ideologies of nationalism, socialism, and third world liberation, emphasizes nativism, a return to indigenous traditional mores, particularly those thought to be Islamic. Finally, "populism" involves seeking justice for the dispossessed (*mostazafan*) and "the bare feet" (*pa berahneh-ha*) of the world against the oppressors of the world (*mostakbaran*) under the charismatic leadership of Khomeini.

Taken together, these concepts spelled out a new "imagined community," an "invented tradition," and a new "Islamicate identity" for postrevolution Iranians in whose constructions the media and cinema played important and constitutive roles. The educational system, too, was mobilized for this purpose. As Golnar Mehran demonstrates, the regime attempted to instill such Islamicate values in pre-university students by incorporating them into uniform nationwide curricula, textbooks, and extracurricular activities. The result was that Iran ranked fifth among fifty-four countries studied in terms of "percentage of teaching time allocated to religious education during the first six years of formal schooling," after Saudi Arabia (31 percent), Yemen (28.2), Qatar (15.5), and Libya (14.3). Significantly, this religious education was "closely linked with identity formation," favoring creation of a "politicized Shi'i identity among schoolchildren" (Mehran 2007:54–56).

Despite the wish for simpler, purer, and more authentic values, these Islamicate values were not absolutist concepts that rejected the modern world. Rather, as a form of dynamic populism, in the sense that Ervand Abrahamian proposes, they were capable of change and of absorbing modernity, "even eventually of political pluralism, gender equality, individual rights, and social democracy" (1993:2). This change was partly because a large portion of the increasingly sophisticated populace resisted, rejected, negotiated, and, in short, haggled with the hailing tendencies and practices of the regime. As a result, these values evolved and even disappeared with changing circumstances. For example, populism as a vibrant part of the Islamicate ideology effectively ended with the termination of war with Iraq and the death of Ayatollah Khomeini, in 1989. Populism was first replaced by clientelism, according to which autonomous parallel groups formed powerful vertical, personal, patron-client bonds with ruling Islamic structures, and then by increasing militarization of the government after the war, during the presidencies of Rafsanjani and Khatami, culminating with Ahmadinejad's presidency, in 2005 (Alamdari 2005:1286).

In one ideological and structural respect the Pahlavi and the new Islamic Republic were very similar, and that was the way both elevated their leaders to transcendent heights, towering over the mere mortals who were their subjects. During the last phases of the "White Revolution," Mohammad Reza Shah Pahlavi's title was changed from the Shah, or the Shahanshah (king of kings), to Shahanshah-e Aryamehr (king of kings, light of Aryans); likewise, after the success of the "Islamic Revolution" and his return to Iran, Ayatollah Ruhollah Khomeini acquired the title of Imam, which in Shiism is generally reserved for the twelve direct descendants of Prophet Mohammad and Ali, and is generally not applied to any other religious leader, as is the case in Sunni Islam. He also acquired the new titles of *velayat-e faqih* (guardian jurist), and *rahbar-e enqelab* (leader of the revolution).[13] These ascending titles confirmed him as the undisputed leader of the Iranian nation and of the Shiite community in general. The Pahlavi regime and the Islamic Republic were also similar in that both were statist and dictatorial. However, there was a key difference between them in this regard. In the 1960s, the Shah shifted from being a dictator to becoming an absolute and arbitrary ruler, who "tried to combine the role of a traditional, arbitrary ruler with that of a modern revolutionary leader"—in essence, he wished to be both Cyrus the Great and Fidel Castro simultaneously. His ultimate tragedy was that "he failed in both those ambitious roles, neither succeeding as a strong arbitrary ruler nor as a popular revolutionary modernizer" (Katouzian 2009:263). Having left no independence for any social classes or persons, the Shah was highly unpopular not only with his opponents, but also, and more important, with his proponents, all of whom abandoned him in short order, including the armed forces, each of whose members had sworn loyalty to the person of the Shah. Thus, unlike Western revolutions, which typically involved underprivileged classes rising against the privileged classes, in the Islamic Revolution of 1979—as in the Constitutional Revolution of 1906—"it was society as a whole that revolted against the state" (ibid.:325). The Islamic Republic, on the other hand, created a strong base of support and loyalty among the formerly downtrodden people and classes (*mostazafan*) and among the browbeaten traditional Muslims and bazaar merchants who were elevated in due course into privileged social classes that were willing to fight for and defend the republic and its regime.

If Islamicate values championed independence for Iran, they did not favor another form of independence that is a hallmark of Enlightenment and modernity: individuality. In this view humans are not autonomous and sovereign but need the paternalistic guidance and guardianship of God and his prophets, imams, and their jurist representatives. At a deep psychological level, this dependence on the guidance and guardianship of an external agency counters one of the chief engines of cinema, which is the targeting and production of individualized subjectivity through its system of suture.

During the savage eight-year war with Iraq, these Islamicate concepts, values, and icons, particularly those that emphasized populism, self-sacrifice, martyrdom, self-defense, violence, and death, became more prominent. A whole culture of self-sacrifice and martyrdom bordering on fascism emerged. This included the aforementioned theatricalization of the public sphere, not only through religious sermons, rituals, and passion plays, but also through continual invocation of such a culture by the clerical leaders in their public pronouncements. Jokesters played with, and on, these pronouncements publicly and privately. Wall graffiti and posters—new revolutionary art forms and important media of expression and communication—also reflected these (Chelkowski and Dabashi 1999). Slogans were often written in dark-red colors to connote blood. Bloody handprints on walls and posters became emblematic, recorded in photographs and films. Fountains of blood (filled with red dye) sprang up in most cemeteries to denote and validate the martyrs' blood shed on the road to revolution and the revolution's defense. Even the colorful, dramatic, government-issued stamps, which Peter Chelkowski (1987) appropriately called "Stamps of Blood," capitalized on these concepts, circulating to the far corners of the world the iconographic messages of the war and revolution. Oversized portraits of the Islamist leaders and martyrs were (and still are) displayed on public walls and on the roads, and tulips of martyrdom were placed in cemeteries, on stamps, and on the national flag. Schoolbooks, including alphabet primers, were not exempt from violent concepts and imagery.[14] Finally, Islamicate values were often invoked by the movies, in their plots, dialogue, characters, and iconography. They were also used both as currency and as criteria in discussing, reviewing, evaluating, proscribing, or prescribing individual movies, filmmakers, entertainers, or the cinema as such.[15]

The ascendancy of these concepts, values, and icons and their integration into cultural fields and cinema were part of the continuing national and cultural contestation and negotiation over Iranian identity and modernity that had been unleashed at least since the beginning of the twentieth century. Except the rise of these concepts was now occurring after the violence of a popular but disruptive revolution, during which the terms of national identity, of alienating identification, and of self and other had undergone a reversal. At least officially, the West and pre-Islamic Zoroastrian Iran were no longer objects of desire and identification. The West, particularly the United States, had become the Great Satan. Two different idealized imaginaries were erected in the places of the pre-Islamic Zoroastrian past and the westernized modern world: first, the good old days of the early Islamic Caliphate with the Prophet Mohammad and the twelve Shiite imams and their families; second, the good future days of life in paradise, which the pious Shiites could expect to enjoy if they behaved themselves. In the long run, however, there was no unanimity on these shifts in the mechanism of identity formation. Official attitudes remained ossified on anti-Western polemics; popular opinion, particularly among educated classes, students, women, and young adults, gravitated to its polar opposite: infatuation with things Western, particularly American, and a steady shift toward values of secular modernity and liberal democracy. A range of opposition and reformist groups arose within and outside the country.

The same medium whose corrupting, poisonous, and immoral products had been employed to discredit and dismantle the Pahlavi regime was now deployed to legitimize the new Islamist regime. This was a new example of the classic violence waged between idolaters and iconoclasts. Having declared the Pahlavi regime and its culture of spectacle, including cinema, as idolatrous justified the violent exercise of iconoclasm that followed. However, the purpose of iconoclasm is never solely to destroy existing idols, but to replace them with new ones that are more to the taste of the new order (Morgan 2005:117). What needed to be done was to evacuate cinema of its corrupt idols (stars, personnel, genres) and to replace them with upright, moral, Islamicate ones.

When Hojjatoleslam Mohammad Khatami was elected president, in 1997, in a landslide, more Western and modernist formulations found their way into the official Islamicate values. This included such secular and modernist concepts as civil society, political transparency, pluralism, tolerance of opposing views, individual rights, women's public presence, equality before law, and rule of law.[16] Most important, these collectively introduced the concept of individuality—individual choice, sovereignty, and autonomy—which had been missing from earlier formulations of Islamicate values. In terms of foreign relations, Khatami replaced the previous "neither East nor West" doctrine with the "dialogue of civilizations," so attractive beyond Iranian borders that the United Nations designated that year as the year of dialogue of civilization. While these syncretic Islamic ideas sounded refreshing and promised much-needed reforms, in practice their implementation was stymied by the peculiar formal governing structures and informal formations of the Islamic Republic. Arrest, interrogation, imprisonment, torture, and murder of reformists, journalists, and "alternative thinkers" or "counterhegemonic thinkers" (degar andishan) increased under the guise of preserving the nation's security, public order, and moral and revolutionary values (Kar 2001:262). Factionalism and clientelism were involved.

In this chapter, I analyze the initial processes of iconoclastic transition, from the Pahlavi's syncretically Westernized culture and its "cinema of idolatry" to syncretically Islamized culture and its "Islamicate cinema," processes that took approximately four years.

The New Iconoclasm

Purification of the Movie Industry and the Mass Media

One of the first iconoclastic processes during the revolutionary period was to rid society of undesirable Western and Pahlavi features. While the term lustration is perhaps more appropriate in its religious connotation of cleansing by ablution, I apply the term purification (paksazi), which has similar religious and political connotations and was in wide use in Iran at the time. Purification was applied not only to the film industry, but also to all social, educational, mass media, industrial, and bureaucratic institutions. Schools and university systems were reprogrammed, and curricula and textbooks revised, under the rubric of "cultural revolution."

Surprisingly, the purification of the press and broadcast media began before the revolution. A good case in point was that of Homa Sarshar, a well-known Jewish journalist, editor of the women's page of Kayhan newspaper, and producer and host of her own twice-weekly primetime television show, Four Walls (Chahar Divari), on NIRT. After the Rex Cinema fire, when Jafar

Sharif Emami became prime minister and banned casinos and cabarets to comply with the Islamist objections to them, NIRT terminated her show. She later discovered that "they wanted all women and minorities out of television and radio" (quoted in Sullivan 2001:141). A similar fate befell her newspaper position: when her routine assignment of translating wire-service reports from the French suddenly dried up and she inquired, the news editor's response was: "You must be crazy to think that anyone would give Ayatollah Khomeini's news to a Jewish woman to translate" (ibid.: 145). She soon left for the United States.

In September 1978, NIRT's chief, Reza Ghotbi, was forced to resign (along with one of his powerful deputies, Mahmud Jafarian), and the institution itself was taken over by "the people" on 11 February 1979 (22 Bahman 1357). That same day Sadegh Ghotbzadeh was appointed the new chief of television and radio networks, which began transmitting the "voice of the revolution." Mirali Hosseini, a young NIRT announcer, read a statement on the air declaring the fall of the Pahlavi regime, which in part said, "Greetings to the nation. Today, a furious and tumultuous nation has returned home. The last vestiges of the dictator's radio and television escaped the premises this morning. At the outset, we the striking employees [of NIRT] offer our greetings to the pure souls of men and women martyrs who helped us and our fellow citizens breathe in the air of freedom. Greetings to all those free-minded men and women who shook the pillars of dictatorship at the height of its power."[17] With that, not only the Pahlavi regime but also over 2,500 years of monarchy came to an end.

Destruction and Cleansing of Movie Houses

The first stage in transforming the Pahlavi era's "cinema of idolatry" into an "Islamicate cinema" was the cleansing of the movie houses by fire. During the mass protests in Tabriz in February 1978, the demonstrators turned their wrath against the Pahlavi economic and cultural systems by destroying symbols of those systems. Statistics released by Tabriz University students revealed that sixty-two banks and three movie houses were burned down, with a total of ninety-seven banks and seven movie houses destroyed in the demonstrations, which were credited with setting off the revolution (*Asnad va Tasaviri az Mobarezat-e Khalq-e Mosalman-e Iran* 1978:37).[18] Soon after, on 27 March 1978, a fire in a poor neighborhood of Tehran reiterated the torching of the movie houses as a new revolutionary tactic (Malek and Mohsenian Rad 1994:87). On 4 August, four motorcyclists firebombed Shahr-e Farang Cinema in Isfahan, the only movie house in that city that showed foreign movies in original languages and thus a favorite of foreign nationals and Westernized Iranians. This action, along with the destruction of the New American Club in the same city, convinced many American consultants in Iran, among them Charles Semkus, to conclude that "someone is trying to scare the foreigners, who are indeed, to a great extent, pillars of support for the Shah" (1979:41). So many movie houses were burned and destroyed on Isfahan's Chaharbagh Avenue, said an eyewitness to me, that it resembled "a burned-out war zone," forcing the closure of the famed leafy avenue for a time (Naficy 1983) (figs. 3–5).

After the destruction, the insurgents' self-justifying leaflets tapped into the anti-cinema discourses, claiming that movie houses had become "centers of corruption" (Sreberny-Mohammadi and Mohammadi 1994:129). They may also have been burned because film exhibition was a lucrative business owned by "the Shah's patrons" (ibid.:145). On the seventh and fortieth days of mourning for those who had died in previous demonstrations, more people died in the affected cities and other cities, with each demonstration or mourning commemoration feeding an escalating cycle of violence that gradually engulfed the entire country and all social strata.

Many people blamed the government for torching public places, such as banks and movie houses, and public property, such as city buses, as a way to discredit the insurgency and to prevent Iranians from joining it, while the government blamed the insurgents. As Robert Safarian shows in his lucid thirty-minute film essay, *Image-Makers of the Revolution: 5 November 1978 Day of Fire (Tasvirgaran-e Enqelab: 14 Aban 1357 Ruz-e Atash, 2008)*, about a momentous day in the history of the revolution on which Tehran entered an unprecedented phase of burning and destruction, determining what happened in these conflagrations is not difficult; what is difficult, perhaps nigh impossible, is identifying the culprits. Memories of those who witnessed the event are faulty or incomplete, and corroborating evidence for the widespread claim by Iranians that the Shah's forces deliberately set cinemas and banks on fire do not exist or are not available (archives must be scoured for small bits of evidence). The evidence people offer are often circumstantial, such as the one by the filmmaker Abdollah Bakideh, who filmed the event on that day and tells Safarian that he thinks the government agents who wore civilian clothes set the fires because they wore boots, not regular shoes.

The Rex Cinema tragedy and its lengthy aftermath exemplify some of the complexities involved in determining who was responsible. They reveal varied personal motivations by the arsonists and governmental complicity, incompetence, and cover-ups by both the Pahlavi and Islamic Republic regimes.

3–5 Burned and damaged
Tehran movie houses.

3 Marquee of Paramount Cinema,
Tehran. Frame grab from Hosain
Torabi's film, *For Freedom*.

4 Marquee of Empire Cinema,
Tehran. Frame grab from Hosain
Torabi's film, *For Freedom*.

5 Marquee of Pacific Cinema,
Tehran. Frame grab from Hosain
Torabi's film, *For Freedom*.

Takabalizadeh and cohorts had personal, political, and religious motives. According to Takabalizadeh's testimony, he was a welder who had been both a heroin addict and a drug dealer before joining an Islamic reading group that studied Ali Shariati's books, audiocassettes, and the Quran. He related that throughout his life he had been made to feel inferior; however, now that the "nation had risen" against the Shah, he was bent on proving that he, too, was a "worthy" person. As his friendship with the Islamist group grew, he kicked his drug habit, attended the Isfahani Mosque in Abadan, read religious books and listened to audiocassettes, and became involved in street uprisings. At the same time, as he told it, a key motivation was to make sure that Abadan joined the anti-Shah uprising, for up to that point this major labor center with a large secular population had been quiescent. There were rumors that to provoke the city, Islamist groups from other towns such as Qom, Isfahan, and Mashhad had humiliated their counterparts in Abadan by sending them women's brassieres. Whatever the motivations or the provocations, the result was catastrophic and criminal.

Some arrests were made and confessions were extracted from the accused. However, the successive governments that the Shah appointed, each weaker than the previous one in the face of mounting protests, were unsuccessful in assuaging the public. According to Dariush Homayoon and Hushang Nahavandi, former high officials of the Shah's government, the last Pahlavi-appointed prime ministers were interested primarily in appeasing the religious leaders and quelling the uprising. That is why they suppressed or diminished the results of their own investigations, which had confirmed the involvement of Islamic zealots and Islamic leaders in the Rex Cinema fire, and attempted to make the tragedy to appear "non-political."[19] Both this government passivity and the active ascription of the tragedy by Khomeini and others to the discredited government sealed the public perception of the Pahlavi regime's complicity in the horrific crime and its cover-up. Rumor, the weapon of disenfranchised citizens, flew once again, pitting popular against official discourse.

After the fall of the Shah's regime, it was left to the Islamic government to investigate the crime. But the new regime seemed unwilling. The slow pace of the official investigation led some of the disenchanted relatives of the victims to stage a sit-in at Abadan's Department of Finance. After 105 days, a dispute, and an attack by revolutionary guards, led to street violence.[20] The trial, two years later, under Hojjatoleslam Musavi Tabrizi, brought out new revelations that further obfuscated culpability for the crime.[21] Takabalizadeh, who was eager to clear his name as a Savak stooge, freely admitted his crime; but he was given no defense attorney, and none of the witnesses and co-conspirators he named were called to testify, perhaps because a professional defense would have turned up the complicity of Muslim religious figures. The court even failed to establish the identity of his dead accomplices, some of whom remained known by only one name.

Two of the accomplices may have died in the fire; Farajollah disappeared mysteriously; and Takabalizadeh, whom Radio Farda in its *Conflagration* of *Rex Cinema* series called the "most reliable" person involved in setting the fire, was arrested, tried, and condemned to death.[22] In addition to Takabalizadeh, five other people implicated in the crime were executed. These included three Savak agents and police figures with little concrete connection to the fire, as well as the movie house owner, Ali Naderi, and the movie house manager, Esfandiar Ramezani Dehaqani, who were condemned on the ground of negligence. Several others were sentenced to jail terms. Indicative of the confusion, sloppiness, and behind-the-scenes political corruption, four people condemned to death—all police and security personnel—managed to escape and remained at large.[23] In addition, several alleged co-conspirators were not only not tried, but also were later rewarded with official government positions. For example, Mahmud Rashidian, the former governor of Khuzestan Province, who was presumably related to the notorious Rashidian brothers—film exhibitors and owners of Rex Cinema-Theater in Tehran, who were involved in the 1953 coup against Mosaddeq—was elected to the Majles in Tehran; Mahmud Abolpur, a teacher, was appointed head of Abadan school district; and Abdollah Lorqaba, an employee of Iran National Airlines who had apparently supplied the jet fuel to the arsonists, became a member of the Islamic society of Abadan Airport. The religious and political leaders who may have either inspired the fire or conspired in setting it were never officially named or punished. On the other hand, those who had contrary information were targeted. One of these was Mohammad Reza Ameli Tehrani, a former cabinet minister and head of NIRT during the Shah's last months, who had been placed in charge of investigating the fire and had collected a massive amount of information about it, some of it apparently pointing to the religious leaders' involvement. He was first arrested by the Islamic government and condemned to twenty-eight months of imprisonment; then, when it came to light that he knew a great deal about the involvement of the religious leaders, Ayatollah Khalkhali, the famous hanging judge, had him summarily executed.

Ironically, the Islamic court sessions were held in the plush Taj (Crown) Cinema, where in years past movies had been screened before oil company employees. Apparently nearly one hundred hours of film and videotape of the trial had been recorded there, but none of it was aired by VVIR national television networks (which had replaced NIRT); only the Abadan television station broadcast segments of it at the time, to a visceral public reaction that was both comic and tragic. According to Radio Farda's *Conflagration of Rex Cinema*, the family members of the victims who attended the trial felt that the trial was intended primarily to cover up the truth and the names of the real culprits, rather than to reveal them. The spectators were "bewildered and shocked" by the trial's conduct and outcome.

Because of the evidence that Islamic forces had been involved with the arsonists and because of the incompetent and politicized trial, an ironic reversal of credibility emerged. The belief took root among some in the public at home and abroad that it was not the Shah's regime but the Islamic revolutionaries themselves who were the real perpetrators of that holocaust. The perception—and perhaps the fact—of a cover-up stigmatized the Islamic government as it had the Shah's. Because of the various cover-ups, misinformation, discrepancies, and manipulations of public opinion by both regimes, there is much more to be understood about this pivotal event, whose complexity and murky politics an observer in Abadan analogized to those of President Kennedy's assassination (Naficy 2005e).

Three side issues need further examination: the choice of the site for the crime, the choice of the movie, and the choice of the date. There are two narratives about the site and the movie. According to Mostafa Abkashak's narrative, Rex was selected not because it was showing the oppositional film *The Deer*, but because it was suitable for the crime. The four culprits had attended Sohaila Cinema earlier that day, armed with bags of thinner fluid, only to discover that the physical arrangements of the hall and the doors did not lend themselves to the job (Abkashak 1985:12). On the other hand, according to Takabalizadeh's narrative in *Conflagration of Rex Cinema*, the arsonists did try to set fire to the thinner fluid, in the Sohaila Cinema's waiting room, but found that it was not sufficiently flammable. By early nightfall, they had obtained highly flammable airplane fuel, with which they revisited Sohaila Cinema. Finding that it had closed, they headed toward Rex Cinema. From these accounts, it appears that the choice of Rex Cinema was opportunistic, not planned. If the choice of the movie were a factor, they likely would have chosen one emblematic of the regime's "idolatrous" culture, to signal the arsonists' opposition to Pahlavi policy. From published testimonies, it appears that their purpose in burning down the movie house was less opposition to cinema as such as it was opposition to the Shah regime. The date of the crime, 19 August (28 Mordad), coincided with the twenty-fifth anniversary of the CIA-MI6 anti-Mosaddeq coup. Given the improvisational intricacies of the incident, though, it is safe to conclude that the choice of the date was coincidental.

The repercussions of the Rex Cinema fire were both local and global. Cinema workers in Tehran declared that they would close their cinemas for twenty-four hours in protest, and Reza Anvari, chief of the Iran Cinema Syndicate, announced that movie houses in Abadan, Isfahan, Mashhad, and Shiraz would close for the remainder of the holy month of Ramadan. In early September, about 150 people were arrested and more than a dozen injured in a demonstration protesting the Abadan fire in Los Angeles. A few days earlier, 193 people had been arrested in a demonstration involving 600 participants, mostly college students, in front of the Federal Building downtown (Semkus 1979:56, 109–10). Back in Iran, the government of Prime Minister Jamshid Amuzegar soon fell. Jafar Sharif Emami, who replaced him, moved quickly to appease the clerics and the religious opposition. He abolished the Ministry of Women's Affairs, created a Ministry of Religious Affairs, lifted press censorship and curbs on political parties, abolished the new Pahlavi calendar, closed down fifty-seven casinos owned by the Pahlavi Foundation, removed high-ranking officials reputed to be Baha'is (such as former Prime Minister Amir Abbas Hoveyda), and removed key czars of culture and media, including Mehrdad Pahlbod and Reza Ghotbi (Ghotbi apparently resigned on 12 September 1978).[24] The volume of religious programming on national television increased exponentially, as did the screening of serious, high-quality commercial movies.

These measures proved to be too little and too late to redress the critical situation. Instead, they speeded up the pace of demonstrations and their vehemence. The deliberate torching of nearly four hundred people in Rex Cinema was by far the worst violence involving movie houses, but other cinema fires caused casualties as well, such as the ones in Mashhad and Shiraz that killed three people and injured three people, respectively, all during Ramadan (August).[25] The police and security forces had some success in preventing the destruction of these establishments. In late August, for example, timely action by police in the city of Yazd scared off arsonists, who had released flammable gas from canisters inside Shahr-e Farang Cinema, before they had a chance to set it on fire. Likewise, in Shiraz, the police were able to defuse two time-bombs, placed next to the gasoline containers on the movie house's rooftop, which were set to go off at six the next morning. When martial law was declared in major cities, such as Isfahan and Tabriz, the movie houses were shut down, preventing their destruction. The martial law authorities in Tehran arrested a rich cleric, Shaikh Yahya Nasiri (a.k.a. Allameh Nuri), whose assets were estimated to be in excess of 100 million rials, on charges of sedition and instigating the destruction of banks, shops, and movie houses (Semkus 1979:59, 67, 144).

As the early morning timing of some of these arsons show, the object of torching and destroying movie houses was generally not to kill the spectators, but to destroy symbols of Pahlavi culture. By August 1978, the month in which the Rex Cinema tragedy occurred, 29 movie houses had been destroyed, from a total of 451 nationwide. By the time the Islamic government was established, less than a year later, up to 180 movie houses (32 in Tehran alone) had been burned, demolished, or shut down, leaving only 271 functioning cinemas.[26] Interestingly, the destruction crippled film exhibition in major cities such as Tehran, Isfahan, Tabriz, and Mashhad, because the level of damage to the cinemas in these cities was much larger than in smaller towns, whose cinemas were largely intact.

The purification campaign did not stop with the revolution. Some of the movie houses that remained standing were converted to other uses. For example, the sole cinema in the town of Ferdows was converted into a hay-storage facility, and one of the few movie houses in Gorgan was converted into a prison.[27] The revolutionary zeal produced bizarre syncretic rituals. The stage of the Rudaki Hall Theater, a major modern performance hall in Tehran, was apparently made to undergo a ceremonial Muslim ablution (*ghosl*) in order to transform it from a "polluted" stage (supposedly because of the immoral shows performed on it during the Pahlavi period) into a religiously clean one. The ablution reportedly damaged and rusted the machinery of the revolving stage (Saedi 1984b:7).

The remaining movie houses underwent a different form of baptism, by having their names changed from glamorous Western names to Islamic, revolutionary, or third-world names. In Tehran, Cinema Atlantic was changed to Cinema Efriqa (Africa), Empire to Esteqlal (independence), Royal to Enqelab (revolution), Panorama to Azadi (freedom), Niagara to Jomhuri (republic), Monaco to Shahed (witness), Taj (crown) to Shahr-e Honar (city of art), Golden City to Felestin (Palestine), Polidor to Qods (Jerusalem), Rex to Laleh (Tulip), and Cine Monde to Qiam (uprising). In due course, some of these were refurbished or rebuilt (figs. 6–8).

Another form of cleansing befell the film prints and film negatives held in archives, both of documentary and fiction films. Footage that could be deemed immoral, pro-Pahlavi, or in some way incriminating was burned and culled, depriving Iranians of important historical records.[28]

Curbing and Realigning the Imports

Immediately after the revolution, uncertain conditions discouraged investment in domestic productions, but encouraged both exhibition of old movies and importation of new ones. Table 1 shows a snapshot of the foreign movies receiving exhibition permits. Comedies and "spaghetti" Westerns came from

6 Efriqa (Africa) Cinema on Vali Asr Avenue, Tehran, 2010. Courtesy of Talieh Shahrokhi.

7 Azadi Cinema on Beheshti Avenue, Tehran, 2010. Courtesy of Talieh Shahrokhi.

8 Qods Cinema in Vali Asr Square, Tehran, 2010. Courtesy of Talieh Shahrokhi.

Italy and karate films from Japan. U.S. imports covered a broad range, from comedies to political movies, with such films as *It's a Mad, Mad, Mad, Mad World, Modern Times, Three Days of the Condor, The Cassandra Crossing, The Great Escape, Cinderella, The Jungle Book,* and *Papillon.*

Soviet and Eastern bloc films—inexpensive to import—also flourished to the point of overtaking the American, Italian, and Japanese films. For example, as the *Iran Times* reported, 74 (or more than a third) of the 213 foreign movies licensed by the MCIG for 1981 came from the Soviet bloc. Sixty-nine were produced in the Soviet Union alone. Italy ranked second, with 38 films, and, surprisingly, the United States came in third, with 27 movies.[29] Of the new imports, those that catered to the revolutionary and violent spirit of the time clearly dominated. The best known of these, banned during the Pahlavi period, included such classics as Costa Gavras's *Z* and *State of Siege,* Guzman's *Battle of Chile,* Kurosawa's *The Seven Samurai,* Akad's *Mohammad the Messenger,* and Pontecorvo's *The Battle of Algiers.* The last, which graphically dramatizes the Algerians' armed guerrilla resistance against the French colonial forces, including images of veiled women carrying guns and bombs that killed innocent people, was so popular that it was shown simultaneously in twelve Tehran movie houses and ten provincial movie houses.[30] A spectator who was appalled by the violence of the movie reported that the audience clapped, whistled, and cheered as the film unreeled, consolidating for him the idea that the nation was "changing with the smell of the blood, revenge, and fire" (Khalili 1990:144). A pro-PMOI spectator, on the other hand, saw in the film's detailed recreation of guerrilla tactics an empowering procedural model for "clandestine guerrilla action against imperialist regimes" (Naficy 1983).

The clerical establishment was concerned but divided on the issue of film imports. Some praised the "revolutionary films," such as *Z* and *The Battle of Algiers,* because they showed "the struggle of people oppressed by colonialism and imperialism."[31] Others condemned them as made-in-Hollywood movies with only a "revolutionary mask."[32] Likewise, Hojjatoleslam Ahmad Sadeqi-Ardekani, a leading clergyman in charge of supervising the film industry in 1981, wrote that Iran was continuing its "cultural dependence on imperialists" by importing Western and Eastern movies into the country, where "millions of people are mentally and culturally nourished by cinema." Updating the language of Navvab Safavi and Khomeini, he predicted that continued "acceptance of Western and Eastern films will lead us to cultural colonization and economic exploitation" (Ardekani 1981:10).

The secular intellectuals, too, worried about the influx of these so-called revolutionary foreign movies, but for different ideological and artistic reasons. For example, Gholamhosain Saedi, a leading dissident writer who went into exile in Paris after the revolution and edited the literary monthly *Alefba*, offered the following definition for the "revolutionary films" shown in Iran: "full of cannons, tanks, rifles, weapons, and corpses, without regards to quality or artistic merit" (1982:7; in English, see Saedi 1984a). The Tudeh (Communist) party, which once again was openly involved in politics, published a letter in its official organ, *Nameh-ye Mardom*, complaining that the nine movie houses in Mashhad were screening one British, two American, two Indian, and four "banal" Iranian movies. The writer urged the government to heavily curb foreign movies.[33] Given that the letter was published in the perennially pro-Soviet Tudeh party organ, it is easy to see that the curb was meant to be applied primarily to Western movies, not to Soviet and Eastern-bloc films.

Efforts both to purify the imports and to help bolster domestic productions began early. In July 1979, a committee consisting of representatives of the Film Producers Society, Society for Theater Owners, Society for Film Importers, the Joint Council of Actors and Workers of Cinema, and the Ministry of Culture and Islamic Guidance decided that in the interest of encouraging domestic productions and cleaning up the film exhibition scene, importing of foreign "karate," "anti-revolutionary," and "imperialistic" movies would be banned.[34] *Variety* reported this decision in its usual colorful argot by stating that the government had "knocked the karate and kung fu films flat on the mat" due to excessive violence.[35] Turkish and Indian movies were banned due to their banality. American movies were the next subset of films to be excluded, as the political relationship between the two countries deteriorated. In fact, corroborating, or justifying, the perceived link between Western films and moral corruption, a larger percentage of Western movies were denied exhibition permit than movies from any other region (see table 2).

TABLE 1 Number of feature movies receiving exhibition permits (1980–82)

Year	Permits Received	Iran	Western Bloc	Eastern Bloc	Third World
1980	121	27	56	36	2
1981	161	18	74	58	11
1982	85	7	56	18	4
Total	367	52	186	112	17

Source: Ministry of Culture and Islamic Guidance 1985, appendix 1, 38–39.

TABLE 2 Number of feature movies denied exhibition permits (1980–82)

Year	Permits Rejected	Iran	Western Bloc	Eastern Bloc	Third World
1980	182	72	87	18	5
1981	326	65	156	97	8
1982	123	19	75	25	4
Total	631	156	318	140	17

Source: Ministry of Culture and Islamic Guidance 1985, appendix 1, 38–39.

Tables 1 and 2 show that a total of 998 foreign and domestic movies were reviewed, 631 of which were rejected. Of 364 movies receiving permission, the largest category was that of Western-bloc movies (186 films), followed by Eastern-bloc movies (112), and Iranian movies (52), the last suggesting the failure of domestic productions to live up to Islamicate values. The largest category rejected was that of Western imports (318), followed by domestic productions (156). The curb, however, was not hermetic, for American movies imported prior to the cutoff, such as *Airport 79* and *High Noon*, continued to appear on the screens even during the highly anti-American "hostage crisis" period.

Reviewing and Censoring of Domestic Movies

A few Pahlavi-era movies that were deemed suitable for the revolutionary and modesty-besieged times were screened in public cinemas, which had become "democratized," in that peoples of all social strata, gender, age, and ethnoreligiosity went to the movies. This is because due to the purification process movie houses were no longer considered a bastion of Pahlavi and Western corruptions. Iranian movies shown included the new-wave movies of Baizai (*Downpour*), Mehrjui (*The Cow*), Naderi (*Tangsir*), and Kimiai (*The Earth* and *Journey of Stone*). The remaining stock of movies had to be purified. To that end, all prerevolutionary films were reviewed. Many were permanently banned, and some were re-edited to conform to Islamicate values. Film producers engaged with the government in a cat-and-mouse game of resistance and submission. Some cut, re-cut, and re-titled their movies. The most interesting of these practices was re-titling, which would suggest an entirely different movie, when all that had changed was the title. Sometimes, these re-titled-only movies were indeed exhibited. When caught, producers or exhibitors would again re-title the movies in question. For example, the title of Amir Shervan's movie, *Freeze, Don't Move* (*Bi Harekat, Tekun Nakhor*), was changed in 1978 to *The Thug and the Student* (*Jahel va Mohassel*), perhaps to attract Pahlavi-era spectators. After the revolution, it was changed again, to *Heroin*, to fit the new times, which no longer approved of Pahlavi-era tough guys but appreciated films that pointed up the social problems of that era, such as drug addiction. These superficial changes, however, apparently did not help the movies' earnings.[36]

Sensing the inevitability of the Islamicization of cinema, film exhibitors attempted to control the damage by voluntarily keeping sex off the screens and recasting film as educational. One exhibitor claimed, "Our contribution to the Islamic Revolution would be made best by replacing dirty films with entertainment of an educational caliber."[37] One method for this transformation was to use magic markers as a tool of censorship, painting over the naked legs and exposed body parts of women in each successive film frame. Even Pahlavi-era movie posters that showed women with provocatively bare shoulders and legs and with uncovered hair were painted over by distributors and exhibitors with magic markers to create artificial dresses, skirts, bras, or scarves (figs. 9–10). When this method failed, other more drastic ones were used. The manager of

9 Damaged poster for Kamran Qadakchian's movie *Bandari* (1973), showing a skirt painted, with magic marker or black ink, on the image of the female star to extend the miniskirt originally depicted. Collection of the author.

10 Poster for Iraj Qaderi's movie *Without Veil* (*Bi Hejab*, 1973), showing a bra cup awkwardly painted, with magic marker, on the image of the female star. Collection of the author.

Rex Cinema in Tehran, for example, stated, "We have to show films in keeping with Islamic standards. When the Magic Marker doesn't work, we cut."[38] Other creative ways were also found, such as re-photographing certain scenes in pan-and-scan so as to eliminate the offensive parts, then splicing the new footage into the film. Extensive cutting, however, compromised the intelligibility of the films. For example, a movie version of Dostoyevski's novel *The Idiot* was not only cut by fifty minutes, but also re-photographed to remove offensive elements from the lengthy banquet sequence at the film's end. The resulting film was unintelligible.[39] The heavy cutting and soundtrack manipulation during dubbing, which reduced a typical 110-minute movie to just 70 minutes, rendered character relationships, plot, and dialogue confusing.[40]

Dissatisfied with the limited changes made by producers and exhibitors, the government threatened to close the cinemas and mandated an exhibition permit for all movies.[41] This necessitated reviewing all previously produced films, with the result that many domestic movies made prior to the Islamic Republic were banned, never to be seen again on public screens. As a result, a great portion of the history of Iranian cinema was off-limits. Only those who had seen the movies during their initial releases under the Pahlavis or read about them in film-history books retained a memory. Table 3 shows the outcome of this review process for Iranian features produced both before and immediately after the revolution. In the first year, when all the films reviewed were made under the Pahlavi regime, an overwhelming majority was rejected, with only 200 of the 2,000 movies receiving an exhibition permit. Even the percentage of the first postrevolution movies receiving exhibition permits in 1980–81 was small. These figures demonstrate the strictness of the Islamicate values and the rigorousness of the review process, and they declared an effective end to the postrevolutionary laissez-faire atmosphere.

Not surprisingly, more prerevolutionary new-wave films were given exhibition permits immediately after the revolution than prerevolutionary commercial movies. The principal reason was the prominent presence of unveiled women in the Pahlavi-era movies, particularly their provocative and sexualized presentation in filmfarsi. Unveiled women also scotched new-wave movies, such as Baizai's *Ballad of Tara* (*Cherikeh-ye Tara*, 1978) and *Death of Yazdegerd* (*Marg-e Yazdegerd*, 1980). The prominent presence of such female characters throughout doomed the films, as without these characters there would be no film. Two movies by the French-educated lawyer-filmmaker Gholamali Erfan, who had returned to Iran after the revolution, *Mr. Hieroglyphic* (*Aqa-ye Hiroglif*, 1981) and *All Three Said So* (*Goft Har Seh Nafareshan*, 1980), were also banned, because of unveiled women and because of favorable treatment of leftist guerrillas during the revolution.[42] A precise listing of the charges against *Mr. Hieroglyphic* reveals the complexity of the internecine power struggle that undergirded censorship: misrepresenting the revolutionary struggle by emphasizing the role of workers' armed struggle, encouraging terrorism, concealing the independence of the revolutionary struggles,

TABLE 3 Iranian feature movies given or denied exhibition permits (1979–82)

Year	Films Reviewed	Permit Granted	Permit Denied
1979	2000	200	1800
1980	99	27	72
1981	83	18	65
1982	26	7	19
Total	2208	252	1956

Source: Ministry of Culture and Islamic Guidance 1985, appendix 1, 38–39. See also "Namayesh-e Filmha-ye Hendi va Torky Mamnu' Shod," *Ettela'at*, 27 Esfand 1358/1979.

and employing characters, symbols, ideologies, and women's costumes that are improper, "imported" from the West (*varedati*), and that reflect the thesis of political groups that are tied to foreigners (Jafari Lahijani 2008b:vol. 2:765).

Other banned new-wave films include Haritash's *Kingdom of Heaven* (*Malakut*, 1976), Aslani's *Chess of the Wind* (*Shatranj-e Bad*, 1976), Kimiavi's *O.K. Mister* (1979), and Mehrjui's *The Yard behind Adl-e Afaq School* (*Hayat-e Poshti-ye Madreseh-ye Adl-e Afaq*, 1980).⁴³ Kimiai's *Red Line* (*Khat-e Qermez*, 1982) and *Blade and Silk* (*Tigh va Abrisham*, 1986) were banned, requiring extensive re-shooting and editing.⁴⁴ Because new-wave films treated social issues seriously, which fit the social mood and enhanced political awareness of the postrevolution society, not all were banned. Among the new-wave films exhibited immediately after the revolution were Kimiai's *Baluch* (1972), *The Earth* (*Khak*, 1973), *Reza Motori* (1970), *The Journey of the Stone* (*Safar-e Sang*, 1978), *Qaisar* (1969), and *The Deer*; Mehrjui's *The Cycle* (*Dayereh-ye Mina*, 1973–77), *Postman* (*Postchi*, 1970), and *The Cow* (*Gav*, 1969), the latter of which Ayatollah Khomeini had praised as an exemplary film; Naderi's *Tangsir* (1973), *Tight Spot* (*Tangna*, 1973), *Harmonica* (*Saz-e Dahani*, 1973), and *Elegy* (*Marsiyeh*, 1978); Baizai's *Downpour* (*Ragbar*, 1972); Taqvai's *Sadeq the Kurd* (*Sadeq Kordeh*, 1972); Shahid Saless's *Still Life* (*Tabi'at-e Bijan*, 1975); Hatami's *Broken Hearted* (*Suteh Delan*, 1977); and Haritash's *Custodian* (*Saraydar*, 1976). The domestic features not banned were often censored. Masud Asadollahi's two-hour film *Quarantine* (*Qarantineh*, 1979) was censored three times and finally cut by one hour before its release, four years later, in 1983.⁴⁵

The composition of the national Council of Film Review at the Ministry of Culture and Higher Education (MCHE), which was initially charged with issuing film production and exhibition licenses, pointed to how political the process was and how, like the film review board of the second Pahlavi period, it was stocked with government officials and military and security people. In 1980, the council drew its members from the following sources: the Revolutionary Guards, the Ideological-Political Bureau of the Armed Forces, the Reconstruction Crusade, the Foundation of the Dispossessed, MCHE's Office of Supervision and Exhibition, clerical representatives, and other independent individuals. According to Hojjatoleslam Sadeqi, the head of the council, the criteria for choosing members were three: a love and a talent for the arts, expertise in matters related to cinema and film industry, and Islamic awareness and commitment.⁴⁶ The composition of the council and the criteria by which the movies were judged evolved. Regarding the censorship criteria, in early 1980, MCHE's Center for Audiovisual and Film Production proposed that the following types of movies be banned: aesthetic films; propaganda films espousing the causes of racism, fascism, and imperialism; and movies in which sex and violence were used merely to attract spectators.[47]

While most filmmakers applauded the curbing of low-grade commercial imports, they did not condone their banning, as Baizai, whose own two movies were banned, observed: "It is the enhanced public awareness which should be driving these trite films off the screens, not government force." What is more, he said, the vacuum created by the absence of imports had to be filled with domestic productions, which were nonexistent because of lack of supportive regulations, mechanisms, and structures.[48]

Even when movies passed through the various filters and received exhibition permits, they were subjected to further scrutiny, criticism, and censorship for not being sufficiently Islamic. Iraj Qaderi's movie *Living in Purgatory* (*Barzakhiha*, 1980), starring tough-guy stars Malekmotii, Fardin, Said Rad, Mohammad Ali Keshavarz, and Qaderi himself, provides a good example. In this film, a group of criminals who have been released from prison by the revolution are fleeing the country via the Iraqi border. Saddam Hussein's forces invade Iran, causing the toughs to change plans: instead of escaping the country, they decide to defend it. In that process, they exhibit bravery and give their lives. That they have died in defense of the country is not sufficient to redeem them, however. One reviewer condemned the film for insulting the "martyrs" and the "sacred beliefs" of the people (quoted in Naficy 1987:453). The movie received an official exhibition permit two years after its release and became very popular, garnering the highest box office in history up to that point.

The right-wing press, however, critiqued the film for turning Pahlavi-era actors into heroic characters. One reviewer called it a "shameful" film, since it had transformed the actors who were the symbols of the previous regime's "infamy and decadence" into heroes of "Islamic epics."[49] Another reviewer contended that even "the martyrs are concerned about the screening of this film," as if the dead could speak. Finally, a critic cast aspersions on the film producer's professionalism and honesty and characterized the screenwriter as the author of the "dirtiest and vilest" Pahlavi-era movies who now presumed to write "revolutionary" screenplays.[50] Reviewers were not alone in condemning the movie. A group managed to put together a massive scroll, eighteen meters long, containing signatures of those who opposed the film, provoking MCIG Minister Hojatollah Ma'adikhah, who supported the film, to call for a stop to "their shenanigans in the name of Islam."[51] (Ma'adikhah was soon removed from his post.) The producer, too, joined the public debate. He defended his Islamic credentials by stating that he had taken 2,500 hours of lessons on Islamology, and he vouched for the selflessness of the stars of the

Men in Purgatory (Iraj Ghaderi = 1982) Mohammad-Ali Batoni.

11 The controversial transformation of Pahlavi-era, fun-loving tough guys into Islamically pious and patriotic toughs. A poster for Iraj Qaderi's action movie *Living in Purgatory*. Collection of the author.

Pahlavi-era cinema, who had acted in the film for a very small fee.[52] Beyond airing legitimate criticisms of the manipulative narrative and politics of the movie, the heated public argument about *Living in Purgatory* demonstrates that three years into the transition, purification was still in process and full of contentious currents and crosscurrents. It also showcases the final visible attempt by the stars of the Pahlavi commercial cinema to enter the postrevolution cinema (see fig. 11).

Muzzling and Purging of Entertainers, Performers, and Filmmakers

Some entertainers and filmmakers were thought to be too closely associated with the Pahlavi state's Westernized excesses, with moral corruption and ethical lapses, with pushing modernity's excesses, with religious waywardness, with political crimes, or with working for Savak. They were prime candidates for purification: they were charged, imprisoned, their property confiscated, their persons banned, and even sometimes executed. Since ethnoreligious minorities, particularly Jews, Armenians, and Baha'i's, were well represented in banking, movie exhibition, and the liquor business, they suffered the most from revolutionary destruction.

The case of the prominent producer and studio head Mehdi Misaqiyeh is complex and tragic. When the revolutionary movement began, Misaqiyeh moved to the United States with his American wife, Suzanne, and their three children; he returned to Iran, however, to liquidate his considerable assets and thus to accumulate sufficient capital to start a new life and career in California. The revolutionaries had burned down his Capri Cinema, in Tehran, and he intended to rebuild and sell it, borrowing money from relatives and friends for this purpose. But before the rebuilding was complete, he was arrested and charged with "insulting Islam by parodying it" (*hajv*) with two movies he had produced, *The Go-Between* (*Mohallel*, 1971) and *A Party in Hell* (*Shabneshini dar Jahannam*, 1957). Made long before the Islamic government took power, these comedies were popular during the Pahlavi period, as they made fun of the religious haji types' greed, parsimony, and duplicity. It appeared that *The Go-Between*, directed by Nosrat Karimi, was considered the greater offense, and Karimi was also arrested. However, he was released after a few months, which suggested that Misaqiyeh was primarily being punished for his Baha'i affiliation.[53] He was condemned to life imprisonment, and his extensive properties and bank accounts were confiscated.[54] According to the producer Ali Mortazavi, who knew the details of his case, Misaqiyeh was released after five years, apparently for having publicly recanted and renounced his Baha'i faith (Naficy 1984a). However, as Misaqiyeh's niece, Badi'eh Misaqiyeh (Eshraghian), told me in an interview, Misaqiyeh had never been confirmed officially (*tasjil*) as a Baha'i by the religious hierarchy and, therefore, was never technically a Baha'i.[55] Whatever the reasons for his arrest, punishment, and release, on being freed from jail Misaqiyeh was in bad shape physically and mentally due to the harsh treatment and beatings he had received in jail. He had been incarcerated with forty other men in a small cell, where they had to sleep like sardines, unable to turn, and he was "mentally confused and many of his teeth were broken or removed." In the meantime, his younger brother, Danesh, had managed to complete the renovation of the Capri Cinema and had restarted his brother's film exhibition business. As Danesh was screening his second movie, however, the authorities confiscated and expropriated the establishment: "They took away the keys to the cinema and told him that if he wanted to see a movie there, he would have to purchase a ticket." After Misaqiyeh was released, the authorities promised to pay him 900,000 tomans—a paltry sum—for the expropriated luxury cinema, but he was never given that money. He died four years later, in 1990, at sixty-seven years of age (Naficy 2006a).

Some movie house owners were arrested and charged with smuggling narcotics, peddling pornographic materials, and supporting prostitution.[56] Others were harassed and intimidated. As the new-wave director Bahman Farmanara told me in an interview, the authorities refused to allow him to leave the country after he had returned to Iran to visit his ailing mother, in 1983. "They interrogated me twenty-five different times, sometimes with a revolver placed in front of me on the desk. They questioned my personal relationships, and accused me of making anti-Islamic films." The Forbidden Acts Bureau banned his allegorical *Tall Shadows of the Wind* (*Sayehha-ye Boland-e Bad*, 1978) as "anti-Islamic" (Naficy 1985a). After being subjected to intense interrogation, he was given papers to leave the country. However, the authorities had the temerity to urge him after this treatment to stay because his country needed him (Klady 1979:91).

Secular writers, too, were harassed, imprisoned, and forced into hiding or exile. The case of Gholamhosain Saedi, whose plays and stories had been made into some of the most searing new-wave films, such as Mehrjui's *The Cow* and Taqvai's *Tranquility in the Presence of Others* (*Aramesh dar Hozur-e Digaran*, 1973), is notable. Saedi offers an eloquent and graphic description of his life under duress, stating that in order to make a living immediately after the revolution, he was forced to write articles for newspapers instead of writing plays and stories.

> After each article I would receive threatening phone calls, to the point that I was forced to avoid my home and for one year live clandestinely in an attic. Most opposition members who were in danger would come to stay with me. We were not silent; we had clandestine publications. And yet the regime's agents were looking for me everywhere. They first called my father and said to him that it is to my benefit to turn myself in, and they constantly phoned my brother who is a surgeon, asking about me. . . . One night they raided my attic, but the wife of a neighbor had already tipped me, so I was able to escape the place from the rooftops and hide all night behind the movie sets of a film studio. The next day, some of my friends came and cut my hair and shaved my mustache; with a changed look and new attire I went to new hiding places. For a while I lived collectively with friends, but had to frequently change my

place. I was in hiding for 6–7 months. One of my hiding places was an abandoned women tailor shop, where I stayed for several months. I lived in total darkness, never turned a light on, and drew close all the curtains. My companions were industrial sewing machines and mannequins. I often wrote in darkness, I wrote more than 1000 pages of stories. In the meantime the regime arrested my brother and constantly threatened my father trying to find me. At last, friends arranged for my escape from the country. I passed through mountains and valleys with tearful eyes, extreme anger, and much evasiveness until I crossed the border into Pakistan, where with the help of the United Nations and a few French lawyers I obtained a French visa and came to Paris. (Saedi 1986)[57]

In the overheated postrevolutionary atmosphere, executions continued for "sexual deviance, pornography, prostitution, political dissent . . . , and even for contact with Israel" (Fischer 1980:219).[58] On 12 July 1979, Mansur Baqerian was accused of corruption, making films in Israel, and importing pornographic movies, and was summarily executed. An Armenian-Iranian, Seth Petrosiants, who apparently worked with a Jewish businessman, was alleged to be a member of a criminal gang that included "anti-revolutionary royalists, hypocrites [code word for PMOI members], and Savak agents" who had formed some twenty companies that bilked the government of huge sums and engaged in immoral and illegal trades. Petrosiants himself was alleged to have headed a multifaceted enterprise that produced and distributed "sleazy" pop music and videos, sold alcoholic beverages, forged documents, and ran a house of prostitution, for which he was condemned to one hundred lashes, confiscation of all his properties, and execution—punishments which were exacted on 27 November 1991 (6 Azar 1370).[59] A month before the execution of Baqerian, the daily *Jomhuri-ye Eslami*, the official organ of the dominant Jomhuri-ye Eslami Party, had printed a letter from a group of Islamist militants demanding the death sentence for a group of seventeen actors, producers, and directors of "pornographic and violent" films.[60]

Involvement in making pornographic films was a serious charge launched against filmmakers and actors not just during the transition period. It ebbed and flowed throughout the life of the Islamic Republic, whose laws provided for Muslim women or men convicted of adultery to be stoned to death if married, or flogged one hundred times if unmarried. While these punishments were rarely applied, two women were nevertheless stoned to death for adultery in 2001, during Khatami's reformist presidency, one of them because she had "helped to produce and distribute a pornographic home movie."[61] Other accounts noted that this unnamed woman had been convicted of "acting in pornographic films" and that she was stoned to death in the Evin Prison, where she had been held for the previous eight years.[62] In 2007, in an attempt to combat the growing domestic porn industry, the Majles passed a bill approving execution for those convicted of producing obscene films. The legislation stated that "'producers' and 'main elements' of such works could be sentenced as 'corrupters of the world,' a phrase from the Quran referring to those considered deserving of the death penalty for their crimes" (Tait 2009b). The law followed an outcry over the widespread distribution of an illicit DVD showing Zahra Amir Ebrahimi, a popular soap-opera star, apparently having sex with her former boyfriend. The fact that she had played religious and morally wholesome characters in TV serials and that the DVD was released during Ahmadinejad's presidency, when cultural policy and policing had tightened considerably, made the film more controversial. Amir Ebrahimi claimed that the film, which had sold on the black market more than 100,000 copies in a short time and was also posted on the Internet, was "a fake made by a vengeful former fiancé who used studio techniques to form a montage of incriminating images designed to destroy her career" (Tait 2006). Amir Ebrahimi's former fiancé, an assistant film producer known publicly only as Mr. X, was extradited from Armenia and faced three years of imprisonment and a 6,000 British pounds fine if found guilty. While admitting that he had taken part in the film, he claimed that it was Amir Ebrahimi who had suggested the film, which was shot inside her home, and which she subsequently distributed. Whatever the truth of the charges and countercharges, the fact remains that one of Iran's best-known television performers was faced with "social ostracism, a wrecked career and a possible lashing after police seized copies of the footage" (Tait 2006).

As late as March 2009, police arrested a group of mostly "beautiful young female" actors who were charged with making pornographic films in a middle-class house in East Tehran. The actors, who had produced several amateur films sold on the black market, were arrested, but the directors were not. Naser Fakouhi, the head of Tehran University's anthropology department, warned that the country's youthful population bulge—constituting 70 percent of those under the age of thirty-five, with no memory of the revolution— had caused an "explosion in Internet pornography and the rapid growth of an underground industry." This trend was exacerbated by a rise in the average marrying age under the Islamic Republic, where premarital sex is outlawed and socially frowned on. A recent survey by the state-run national youth organization showed that the average marrying age had risen to forty for men and thirty-five for women, well above the government's recommended guideline of twenty-nine (Tait 2009b).

In addition to various charges involving moral, criminal, and ethnoreligious affiliation, politics and political affiliations provided reasons for prosecution and execution. Two high-ranking personnel of National Iranian Radio and Television were executed by firing squad on 13 March 1979, on political grounds. During the Shah's period, Mahmud Jafarian was simultaneously the powerful deputy director of political affairs for NIRT, head of Pars News Agency, and deputy to the general secretary of the Rastakhiz Party. He had apparently been the main conduit between NIRT and Savak, and possessed a feared and formidable personality. In addition to holding these prominent political posts and connections with the deposed regime, during the run-up to the revolution he had spoken forcefully on television against the resurgence of leftist opposition and had warned of the dangers of "red imperialism" (Sreberny-Mohammadi and Mohammadi 1994:142). Parviz Nikkhah had been involved in televised recantations and had named underground leaders and opposition intellectuals; the Revolutionary Court charged him with renouncing the struggle against the Shah's regime, placing his knowledge and competence in the service of "reaction," playing an important role in the imperial regime's censorship apparatus, and cooperating with Savak.[63] Like Nikkhah, Jafarian had been a communist—a member of the Tudeh Party in the armed forces—who had been arrested, tortured, and co-opted into working within the system. The court's death sentence against the two was carried out less than two hours after the verdict (National Movement of Iranian Resistance 1983:115–16).[64] The first head of the Revolutionary Court system, Sadeq Khalkhali (a.k.a. "the hanging judge"), apparently presided over the verdict (Khalkhali 2001:357).

In addition to individuals executed because they were part of the Pahlavi apparatus, other public figures were assassinated due, it seems, to their mediawork in support of the regime. One was the golden-voiced Seyyed Mohammad Javad Zabihi, the famed reciter of the Quran and of Ramadan religious chants (*monajat*), whom Khalkhali dismissed as the "Shah's singer" (*khanandeh-ye shah*); another was the renowned broadcast-news reader Mohammad Taqi Ruhani, who read pro-regime political commentaries on NIRT radio and television.[65]

The atmosphere of terror expanded. In May 1979, the managing board of the employees union of Voice and Vision of the Islamic Republic (VVIR) reiterated its earlier call for management to reveal the identities of former Savak members, so as to prosecute them. Subsequently, vvir's public relations office published its own threatening announcement, asking those who had worked for Savak to voluntarily come forward or their names would be printed in the newspapers, that they might become subjects of vigilante justice.[66]

In the years after the consolidation of the Islamist regime, more television officials and prominent artists who dared to oppose the regime and its total Islamicization and panoptic control of society and culture were also executed, even those who had been card-carrying revolutionaries. This included Said Soltanpur, a Marxist poet, playwright, theater director, and a member of the pfoi (Minority Faction), who staged plays such as *Death to Imperialism* in the streets, and Sadegh Ghotbzadeh, a powerful protégé of Ayatollah Khomeini, former head of vvir, and former foreign minister, who was executed in 1981 on the charge of organizing a coup against Khomeini.[67]

The film producer Feraidun Zhurak and the actress and singer Marjan, according to the producer Ali Mortazavi, were imprisoned for two years on charges of associating with pmoi (Naficy 1984a). Giti Naziri, a twenty-six-year-old female film student at nirt Cinema and Television College, whom the Mojahedin publication identified as a television reporter-presenter, and nine of her coworkers were tortured and executed on the charge of belonging to pmoi.[68] Rumor had it that when Naziri was arrested and urged to confess, she refused; instead, she spat into the face of the judge, a mullah named Hejazi. This action apparently sealed her fate, for she was said to have been raped before being shot to death. Subsequently, officials went to the home of her parents, asking them to pay for the costs both of firing the bullet with which she was executed and of marrying her before execution. Under the Islamic Republic, the execution of a virgin woman is regarded as a sin, and it is believed to send her to heaven, which the government does not wish to facilitate for members of the opposition. Victims were therefore reputedly married to their executioners, who raped them before murdering them. This case of Naziri and her coworkers raised an international outcry when, in 1985, Alice Lidderdale, representing the British Actors Equity Association, used it to condemn at the annual conference of Britain's Trades Union Congress the human-rights violations of the Islamic Republic. In introducing her condemnation motion, she stated,

Six years ago, delegates, you were probably rejoicing over the revolution which brought liberation to Iran, but the regime that rules Iran now is one of death. . . . My union brings the motion before the conference because it believes that although the suffering in Iran is universal, the communicators have suffered more than many. . . . We have with us some representatives of the Iranian opposition in exile. . . . I ask you, delegates, in their presence to give the motion your overwhelming support.

Her motion was passed and the congress called on the General Council to do "all within its power to campaign for the restoration of human rights in Iran."[69]

Indeed, movie stars, performers, and actors suffered disproportionately from the purification and Islamicization processes because their voices and faces were very public, recognizable, and admired. They could not work incognito or under pseudonyms, as writers could. The veteran film director and writer Nader Ebrahimi was apparently officially prohibited after the revolution. However, he wrote the screenplays for Kumars Purahmad's childrens' television serial *Next Year's Summer* (*Tabestan-e Sal-e Ayandeh*, 1980), which was aired a year later by VVIR's First Channel. Ebrahimi mixed up his wife's name, Farzaneh Mansuri, to create his own pseudonym, Mansur Farzaneh, which appears in the serial's credits (Purahmad 2001:362).

As I have described elsewhere, in a discussion on tough-guy movies, in March 1980 the Revolutionary Court published several orders in national dailies, summoning some thirty actors and actresses before the court for "preliminary investigation."[70] All had starred in commercial movies, particularly in stewpot and tough-guy movies. Among them were Mohammad Ali Fardin, Naser Malekmotii, Behrouz Vossoughi, Simin Ghaffari, Puri Banai, Reza Baikimanverdi, Iraj Qaderi, Manuchehr Vosuq, Morteza Aqili, Shahnaz Tehrani, Gholamreza Sarkub, and Foruzan. To reassure them, the ad stated that other actors who had been summoned had been released after guaranteeing proper Islamic behavior. The renowned tough-guy character actor Mohammad Ali Fardin and a beloved singer of ballads, Akbar Golpaygani, were arrested for drinking, dancing, and gambling in a home in north Tehran, and the famous singer Nemat Aghasi, whose tough-guy song was used in a café sequence in *Dash Akol*, was arrested and flogged publicly fifty times for gambling and drinking. In the same house in which Fardin and Golpaygani were arrested, an unidentified German "spy" was also arrested and charged with "trying to get close to anti-revolutionary (*taquti*) actors and singers in order to take advantage of the situation for their own [German] ends."[71]

Being sidelined and banned from a profession that had made some of the actors beloved superstars was very difficult for them financially and psychologically. Many of them tolerated these conditions with dignity. But they suffered and struggled nonetheless. Fardin described this situation succinctly to the postrevolutionary movie star Reza Kianian: "I am an actor, but I am not acting. I am like a fish out of a fishbowl." A fishbowl is an apt metaphor for the movie screen, as both are places where spectators can view and admire other lives on display. Kianian adds a dramatic coda to Fardin's comment: "That fish [Fardin] leaped into the air so many times and landed on dirt, he struggled so much, that he finally died outside the fishbowl" (Kianian 2008:48). Iren Zazians, a sexy Armenian-Iranian movie star, describes in Shoka Sahrai's brief film *Iren, Iran's First Movie Star* (*Iren, Nokhostin Setareh-ye Iran*, 2010) her postrevolution purification with a touch of irony, "I was honored with purification." Then she continues: "For me this was a very high price to pay psychologically. Just think: I had worked in this field for almost a quarter of a century, a profession that I loved, had expended my energy and youth on it, and had reached a certain level of professional experience. I was forced to give that all up." Unemployed and unemployable, she sold her valuables, traveled abroad, and finally attended a cosmetics school in Frankfurt, Germany. Returning to Iran, she opened a beauty salon. In this way, she said, "I stayed on my feet and earned a living, without complaining." Her assessment of her life as a former movie star is sobering and sad, but probably common among Pahlavi-era stars: "I am not happy, but I continue my path."[72]

Although these excessive measures eased gradually, the purification process became institutionalized. Near the end of 1980, Hojjatoleslam Hosain Ansarnia, head of the Forbidden Acts Bureau (Edareh-ye Monkarat), declared that the cases of ninety additional performers belonging to the previous regime were still under review.[73] In addition to legal actions against the performers for their various moral and legal lapses, most of the performers were banned from performing in cinema and television. The ban was total and outright for most of them, applying to their person entirely. Sometimes the ban, however, was ingeniously partial, applying only to faces or bodies, for example, which meant the performers could work as dubbers, voice-over artists, and radio actors, or applying only to voices, which meant that singers could act but not sing in the movies. A performer whose face, body, and voice were banned could potentially become a behind-the-scenes crewmember or a writer, director, or producer. These were rare, but one case can be cited. Iraj Qaderi, who had directed and acted during the Pahlavi era, was banned for over a decade. However, after publicly admitting to and repenting of his "sin" of participating in the "pseudo-cultural . . . and calculated propaganda" of Pahlavi cinema, he was allowed to return to the country, but only to direct movies, not to act in them.[74] The ban could also be medium specific, as in the case of Shabnam Toloui, an actress in the television serial *No Comment* (*Bedun-e Sharh*). When she was asked to fill out a detailed employment form, containing many personal questions, including religious affiliation, she identified herself, against the advice of friends, as follower of Baha'ism, a faith to which she had converted, as she had been born in a Muslim family. She was therefore banned from working at VVIR. However, she continued to act in theater and cinema, including in Marziyeh Meshkini's film *The Day I Became a Woman* (*Ruzi keh Zan Shodam*, 2000), until she was banned from work in all the performing arts. "I could not do any other work. All doors were closed to me," stated Toloui in an interview with Voice of America. "In my private life, too, I had somehow reached the end point—the point of zero—a lone woman without any possibility of making a living." Like many other performers, she was forced to choose exile, in France.[75]

Susan Taslimi, an accomplished and versatile actress, was forced to leave the country because of the impediments the government placed in her professional life. In 1980, she was expelled from the City Theater after she wrote a letter objecting to a reduction in actors' pay and to forced Islamicization of the theater, which required, among other things, the use of revolutionary stories, topics, and characters—ones who were more stereotypes than individuals with subjectivity. The two revolutionary-era movies she made with the director Bahram Baizai—*Ballad of Tara* (*Cherikeh-ye Tara*, 1978) and *Death of Yazdegerd* (*Marg-e Yazdegerd*, 1980)—were both banned permanently (they are still banned), while the screening of two later films she made with Baizai—*Bashu, the Little Stranger* (*Bashu, Gharibeh-ye Kuchak*, 1985) and *Maybe Another Time* (*Shayad Vaqti Digar*, 1987)—encountered many difficulties with the censors. Finally, when Farabi Cinema Foundation authorities viewed some of the preliminary rushes of Ali Zhekan's movie *Madiyan* (*Mare*, 1986), in which Taslimi had starred, they objected to her colorful costumes and her "powerful presence and penetrating eyes," adding, "This woman has become too powerful, she has become dominant." Her physical beauty, which magnified her presence, proved to be an additional drawback. The authorities assigned a minder to monitor her acting and costumes during subsequent filming. Taslimi narrated what followed.

> They told me not to look into the eyes of my male counterpart, to look down when I talked to him. I replied, "How is this possible? I can't look away from the person to whom I am speaking." They replied, "No matter, you should not look." My minder kept an eye on this situation as well as on my costumes. He even dictated that the camera angle be ugly

and the color of my costume be dark and drab, all of which you see in the film.

Thus hemmed in by tightening rules and narrowing possibilities, she emigrated to Sweden, where, after a period of confusion and recuperation, she established herself as a successful Swedish theater and film actor, director, and cultural administrator.[76]

The theater and film actress Farzaneh Taidi, who had acted in Hosain Rajaiyan's upper-class angst film, *The Eighth Day of the Week* (*Hashtomin Ruz-e Hafteh*, 1973), and in Masud Kimiai's anti-imperialist movie, *The Earth*, relates another story of disorientation, harassment, and escape from Iran. Her narrative begins two years before the revolution, when "low employment surfaced, first in cinema and then in theater. Because of this and the resultant anomie, a certain kind of confusion emerged, followed by distrust. . . . The atmosphere was so confusing, chaotic, and full of ambiguity and doubt that people were distrustful of each other and of the future" (quoted in Rusta, Matin, Javidi, and Mohajer 2008:378, 381). In 1980, Taidi was subjected to the purification process: the Ministry of Culture dismissed her from her position as an actress after eighteen years of employment as such, the ostensible reason being that "she was no longer needed." She received this verdict after two years of inquiry conducted by an official who, in the emerging fashion of Islamic mannerisms, averted his eyes from her during the dismissal process but gazed at an imaginary point in the space near her. As it turned out, she was dismissed not because she had played immoral and sexual roles in the Pahlavi-era movies, but for her alleged Baha'ism. She had been born to a Baha'i father, who was an army officer, both associations having come to be regarded with suspicion; she was not a Baha'i herself, however, and she refused to recant in the daily papers or to state that she rejected this "despicable sect," as the authorities demanded (ibid.:387). To ward off the state's further incursion into their private affairs, she and her male live-in companion, Behruz Behnejad, engaged in an unusual ninety-nine-year "temporary marriage" contract. Soon, her face was banned, depriving her of employment in theater and movies. Unemployment, harassment, humiliation, poverty, and inability to obtain an official passport forced her after seven years to plan an escape from the country. "This was a forced exile. They gradually pushed us into it. We had no place, no money, nothing" (ibid.:399). Under the pretense of making a documentary film in southern Iran, having obtained fake official permits from the broadcasting authorities and traveling in disguise, she was smuggled into Pakistan, where she obtained a visa for Britain, where she joined her son and father, now deceased, in exile. Her partner joined her soon thereafter. That she later acted in Brian Gilbert's notorious anti-Iranian and anti-Islamic Republic movie, *Not Without My Daughter* (1991), may be understood in the context of this terrible back story and forgiven as a kind of revenge.

By banning the actors' and stars' voices, faces, and bodies and by legal and illegal harassments, impediments, lashings, and confiscations of their persons and properties, the new regime was not only going after the Pahlavi-era stars but also essentially dismantling its star system. It would take many years before newly minted postrevolution stars appeared in the cinematic firmament.

Technical and production crew also suffered purification, although not as severely or systematically as the performers. In mid-1982, a pro-Mojahedin group of "committed and combating" filmmakers complained in a letter to the PMOI leader Masud Rajavi that due to the policies of the regime, the "toiling workers of cinema" had become unemployed and were forced to make a living by selling cigarettes and chewing gum in the streets.[77] This atmosphere cast a pall of despair and uncertainty over the entire entertainment industry, forcing many of its members to seek either internal seclusion or external exile.

The Politics of Transition to an Islamic Republic

With the departure of the Shah from Iran on 16 January 1979, and the installment of a civilian interim government headed by Prime Minister Shapur Bakhtiar, filmmaking activities commenced in earnest. The dreaded and despised Savak was dissolved. However, Bakhtiar's official secular government existed side by side with a parallel, more powerful, informal, religious government, headed by Khomeini, which eventually overpowered and outmaneuvered it. In February 1979 the Bakhtiar government fell and he escaped to France, where, it is alleged, Iranian government agents eventually assassinated him. The Islamic Republic was officially formed in April, based on a national referendum, which allowed only a yes or no vote. Summary executions of Pahlavi-era officials followed.

On 3 March—that is, even before the establishment of the Islamic Republic—Khomeini announced that women could not serve as judges; on 6 March he ruled that women were to wear the hijab in the workplace. Women, whose active participation had been instrumental in the success of the revolution, now demanded in growing demonstrations that their equal rights be respected. However, two days after Khomeini's hijab declaration, one such demonstration was famously disrupted by Islamist roughnecks and others who rushed the women, shouting, "Ya rusari, ya tusari!" (Cover on the head, or a blow to the head!).

Sartorial reforms included the imposition of the hijab for women. In general, male attire became both militarized, due to the war with Iraq, and pauperized, due to the antimaterialistic and populist Islamicate values and the rise of the dispossessed and the barefoot as the champions and symbols of the revolution. Military jacket, camouflage outfit, unkempt beard, and disheveled appearance became popular with young males, a sartorial fashion that was reflected in fiction movies. For at least a decade, the modern "Westernized dandies" gave way to "scruffy chic," the Islamicate dandies. Over the years all sartorial rules, including the official ones dealing with the veil, underwent major modifications toward liberal interpretations, particularly with the end of the war, the death of Ayatollah Khomeini in 1989, the cooling down of revolutionary ardor, and the failure of successive Islamist governments to deliver on their social promises.

With the admittance of a privately ailing Shah, who was suffering from an advanced case of non-Hodgkin lymphoma, to the United States, in October 1979, the Iranians, fearful of another American-engineered coup to return him to power, took over the sprawling American embassy compound in Tehran on 4 November and held some fifty diplomats and others hostage—an ordeal that lasted 444 days and toppled Mehdi Bazargan's secularly Islamic interim government. This was a turning point. Internally, it was tantamount to a second revolution, or a creeping coup, which ensured the Islamists' hold on power. Externally, it led to Iran's isolation, which lasted for the rest of the period under study here, with unforeseen positive and negative consequences for culture and cinema. By the end of 1979, border clashes with Iraq escalated into an all-out war when Iraq invaded Iran, a war that lasted eight years, reportedly causing half a million casualties on each side. Meanwhile, the exiled "homeless" Shah was forced to travel from country to country seeking what he hoped would be temporary residence. He succumbed to complications from his cancer in July 1980, in Cairo, Egypt, at the age of sixty.

For those prerevolution filmmakers who did not go into either external exile or internal exile and who wished to revive their professional careers, the situation was complicated. The attempts by Reza Safai, the veteran director, producer, writer, editor, and actor of filmfarsi movies, to revive his career is illustrative of the period. As he tells it in his autobiography, soon after the revolution Mohammad Ali Najafi, the head of MCIG's Cinematographic Affairs Office, invited him to jumpstart his career by making *Uprising* (*Qiyam*, 1979–80), about a revolt against a feudal landlord with connections to the Savak. Surprisingly, his troubles began not with the production of the film, but with its exhibition.

The review committee, on which Pahlavi-era filmmakers such as Abbas Shabaviz and Manuchehr Mosairi served, refused to give *Uprising* an exhibition permit, on the grounds that it was a copy of the despised prerevolution filmfarsi movies, with added revolutionary slogans (Safai 2001:179). Soon, articles attacking him appeared in newspapers, and he was summoned before a revolutionary committee headed by Haji Tehrani, a friendly interrogator who was subsequently assassinated. Months later, a committee that included Student Followers of the Imam Line (the group that took the Americans hostage) and was headed by Hojjatoleslam Moini Shirazi, and that was responsible for reviewing the suitability of pre- and postrevolution movies, approved the film. However, without MCIG's exhibition permit, the film could not be screened in public movie houses. Moini Shirazi interceded and an official permit was issued. This resulted in wide screening of *Uprising*, which appeared in twelve movie houses in Tehran and which generated a respectable twelve million tomans box-office (indicating that some six hundred thousand spectators had seen it).

The honeymoon was soon over, however; by 1982 the exhibition permit for Safai's movie and those for 790 other movies were canceled (Safai 2001:188). Obtaining a new permit sent Safai, with his prerevolution commercial movie record as a liability, into the evolving Kafkaesque bureaucracy of the Islamist regime. Apparently, he was not officially charged with ideological, political, or criminal wrongdoings. Nevertheless, because of the negative regard in which commercial movies and moviemakers of the Pahlavi period were held, Safai was unable to absolve himself, despite his perseverance and appeal to influential ayatollahs, law courts, the Majles, the minister of Culture and Islamic Guidance, and even the president's office.

It took years for the doors to open to him again. When they did, it was not at MCIG but at its rival, the Voice and Vision of the Islamic Republic, where in the 1990s he was put in charge of producing two film serials, *Springtime* (*Baharan*) and *Future* (*Atiyeh*), and a feature TV movie, *Mission* (*Mamuriat*) (his Hajj pilgrimage to Mecca may have helped). By 1996, the prohibition against the former regime's filmmakers had reportedly been lifted, but Safai did not receive his official clearance until 2000 (Safai 2001:257–59). The new-wave filmmakers did not carry the same moral and political stigmas. Because of their history of dissident moviemaking, they were regarded highly—though suspected of secularism, communism, or agnosticism. Those new-wave cineastes who stayed behind—Taqvai, Baizai, Kimiai, Shirdel, Sinai, Naderi, and Kiarostami—became instrumental in creating a dynamic postrevolution art cinema. Those relatively apolitical new-wave directors who went into external exile and returned within a few years, such as Kimiavi and Mehrjui, were also revived and contributed to the new art cinema. Even Farmanara, who on his return was initially harassed and threatened, was later allowed to make films that garnered the top film awards of the country.

After their restoration, however, each of these directors faced his share of individual difficulties under the new Islamist regime. There were new-wave directors or dissident filmmakers who went into exile voluntarily, or were pushed out legally or illegally, and who sought political asylum or residence in Europe and North America: Parviz Sayyad, Barbod Taheri, Amir Naderi, Masud Asadollahi, Asadollah Niknejad, Rafiq Pooya, and Reza Allamehzadeh. Myriad producers, performers, entertainers, talk-show hosts, and technical personnel also emigrated, together forming the backbone of a new deterritorialized cinema and culture—an Iranian accented cinema and culture.

Finally, the politics of transition and consolidation to an Islamicate society, culture, and cinema did not end with the transition period examined in this volume. It had to be reiterated over and over during the lifetime of the Islamic Republic in the next thirty plus years because the opposition to such panoptic control of society and culture kept emerging and evolving. This opposition took different individual and group forms, and it came in fits and starts and in waves. As a result, the muzzling, purging, censoring, harassing, imprisoning, torturing, and exiling of intellectuals and filmmakers continued, escalating into a pitched social and cultural battle in the aftermath of the disputed reelection of Mahmoud Ahmadinejad to the presidency, in 2009.[78]

DOCUMENTING THE UPRISING,

THE REVOLUTION, AND THE

EMERGING OPPOSITION

In the initial phase of revolution, when Pahlavi-era film culture was under attack, a movement to document the anti-Shah uprising emerged. Freed from censorship and fired by revolutionary ardor, a "spring thaw" ("spring of freedom," in Persian) came about. Imagination became a fact of life. While filmmakers were united in their opposition to the Pahlavi regime, they differed in their ideologies, modus operandi, and political affiliations, resulting in a wide variety of films. This chapter focuses on the documentaries that were made during the uprising and the full-blown revolution as well as in the immediate aftermath of these social upheavals, as opposition to the Islamicization of the revolution grew. Several major issues and genres of documentaries that emerged in this period are identified and examined.

International journalists and domestic filmmakers blanketed the incipient revolution with media—the latter using equipment and raw stock "liberated" primarily from NIRT's networks and its film subsidiary, Telfilm, and from MCA—to record strikes and demonstrations. The official logos of these state institutions on the equipment gave the filmmakers cover and opened doors to them. There was a great deal of excitement in the air and much danger in covering this once-in-a-lifetime occurrence. Cinematographers used any and all raw film stock they could get their hands on and any gauge of film and video from any source. The lower-gauge formats dominated. Scores of films were made, many unaccounted for. Majid Jafari Lahijani in his extensive work on filming the revolution discusses over two hundred documentaries that were made between fall 1978 and fall 1980 (Jafari Lahijani 2008:vol. 1:149). Some of the filmmakers formed groups reminiscent of the "film committees" during the 1917 communist revolution in Russia. Late at night and early in the morning, they made plans using information from revolutionary groups, including from NIRT's "revolution committee." Small film crews were then dispatched to cover ongoing events nationwide, creating spontaneous, collective coverage.

Television Cameramen and Others Cover the Uprising

As the documentary cameraman Manuchehr Moshiri told me in an audiotaped letter, a NIRT cinematographer named Mahmud Bahadori was perhaps the first professional cameraman to begin filming the rising tide of the revolution. Moshiri, then a cameraman at NIRT, assisted him. Using NIRT's 16mm Éclair cameras and negative film stock, smuggled out thanks to sympathetic producers, they filmed the demonstrations leading to the 8 September 1978 tragedy known as the Zhaleh Square Massacre or Black Friday.[1] The massacre itself, documented by a cameraman from a nearby high-rise, galvanized anyone who saw the footage of people being mowed down by gunfire. With the widening of the uprising and quickening of its pace, Moshiri and Bahadori decided to break into two film crews to better cover events. Late in October, Bahadori filmed the release of political prisoners from the notorious Qasr Prison to their jubilant relatives. The most historically valuable footage was his interview with Safar Qahremani, who was reputed to have spent the longest time in jail as a political prisoner—some thirty years. "He was a young man when he went in, and now he was an old man. I remember while he was being taken to his daughter's apartment from jail, he asked in a bewildered state, 'What is this apartment thing you are all talking about?' He had not seen one before." In the course of filming, Moshiri and Bahadori encountered Asghar Shahdust (Fardust), an Educational Television (ETV) cameraman, who was also filming the uprising, using ETV's equipment. "In a meeting in a coffeehouse, we decided to join forces and to create a third film group."

Another NIRT news cameraman, Parviz Nabavi, filmed the massive anti-Shah demonstrations near Tehran University on 4 November 1978 (13 Aban 1357), in which a student was shot dead. NIRT's First Channel aired 7.5 minutes of footage of the incident, known as the University Event (Hadeseh-ye

Daneshgah), on its flagship national newscast. Allocating so much news time to an incendiary event was highly unusual; some thought that this was because the regime's ironclad control of both country and media was slipping. However, it appears that it was instead due to a policy of openness by the new director of NIRT, Nasereddin Shah Hosaini, who wanted no censorship by the broadcast agency. Nevertheless, the film was so incendiary for its time, particularly because of the directly anti-Shah slogans, that Shah Hosaini did not allow the full film, which reportedly was either thirteen or twenty minutes long, to be aired. The reactions to this broadcast containing the first shooting death at the university was swift and at a high level. Abolfazl Qazi, minister of Science and Higher Education, resigned in protest over the treatment of university students by security services, and the mayor of Tehran, Javad Shahrestani, wrote a scathing letter to Prime Minister Jafar Sharif Emami, accusing him not only of being unable to control the affairs of the state, but also of lacking "understanding [of] the actual conditions of the country and the public opinion." Savak confiscated the only full copy of the reversal film, which was never to be seen again, and arrested some of the television personnel who had worked on it. Apparently, it was due only to the NIRT director Reza Ghotbi's intersession with the Shah that the five arrested personnel were released (Jafari Lahijani 2008:vol. 1:405–8).[2] To regain control, the Shah two days later appointed a military government headed by General Gholamreza Azhari and made a remarkably humble speech on national television, addressed to the "dear nation of Iran."

> In the name of your monarch, having sworn to protect the country's territorial integrity, national unity and Twelver Shia religion, once again I repeat my oath in front of the people of Iran and make a pledge that past mistakes will not be repeated. I further pledge that past mistakes will also be remedied in every way. I pledge that, after the restoration of order and peace, as soon as possible, a popular government for the establishment of fundamental liberties and holding of free elections will come into being so that the constitution which is the price of the blood spilt in the Constitutional Revolution will come into full application. I too heard the message of the revolution of you people of Iran . . . I guarantee that, in the future, Iranian government will be based on the constitution, social justice and popular will, and free from arbitrary rule, injustice and corruption. (Quoted in Katouzian 2009:319)[3]

A second remarkable feature of this nine-page speech—which fell on deaf ears and, at any rate, was never implemented by the Shah—is that it was written by none other than Reza Ghotbi, director general of NIRT and a close cousin of Empress Farah (allegedly aided by the philosopher Seyyed Hosain Nasr). The Shah apparently read from Ghotbi's handwritten manuscript, bearing many emendations, which is available on the Internet.[4]

One time, Moshiri, Bahadori, and Shahdust traveled to Qazvin, an ancient city west of Tehran, to cover a demonstration. The army had apparently attacked a line of people waiting for heating oil and had injured many. As soon as the film crew arrived on the scene, they began filming the melee, but they were quickly arrested. What saved them were the NIRT logos on their equipment and their cover story of an assignment valorizing security forces. Convinced that the film group was on their side, the soldiers and police let down their guard and spoke of their own moral quandary: they wanted to perform their professional duties by quelling the demonstrators, but some were sympathetic to the demonstrators' cause. "We became friends with them and began to understand the point of view of the military and police forces. We were surprised by the degree to which they were afraid. They were so fearful of public reprisals that they had removed their families from their homes and moved them into military dorms and barracks."

By the end of December, the troika filming groups decided to explore the possibility of exhibiting their extensive footage as unedited rushes. Informal guerrilla exhibition spaces had opened everywhere, in hospitals, mosques, and even in the streets. They turned to Filmsaz Studio, a well-known professional film lab, which had been shut down for several months due to lack of work. The studio director Masud Kalantari was sympathetic and he agreed to develop their footage.

Public fear seemed to have evaporated, presenting cinematographers with a quandary: to participate in the revolution or to film it. Mahmud Oskui, who filmed with Barbod Taheri *The Crash of '78* (*Soqut-e '57*, 1980), about the unfolding revolution, explained: "I first wanted to join the people and like them to shout slogans and participate in demonstrations. But after a bit of thinking I reached the conclusion that it is best to film these scenes so that they remain recorded in history. I think you can call me 'the cinematographer of the revolution.' I am proud that I visualized over three-and-half years of the history of that incredible time" (quoted in Jafari Lahijani 2008:vol. 1:299). In addition to professionals, many amateurs, most very young, filmed the streets with Super 8 cameras or took photographs (figs. 12–14). On the day the Shah departed Iran (16 January 1979), the troika was in a restaurant, and a shout from the street brought them out. "People outside were shouting that the Shah had 'escaped,' the entire street was jubilant and jumping with

"God has promised us victory
Down with the Shah!"

It's our day of victory today
though our martyrs are no longer with us

12–14 Professionals and amateurs filming the revolution. Frame enlargements from Hosain Torabi's feature documentary, *For Freedom*. The subtitles are from the film's soundtrack, which contains the speech Ayatollah Khomeini delivered after his return from exile.

do not spend a moment
in oblivion because

happiness. Naturally, we had our cameras with us or in our cars." Bahadori, Shahdust, and Moshiri filmed the overwhelming emotionality of the public at the Shah's departure.

Everyone impatiently awaited Ayatollah Ruhollah Khomeini's arrival from his exile in France. Moshiri filmed the city center, from Azadi Square to Behest-e Zahra Cemetery. In the square he filmed the hundreds of thousands of anxiously waiting people. They were very orderly, wanting things to go well. "As soon as Imam's motorcade entered the square it was as if an explosion had taken place. It became a special situation, all the ropes and railings were pulled off and people rushed to his car, creating a dramatic scene that I filmed," Moshiri recalled. The striking Muslim members of NIRT began broadcasting Khomeini's airport arrival on live television using three mobile units, but the transmission was stopped midstream due to internecine sectarian conflict with leftist members, auguring the larger social power struggle that was to come after the fall of the Shah. Interestingly, the live transmission of the event to the outside world was unaffected by this domestic squabble, thanks to NIRT's contract to supply the American television network ABC with a live feed (Jafari Lahijani 2008:vol. 1:42). In the meantime, the filming troika continued its documentation of the rising tide—including the revolts in the barracks, violent street fighting, and Khomeini's temporary headquarters at the Refah School—until the victory of the revolution on 11 February 1980 (22 Bahman 1358). A makeshift low-power local television studio, which used NIRT's liberated production equipment and a portable transmitter, was set up at the school, where Khomeini's pronouncements and interviews were filmed and aired. It was dubbed "Revolution Channel," a station that at first reached only the neighborhood around the school, but later expanded its coverage to Tehran; soon after 11 February it was integrated into the new Voice and Vision of the Islamic Republic (Jafari Lahijani 2008:vol. 1:52).

After that Moshiri and his cohorts filmed less and devoted more time to trying to release their footage from Filmsaz Studio, which was awaiting payment for the work it had performed. They approached Sadegh Ghotbzadeh, new head of the successor to NIRT, VVIR, proposing that the television organization pay for the cost of processing so that the valuable historical footage they had filmed could be transferred to its vaults for safekeeping and for use in future films. "No one was taking this seriously," intoned Moshiri. In the meantime, foreign broadcasters and filmmakers from around the world congregating in Iran were interested in purchasing their footage. However, Moshiri comments, "I was insulted by the suggestion that we sell our valuable documents, even though we needed the money to gain their release." Torabi also states that a reporter for CBS News in the United States offered to purchase, for $100,000, his footage of the Shah's tearful departure from Iran, which appeared in his film *For Freedom*, but it was an offer he refused (Jafari Lahijani 2008:vol. 1:174). Moshiri's sense of outrage stemmed from his notion—shared by many documentarians of the revolution—that what he and the others had filmed was not ordinary footage belonging to individual filmmakers, but a set of historical documents, almost sacred icons of a great heroic act of the nation, which should be preserved, not sullied by mundane capitalist exchanges. After months of perseverance, VVIR finally paid for the processing: "Bahadori and I stuffed nearly forty hours of our negatives into gunny sacks and delivered them to the television lab."

Not all filmmakers had the same reverential sentiments about their footage. Oskui, who filmed with Taheri *The Crash of '78*, states that most of the footage of the revolution he filmed for over three years was sent to Visnews and Reuters, for whom he worked as a stringer, receiving $250 for each assignment. He later became a Visnews employee and emigrated to Britain, where he worked in the editing department (Jafari Lahijani 2008:vol. 1:299, 302, 312). News reporters and technicians of American broadcasting networks, CBS, ABC, and NBC, each established their headquarters in the Intercontinental Hotel (now Laleh), where they would edit the news footage of their own camerapeople and their local stringers (shot on reversal film stock) and send them via VVIR satellite uplink to their home organizations.

The fall of the Evin Prison, in February 1979, to the revolutionaries became an occasion for a film that demystified this notorious and horrifying prison, the site of interrogation, torture, and execution of scores of dissidents. Parviz Nabavi directed and filmed *Pahlavi's Justice (Adl-e Pahlavi,* 1979), a forty-one-minute film that for the first time entered the prison complex to show what its various spaces and departments looked like. Majid Moini, a PMOI member who had been tortured and spent years in the Evin Prison, acts as the on-camera tour guide, buttressing the visual documentation of torture chambers and residence halls with his own graphic recollections of the horrors of prison life under the Shah.[5]

As is common in collective filmmaking, particularly one as ad hoc as this, division soon surfaced. Shahdust wished to edit the footage into a long film and cut the negatives to prepare a release print for screening in movie houses, which had been closed down; he thought that this would make a great opening film for the revived cinemas. Moshiri and Bahadori disagreed vehemently with the idea of tampering with the negatives. Nevertheless, Shahdust brought in the ETV editor Davud Kan'ani, forged ahead with editing and cutting the negatives, and made the 144-minute compilation film *The Pulse of History (Tapesh-e Tarikh,* 1980), which covered the revolutionary events from 8 September 1978 to February 1979, using a politically strident voice-over narration, which does not match the relatively evenhanded visuals and editing. Shahdust states this about the editing process of the film: "[Kan'ani and I] lived a full four months in the editing room, where we sometimes slept the night. During this time, we did not have a normal life. Of course, we did all this, whether during or after the revolution, on a voluntary basis, without getting paid or being sponsored by anyone" (Jafari Lahijani 2008: vol. 1:209). This film, too, like *For Freedom*, contains much unique historical footage, such as the Shah's mea culpa broadcast. However, as Moshiri narrated to me, "Bahadori and I disagreed with what Shahdust had done intensely, and we asked him not to use our names as co-directors, but credit us only as cinematographers. It was not a good documentary anyway, and had a very cursory interpretation of events; it was only good for filing away on the archive's shelf. I am sorry that such important historical records were cut and mutilated. All that remains of it for me is the memory of an exciting and important period in our lives." According to Moshiri, Bahadori agreed with his assessment of the situation when he was alive.[6] Apparently, *The Pulse of History* was not aired on television and was rarely screened in its entirety in public (and only in high-art institutions). Kan'ani stated that this was because a panel in the international-relations department of NIRT had decided that "the Islamic aspect is not sufficiently emphasized in the film" (quoted in Jafari Lahijani 2008:vol. 1:248), while Shahdust noted, "Every week, every day, or every minute that passed beyond the revolution, the screening of such films faced additional difficulties." The political situation was changing so fast that the film could become a liability for them. "We decided not push the film or to reveal our participation in it, because we saw that there was a real risk of death in doing that" (ibid.:216). Nevertheless, various television channels showed excerpts from *The Pulse of History* on the regularly celebrated anniversaries of the revolution.[7]

Many of those who filmed the revolution knew each other, or knew of each other, and in some cases they collaborated or even exchanged footage with each other. Asghar Shahdust, for example, states that while editing *The Pulse of History* he exchanged with Barbod Taheri, the director of *The Crash of '78*, some footage that each needed. He gave Taheri footage of fires in Tehran on 14 Aban 1357 in exchange for Super 8 footage of the massacre of the Black Friday on 17 Shahrivar (Jafari Lahijani 2008:vol. 1:202).

Non-NIRT cameramen also filmed the tumultuous events widely across the nation, some turning them into films inside the country and some outside.[8] In early 1978, Asghar Rafii Jam, a cinematographer for Ayat Film, shot the rising revolution on nearly 30,000 feet of 35mm film (Haidari 1997:429), and another Ayat cinematographer, Hojatollah Saifi, took many hours of 8mm film. Mohammad Ali Najafi, at the head of Ayat Film Studio, released the eighty-five-minute film *The Night of Power* (*Lailat al-Qadr*, 1978), about the roots of the revolution, which included compelling compilation footage of the early revolutionary days that he, Rafii, Saifi, and others had filmed, much of it with Super 8 and 8mm cameras, such as the powerful scenes of people performing their ablutions in the street gullies and praying in massive numbers in the streets, sidewalks, and squares of Tehran (in addition to covering all the dramatic milestone events of the revolution).[9] When the Shah declared martial law, Najafi, the writer and cinematographer Fakhreddin Anvar, and the producer Mostafa Hashemitaba took all their exposed Super 8 footage to London, where they processed and edited it, adding to the film's soundtrack the many rhythmic chants that demonstrators had shouted, recreating both the powerful soundscape of the oncoming revolution and the poetic sensibility of Iranians. They returned home with an intermediate print after they heard of the unexpected triumph of the revolution. Ayat Film members Najafi and Anvar were appointed to high positions within MCIG and VVIR, respectively, and they hired a powerful film distributor, who duplicated and distributed the film widely to urban and rural cinemas (Jafari Lahijani 2008:vol. 1:313–20).

One cleric who filmed the revolution was Abbas Salehi, who headed the Thar Art Group in the city of Arak. He codirected and coedited *Till Victory* (*Ta Piruzi*, 1979) with Mehdy Haqqi. The codirectors and other cinematographers of the group filmed the revolutionary events with half a dozen Super 8 cameras, which after editing and transfer to 16mm, was exhibited in mosques in Qom and Tehran and broadcast by VVIR. By all accounts, Salehi was a brave and agile cinematographer, who had been shot at several times and was arrested by the Shah's forces. After the success of the revolution, he and the Thar Art Group moved from clandestine activity to open engagement, organizing filmmaking classes for the youth under the tutelage of the education ministry. In 1980 he was killed in the Iraqi war front, becoming the third martyr of his group (Jafari Lahijani 2008:vol. 1:388–90).

Very few professional women are known to have filmed the revolution. One was Mehrnaz Saeed-Vafa, who against the wish of her conservative father had gone to the London Film School and become a film professor at NIRT's College of Cinema and Television. She took photographs and shot 8mm films of the burning tires, scattered demonstrations, revolutionary banners, destroyed movie theaters, liquor shops, newspapers of the time, and television programs. As she told me, "I walked every day along with demonstrators on sidewalks, mainly going toward Azadi Square [previously Shahyad Square]. Sometimes to get a high angle view, I would ask young men (Islamist guards or demonstrators) who were on top of trees to get a shot for me. At other times, such as during the women's demonstrations and *Ayandegan* newspaper demonstration at Tehran University, I had to run away to save myself from oncoming brick attacks" (Naficy 2006d). She often hid the camera under her chador. Since her 8mm camera was silent, she recorded the sounds of revolution, including chants, on a separate cassette recorder. She was shot on the day in which the army surrendered and the people ransacked the police stations and military barracks and took away their arms and ammunitions. The people rode around Tehran streets in minivans and pickups, brandishing their newly acquired arms, showing off, and celebrating by shooting into the air, "just like the wild west." That day, one of the stray bullets ricocheted off a building and wounded Saeed-Vafa in the back.

To consolidate its rule, soon after the success of the revolution the new government required that all civilians return their arms to the government and more remarkably, to turn in all the footage they had filmed of the revolution. Many filmmakers did so, among them Mohammad Bozorgnia, who turned in some 20 rolls of 16mm film (about 30 minutes) (Jafari Lahijani 2008:vol. 1: 447). Saeed-Vafa, however, sent some of her footage and audiocassettes out of the country and hid the rest in her home, where they were lost when it was sold in absentia (Naficy 2006d). The only legacy of her filming is the footage she used in her documentary *A Tajik Woman* (1994), made in exile, showing women demonstrators marching and chanting pro-Khomeini slogans and unfinished high-rise buildings with their wall-less floors stacked with thousands of demonstrators and onlookers.

The French-trained new-wave filmmaker Parviz Kimiavi, who worked for NIRT, also filmed hours of the uprising. His troubles began, as he told me in an interview, immediately after the revolution, when he participated in demonstrations and strikes at the station against the new regime. He has also claimed that these troubles were due to a personal hostility that Ghotbzadeh had toward him, which was rooted in the fact that Kimiavi had challenged Ghotbzadeh's authority as the gatekeeper of Khomeini during his exile in France (Jafari Lahijani 2008:vol. 1:95). Whatever the real motive, the nascent Islamic Republic imprisoned Kimiavi, until pleas by famous leftist international film directors and stars, such as Constantin Costa Gavras, Simone Signoret, and Yves Montand helped lead to his release. Soon after, in 1981, he left for exile in Paris, where he worked in French television for over a decade before returning to Iran (Naficy 1989:92–93).[10]

Using 16mm film stock and equipment borrowed from NIRT's Telfilm, Dariush Mehrjui and his cameraman Shahrokh Majidi filmed hours of street demonstrations, movie house burnings, and hit-and-run street battles between revolutionaries and security forces, including the aftermath of the Black Friday. As Mehrjui told me, Telfilm processed all the footage, but it was never edited or screened publicly, because "by the time I was finished filming I had become disappointed by the outcome of the revolution." He noted that this historic footage now resides in the VVIR archive. During filming, his crew ran into others filming the events, including Kamran Shirdel. "Everyone was filming," he said. Mehrjui and Kimiavi had had an earlier filmic encounter with Ayatollah Khomeini that is worth noting. While Khomeini was residing in exile in Neuphle le Chateau, outside Paris, Mehrjui and Kimiavi interviewed him several times, with Kimiavi filming and Mehrjui interviewing. "Parviz slated the film by clapping his hands in front of the Ayatollah's face, holding one finger and saying, 'Ayatollah Khomeini, take 1.' Because we were not fully ready we had to slate the scene three times very close to the Ayatollah's face, who held a quizzical but bemused smile about our filming ritual" (Naficy 2008). Khomeini would soon become a master user and manipulator of the media.

Other new-wave feature filmmakers documenting the revolution were Shirdel, Mohammad Reza Aslani, Barbod Taheri, and Khosrow Haritash. Haritash told me that he preferred to work alone with a hand-wound portable Bolex camera, because that way both he and the camera were more "mobile," not having to coordinate his filming with others (Naficy 1979d).[11] In addition, according to Moshiri, Haritash used the revolutionary demonstrations and activism as background for his features: he placed actors into crowds of anti-Shah demonstrators and filmed them as part of his fiction movies (Naficy 2005d). Shirdel, on the other hand, worked both alone and in collaboration with others, clandestinely and openly. Of his hit-and-run style of shooting, Shirdel remarked to me: "I can't believe how I came out of that experience ALIVE!" (Naficy 2005c; original emphasis). He filmed the events that led up to the revolution and some of the important political happenings that followed, including American hostages that were being held in the U.S. embassy in Tehran.[12]

Kamran Shirdel Films the Revolution
and the American Hostages

Thirty-nine at the time of the uprising, Shirdel later stated that the revolution "was not a strange event for me, as I expected it and even welcomed it, but there was also this fear that it may turn into a civil war." This is how Shirdel began his narrative to me. Going into the streets to film the rising tide of revolution had become a daily, "precise" routine for him. "Perhaps never in my life have I performed a job with this degree of precision: I was constantly worried that I might miss something by losing a piece of film." The birth of the revolution and the birth of his daughter coincided, forcing him to make a difficult choice between personal and social responsibility. He and his wife hoped that the baby's birth would not coincide with martial law hours. Luckily, they were able to get to the hospital early in the morning, but he was forced to make a choice: after delivering his wife to the hospital, he headed out to film. Only later did he return to see his newborn. He often carried with him one Super 8 film camera and two still cameras with many rolls of exposed and raw films bulging from his various pockets. As he followed the paths of demonstrations, mass prayers, and police actions, he would run into other filmmakers with cameras. That was how another revolutionary film group was formed, consisting of Shirdel, Mohammad Reza Aslani, and Mohammad Reza Moqaddasian.

Group members were both cameramen and participants in the revolution, rather than disinterested observers. They made history at the same time that they wished to document it. Like the other film groups, Shirdel and his group would meet early each morning to decide what to cover. Sometimes proximity or interest determined this, but many times the choices were ad hoc. Shirdel was assigned to film the Eshratiyeh military base in Tehran, as it was near his home. He filmed the dramatic fall of the base to the revolutionary forces from the roof of an adjoining house, where he shared the space with two revolutionary groups, one of them all masked, who were shooting at the base.

Rumors and informal networks of information were often reliable in pointing the cameramen to the sites of action. One morning, while in the Revolution Square, Shirdel heard that Tehran's infamous red-light district, the New City—also known as Fortress (Qal'eh), about which he had made Fortress: The Red Light District, which had been banned in the mid-1960s—had been torched.[13] He and Aslani were working together that day, and they began running down the street, south toward the New City, passing a ransacked brewery, all of its bottles and casks spilled, broken, and piled high in the street, creating a deadly and foul-smelling scene. Arriving at their destination, they found the New City under siege by the army, a siege that seemed to Shirdel to be politically motivated to arouse the anger of the revolutionaries. New City was a veritable small city, with residential homes, houses of prostitution, shops, mosques, movie houses, clinics, and burlesque houses, all aimed at entertainment and prostitution. "Here, I witnessed one of the most painful and bitter scenes of my life," Shirdel told me. "Poor, old women with tattered clothing, who were working as housekeepers in the New City's whorehouses, were running away from the fire with the only things they could carry with them—old, decrepit mattresses. As they were escaping the place, some bystanders kicked them, threw stones at them, or hit them over the head with sticks." A neighboring movie house was also on fire, with flames leaping through its box-office window. Brief, grisly scenes of the charred bodies of the prostitutes that Shirdel filmed at this time were later incorporated into compilation films of the revolution. This theater fire was another shameful act, like the Rex Cinema fire in Abadan before it, which was allegedly set by Islamist zealots to speed up the Shah's downfall and to purify society.[14]

Another memorable filming involved the story of a twenty-seven-year-old university professor, Kamran Nejatollahi, whom Savak had shot and killed on 23 December 1978 on the balcony of a Ministry of Higher Education building during a strike. Revolutionaries had smuggled his bloodied body in a rolled-up carpet and hidden it to prevent it from falling into the hands of security forces. Shirdel and cohorts, who were interested in making a film about Nejatollahi's murder, had filmed a re-creation of the murder scene with the help of university employees, but were now waiting to film the body. The revolutionaries, who intended to stage a proper public funeral for the body, were also waiting. However, no one seemed to know where the body was. Private contacts led Shirdel and Aslani to Imam Khomeini Hospital, where Shirdel alone was smuggled through a huge waiting crowd onto the hospital grounds. He was hidden inside the trunk of a car manned by a hospital driver who slipped through the security cordon around the hospital. With his heart in his throat, Shirdel listened to the security officers as they stopped the car, talked with the driver, examined his papers, then let him through without checking the trunk. Later, Shirdel declared this to have been "one of the most exciting moments of my entire life, before or since." After kissing Shirdel goodbye, the driver discharged him in the tree-lined grounds of the hospital where, alone, from behind the trees, he could film the arrival of Ayatollah Taleqani, who somehow managed to broker a peace that allowed the gates to open and let in the crowd. Finally, Shirdel was led into the morgue where Nejatollahi's body was being autopsied. He took a risky but effective tack: holding the camera to his eyes, he kicked the iron door of the morgue. Someone inside asked, "Who is it?" Shirdel confidently responded, "Open up, it is an insider." Suddenly the door swung open, "And I saw the beautiful face of that young man lying on the bed. It all happened in one instant. I entered the room as I pressed the camera button and filming. Just as soon, however, the doctor in the white smock who was conducting the autopsy shouted, 'Throw the son of a bitch out,' whereupon they kicked me out. I filmed the scene of my being thrown out and the door slamming into my face."

The historian Afshin Matin-Asgari witnessed what happened outside when Nejatollahi's body was released for the funeral procession to Behest-e Zahra Cemetery: "Army helicopters were flying above, tanks were stationed around hospital gates and soldiers were standing guard everywhere. We started our procession behind the slain hero's coffin, reminiscent of the scene of General Lamark's funeral in *Les Misérables*. . . . As the front lines approached the 24th Esfand Square [now Revolution Square] from the north, the soldiers opened fire. The crowd split up, with people fanning out in all directions into side streets. . . . I was in first row and directly in the line of fire" (2000:172–73). In the melee that followed, some 250 people were killed, including the *Los Angeles Times* reporter Joe Alex Morris Jr., providing another bloody milestone on the road to revolution. As Shirdel filmed the demonstrators walking and running alongside the ambulance containing Nejatollahi's body, soldiers opened fire on the demonstrators, scattering them, and Shirdel was thrown into a muddy gutter while still filming.[15] Taheri's *The Crash of '78* contains some footage of this vicious attack on the cortege.

Ordinary people, knowing the importance of recording for posterity the historic events, were helpful to the filmmakers. They hid them, fed them, and helped them escape over the rooftops and back alleys. A photo shop owner near Revolution Square gave away all of his raw film stock, providing it gratis to anyone who was filming the revolution, including Shirdel. Shirdel's encounter with one old lady echoes Moshiri's conception of his footage as sacred. Shirdel had been trying unsuccessfully to climb onto the roof of a bus-stop shelter in order to film an altercation a street away, when an old lady wearing the hijab arrived. Realizing his predicament, she told Shirdel: "Young man, go ahead and climb onto my shoulders." He demurred and thanked her, causing her to utter an obscene expletive followed by an authoritative command: "I am telling you to get on my shoulders and film the damn scene." This encounter shook Shirdel, for her passion and commitment to record that moment equaled his own. Thanking her profusely, he refused again, offering as excuse his strapping size and the fact that he was loaded with equipment. He was "astonished" by this and similar encounters, which demonstrated the people's historical consciousness and their forbearance, good humor, and unity during the uprising.

Twice he was arrested while filming in the streets, but each time he was released by claiming that he was a NIRT employee, similar to Moshiri and other television cameramen. As the fall of the Shah neared and chaos increased, Shirdel asked a revolutionary committee to issue him a camera press card so as to avoid being arrested and harassed. Although the committee did not have a press card for cameras, like everyone else in those days they improvised: they took a picture of Shirdel and attached it to a card permitting its owner to carry weapons. Then, they crossed out the word "weapon" on the card, replacing it with "camera." The camera had literally replaced the gun, making real one of the stated dreams of the 1960s revolutionary filmmakers!

For a while, the Kodak Film Lab in Tehran processed Shirdel's and company's footage, but when the lab was closed, they turned to another technically proficient film friend, Homayun Paivar, who agreed to create a home film lab. Badie Film Studio's chief, Fuad Badie, told me that some of Shirdel's footage, which was stored at Telfilm, was lost when the Islamic Revolution committees took over Telfilm and imprisoned its director, Sassan Veissi, for a few months (Naficy 1979a). As a result, much of the 16mm footage that Shirdel had filmed at such great risk, using Telfilm's equipment, and stored at NIRT (Telfilm's parent organization) for safekeeping and later editing, was confiscated with the takeover of the company (perhaps that filmed by Mehrjui, also).[16] Neither the Islamic committees nor the network officials would later release the footage to Shirdel, claiming that he could not prove provenance. Some of Shirdel's 16mm footage later found its way, without proper credit, into other people's documentaries about the revolution. The fate of his Super 8 footage is another story, as it was processed in the makeshift lab that Paivar created in his house. He washed and developed the footage in tubs normally used for washing clothes, after which he hung the filmstrips on the clotheslines to dry, similar to what Moradi and Motazedi must have done at the dawn of cinema, during the Qajar period. As a result of these artisanal conditions, the image quality was not uniformly good, particularly for blowing up to larger formats for public screening. However, according to Shirdel in an e-mail interview, the footage was "superb," containing "great revolutionary scenes." In the meantime, he sifted through it with primitive equipment at home, discarding ruined scenes and cleaning, sorting, and storing the remaining lot for some future use, and perhaps for storage at the National Film Archive. Some of the Super 8 footage was shown only once, as part of the "Cinema of Revolution" program during a documentary film festival, with Shirdel present.

Shirdel's sympathetic filming of the uprising and the postrevolutionary events took him into some strange waters. Few people know that it was he and another cameraman who filmed the American hostages' "Christmas party" in 1979, when they were visited by three Christian clergymen from the

United States and one Algerian cardinal and were paraded before the cameras. The scared hostages announced to the world for the first time that they were alive, and with considerable unease denounced U.S. policies in Iran—as they had been instructed by the captors to do. Shirdel prefaced his story to me, which is being published for the first time, with this account.

> Of course the whole story as to *how* and *why* I was selected, where I was picked up to be guided to the American embassy where the hostages were kept, and then led into the room, where there was this tall but very poorly decorated Christmas tree, a table with some sweets (maybe also some candles and fruit), and the three young [American] clergymen who entered after we prepared the lights and positioned the cameras, is itself a very emotional and touching story!

Shirdel and the cameraman Mohammad Zarfam were blindfolded and led into the American embassy, then called "the nest of spies," and guided to the room where the Christmas "party" was to take place. Each was carrying a 16mm film camera. Once there, their blindfolds were removed, but they were told not to exchange any words with the hostages.

> I have to be precise and try to remember exactly what went on. As I remember it, each time a couple of the clergies went out of the room and returned with two or three hostages, whom they sat in the chairs at the table facing the cameras, exactly as we had instructed them. All the hostages were blindfolded when they entered the room. They were immensely agitated, pale, and nervous, with panic and tears in their eyes, especially the very young marines! I had the feeling that they thought they were being taken before a firing squad!
>
> There were no interviews or questions and answers! A Christian rite of Christmas Eve was held for each group. There were few Jews among the hostages who remained silent or very pensive during the ceremonies. After having some sweets and beverages, they introduced themselves and said a few words and, then, the whole sequence was over. We cut, but started filming again as soon as a new group was brought in and took its place. The process was repeated until all the hostages had been filmed. The last group consisted of women who seemed to have just been woken up, as they were very sleepy and tired. It was around 4:30 or 5 A.M. when the program was over.
>
> We filmed on 16 mm reversal stock, which we were given. After the filming, the captors took the film from us and, as I heard afterward,

the footage was taken under special escort to the VVIR's film lab for processing.

Immediately after the filming I walked to my house on Bahar Street, which was near, and went to sleep! I was tremendously shocked and was both sad and elated to have succeeded to do the job, as I knew the families of the hostages would soon see and try to TOUCH their children and relatives, although through the cold television screens!

The next day, at 4 P.M., I was picked up to go and assist in assembling and editing the footage and the sound tracks, which we did with precision and care (the editor was Manuchehr Oliai). It was late in the afternoon when we finished our task and the completed film was handed over to the person in charge of the "film chain" both to broadcast and to convert to video.

In the meantime, rumors were flying that there was a deal in the works between the head of Iranian broadcasting organization Sadegh Ghotbzadeh and his aides and the international news companies to sell the television rights of the film. I heard that the film was sold for a fantastic sum. Me, of course, I didn't receive a penny. I never thought in financial terms when it came to these kinds of assignments, never in my whole life! (Naficy 2005b)

The fifty-minute film was transmitted worldwide, with much fanfare, particularly by the commercial television networks in the United States, which aired segments of it in their nightly newscasts, identifying it as a film shot by Iranian TV. Longer versions were aired in their news specials, devoted entirely to the film and to its debunking. The NBC news special *Crisis in Iran: The Hostage Christmas*, hosted by Edwin Newman, aired the film on 31 December 1979, the same night as CBS's news special *The Hostages at Christmas*, hosted by Dan Rather, was aired. NBC called the film a "dog and pony show" and a "propaganda ploy" by hostage takers, while President Carter characterized it as "exploitative." CBS showed eighteen minutes of the film, in which American hostages read statements such as "The Shah was a puppet controlled by the U.S. government" and "U.S. was sabotaging Iranian agriculture by selling it the kind of fertilizer which destroyed the land on which it was used." On this special, a UCLA psychologist speculated that the hostages were under "persuasive coercion," while their family members claimed their loved ones were sending private signals to the effect that the whole thing was staged.[17] The film, which also included a statement by "Mary," who represented the "student" hostage takers, created controversy in the United States not only about its status as a "cynical propaganda ploy" to divert attention from the fact of hostage taking, but also about the number of Americans held captive, as only forty-three people had appeared on camera, not fifty, which was thought to be the tally (Naficy 1984b:61–63).[18]

Iranian state television, too, engaged in its own manipulative mediawork about the hostages. It frequently showed the blindfolded hostages in its newscasts. The former American embassy, the "nest of spies," had been turned into a center of anti-American demonstrations and a bazaar selling food, souvenirs, and literature. VVIR broadcast interviews with the students who supported "the Imam's line," showing also embassy interiors, luxurious quarters, high-tech intelligence equipment, and groups of students painstakingly pasting shredded diplomatic and confidential documents into readable books, which were published and sold outside the embassy compound. Nader Talebzadeh Ordubadi, an Iranian graduate student in film at New York's Columbia University, who was drawn to Iran to film the revolution, made the thirty-five-minute film *Reality* (*Vaqeiyat*, 1979), about the hostage crisis. It analyzes the sensationalist and negative news reportage about the hostages that the American television networks broadcast, using interviews with American reporters, Iranian student of the Imam's line, clerical leaders such as Ayatollah Beheshti, and viewers in the United States. This was one of the few intercultural films and was made possible by Talebzadeh's earlier media experiences. Because of his command of English and filmmaking, Talebzadeh had become a fixer for American television networks such as CBS News. According to him, these networks maintained large crews in Iran at the time, with CBS's group consisting of between thirty and forty members in addition to translators and guides. Their editors edited the day's news footage in the Laleh Hotel rooms, and uplinked them via satellite for broadcast in the United States the same day. Some of the CBS cameramen, like Tom Aspen, who later became a CNN reporter, were daredevils whom Iranians nicknamed "cowboys with cameras," an appellation that might have suited Shirdel as well. Talebzadeh made *Reality*, after he left CBS, due to his personal disenchantment with the way Western news media had turned sour on the revolution, which had acquired a hard-line Islamist character. He used his contacts with American networks to interview their reporters about their news coverage, and he used his contacts with VVIR and MCIG to gain access to these reports (a copy of which they were mandated to deposit with MCIG's international division). By juxtaposing the aired reports with his interviews with the reporters he revealed contradictions and biased views (Jafari Lahijani 2008:vol. 1:424–27).

Shirdel continued to make commissioned films as an independent filmmaker, mostly industrials. He made two "oil films"—*Gas, Fire, Wind (Gaz, Atash, Bad,* 1985–86) and *The Genaveh Project (Tarh-e Genaveh,* 1985–89)— both for the Oil Ministry.[19] His *Pars Wagon Factory (Vagon-e Pars,* 1987), *Exploring Foundation of Dispossessed and Veterans' Industries (Negahi beh Sanaye'-e Boniad-e Mostazafan va Janbazan,* 1988–89), *Exploring Panzdah-e Khordad Industries (Negahi beh Sanaye'-e Panzdah-e Khordad,* 1991–92), and *Mobarekeh Steel Company (Fulad-e Mobarekeh,* 1995–97) were all commissioned by the respective industries and organizations. Some of these industrial units became major supporters of documentary films. For example the Mobarekeh Steel Company established a documentary film center in 1983, which in the past two decades produced over twenty-five documentaries and many more news films, and it sponsored perhaps the first "industrial film festival," in the mid-2000s, in Isfahan, as a component of the city's International Short Film Festival (Mohassesi 2008).[20] These Shirdel films were industrial and institutional documentaries mostly in the "official style" of the Pahlavi era: an omniscient, unseen, male voice-over narrator provided information and historical context. Modeling Golestan and Pendry's oil movie, *Wave, Coral, Rock,* they sometimes waxed poetic. In fact, the more the visual register emphasized modernity, industrialization, steel, oil, iron, fire, and cement, the more the film's soundtrack veered to the softness and malleability of oral tradition and poetry.

In addition, Shirdel made at least two films for the Kish Free Trade Zone Organization. *The Sun's Cradle (Gahvareh-ye Khorshid,* 2000) is another institutional documentary, offering a treatise on the rich and long history of the ninety-square-kilometer Kish Island by invoking historians, poets, and archaeological sites and artifacts, from a millennium before Christ to 1989, when the first free-trade zone was created.[21] It also documents the industrialization of the island and the tourist industry. In the opening sequence a mysterious air cargo is delivered to the island; the treatment implies that the cargo is top secret: Soviet President Gorbachev, perhaps, or enriched uranium, or missiles. This is tongue-in-cheek, as the mystery cargo turns out to be dolphins and seals for the island's water park. *Solitude Opus 1 (Tanhai-ye 1,* 2000) is a shorter film shot on Kish, and not an institutional film. Rather, it is Shirdel's affectionate homage to the late director in exile Sohrab Shahid Saless, filmed in Shahid Saless's austere style—without narration, music, or words. It concerns the daily routines of Ali Rejai, the eighty-year-old bespectacled guardian of the island's Hur Hut (Kolbeh-ye Hur). It appears that while he is waiting by the seaside (like the characters in Shahid Saless's films), he is imagining other lives, such as one in which he is in charge of a complex for alternative energy. In true artisanal fashion, Shirdel wrote, filmed (with Siamak Pourafshar), recorded the sound, and edited the film.

Some of these films were censored, and with the rise of Islamist hardliners, most of them received only limited exhibition. Shirdel shared with me his analysis of his postrevolution career.

> I have not been very active as a social filmmaker anymore after the revolution, though I had great plans and projects at the start of the revolution! So far I have made many so-called commissioned industrial films for national oil, gas, and steel companies as well as for government ministries, in which I tried to bring the films as close as possible to my taste and to my way of thinking and make the films' sponsors to see the world from content and formal viewpoints. Some of these films encountered serious censorship problems and part of them were cut for their public screenings, such as *Gas, Fire, Wind* and *The Genaveh Project*, both of which were filmed during the Iran-Iraq war.[22]

Almost all of Shirdel's prerevolution social documentaries were both commissioned *and* banned by state agencies, so this situation was familiar. Nevertheless, the postrevolution difficulties were more disheartening for him, even though he maintained his critical irony: "In my self-imposed solitude and because of a very rooted and severe form of psychological deformation (this is my last diagnosis of my condition!) I chose to shoot and make my personal films in my mind and leave them on my mind's shelves; rather than have them banned, confiscated, and shelved by the Ministry of Culture and Islamic Guidance" (Naficy 2005b). His many years of making commissioned documentaries may have softened his oppositional ardor, for in some of his later films, such as *Mobarekeh Steel Company* and *The Sun's Cradle*, this filmmaker who had always questioned authority produced works that, if not exactly propagandistic, were at least positivistic. The dulling of his cutting edge was perhaps the ultimate price of his commissions. Ironically, during this same period, he began to be recognized widely, not only in Iran but also internationally, as the serious, creative, and incisive documentarist that he was.[23]

The revolution had turned the country into a fascinating, exciting, and turbulent "social laboratory" for filmmakers. The new-wave director Bahman Farmanara expressed this when, in May 1979, he told *Weekly Variety*, "I am part of a whole generation that never knew what freedom meant until the Revolution took place and we don't want to lose that freedom. For the intellectuals, the Revolution is just beginning; we have just removed the first obstacle. Our aim is to rebuild the culture of the country that was almost obliterated. . . . Iran is at last standing on its own feet with pride and once the situation settles down we can look forward to great cultural achievements" (Werba 1979:5). The revolution and the social changes that it brought were transformative, affecting its witnesses' personal lives, identities, and artistic work. Its impact was inscribed in all postrevolution films, fictional or nonfictional, about the revolution or not, and in all types of films discussed in these pages: official films, populist films, Savak films, art films, documentaries, war films, experimental films, women's films, and accented films. The revolution—and, later, the war with Iraq—haunted the movies in various forms, as documentary footage, documentary photographs, animated films (surprisingly, there were many of these), film re-creations in which actors played real people, film re-creations in which real people played themselves, films in which actors played fictional parts during the unfolding revolution, fictional films based on real events, or completely fictional stories inspired by revolution and war. The result of these hauntings was the mixing of real with imagined and fictional with nonfictional, which gave Iranian cinema one of its national cinema specificities.

Much of the documentary footage filmed with such euphoria remained just that—raw footage, or rushes, never edited into completed films. The footage that was edited encountered television's "purification" and Islamicization. vvir curtailed not only the secular and leftist filmmakers themselves, but also their films, many of which were opposed to the Islamic Republic. Films of the events that opposition groups staged and non-Islamic cameramen filmed either would not be broadcast or would be tampered with. For example, in early 1980, Mohammad Sadrzadeh, an experienced documentarian with leftist tendencies, objected publicly about the mutilation of his film *Battle of Sanandaj* (*Jang-e Sanandaj*), about the armed struggle of the People's Fadaiyan guerrillas (PFOI) against government forces in Gonabad. In a published letter vvir officials accused him of one-sidedness and promised to use his footage in a larger "comprehensive" documentary.[24] Similar limitations were enforced against news films about Kurdish guerrillas and the People's Mojahedin guerrillas (PMOI).

Television coverage by foreign broadcasters was also subjected to censorship, particularly as many relied on Iranian domestic satellite facilities. The massive women's demonstration in Tehran on 15 March 1979, to protest the imposition of the Islamic dress code, was not broadcast by vvir itself. Attempts by correspondents of the three American commercial television networks—ABC, CBS, and NBC—to transmit their reports of the event via satellite also encountered "technical difficulty" (Charles T. Powers 1979). Nevertheless, foreign reporters and cameramen were generally able to transmit much of what they filmed in Iran in the form of daily newscasts and periodic news specials and documentaries, which gave some sense of the revolution, a sense that grew both in volume and urgency with each event to create a massive, seemingly orchestrated antigovernment mediawork, particularly when the events involved American citizens.

Compilation and Historical Documentaries

Some of the diverse news footage that Iranians filmed during the early days of the uprising was compiled into raw sound and vision pieces that gave an inside view of unfolding events, countering naïve, prejudiced, stereotypical, or jingoistic Western mediawork. The Iranian footage, in turn, exhibited its own brands of naïveté and partiality. Some of this footage was broadcast by NIRT, now christened Voice and Vision of the Islamic Republic (VVIR, a.k.a. IRIB). A key requirement of the compilation genre is the availability of preexisting footage shot by multiple camerapersons at different times and places without prior planning and coordination. Compilation films are thus more dependent on editing than on planned filming. In fact, they are "made" during postproduction. The job of the film compiler is to locate, select, edit, and shape a vast trove of existing footage and sound—with some additional filming—into a coherent presentation according to an overarching idea. According to Jay Leyda, who coined the term *compilation film* (*film de montage*, in French), the term "would have to indicate that the work begins on the cutting table, with already existing film shots. . . . [It could] also indicate that it is a film of ideas, for most of the films made in this form are not content to be mere records or documents" (1964:9). The compilation genre came into its own in the West during wartime, particularly during the two world wars, and in filmic biographies of prominent figures, and it became a familiar form through television.

The diversity of events leading to the Iranian revolution and the plethora of filmed coverage created a situation suitable for the compilation genre and for its allied genre of historical films. I apply the term *compilation films* to those films that dealt strictly with the contemporary events of the revolution and the term *historical films* to those compilation films that ground their coverage of the revolution in the longer history of Iran. Many of the compilation films were no more than collections of amateur news films of various strikes, demonstrations, attacks, and counterattacks put together by novices or political groups without much film training and without much historical context. The emphasis was on the visuals of raw history in the making, accompanied by a soundtrack of live audio—the chanting and shouting of demonstrators, gunfire, and speeches—sometimes buttressed by a highly partisan and rhetorical off-camera voice-over by an omniscient male narrator. This emphasis on synaesthesia and on the phenomenology of the immediate experience was similar to the revolution's "Xeroxed literature," notable for "its tendency to paint the scene, to gloat in the sight, [and] to celebrate the event" (Ahmad Karimi Hakkak 1983:153). The overarching idea was the inevitability of the uprising, the success of the revolution, and the celebration of its success.

The historical films, on the other hand, took a chronological approach, contextualizing the uprising against the Shah and the unfolding revolution in the history of the nation's grievances. These relied on historical, archival, or library footage from internal and international sources. Some took a comparative approach, like prerevolution commercial movies, comparing the lavish life of the upper classes, including that of the royal family, with that of the poor and of shantytown dwellers, justifying revolutionary anger.

The compilation and historical genres were transnational in sources and circulation, reaching, particularly, Southern California, which became the center of Iranian exilic and diasporic media and pop culture. The transnational circulation of films and videos was the beginning of the process of horizontal and transverse exchange relations among Iranians in various countries and cities, which gradually transformed them from strict exiles, with cathected vertical relations to the homeland alone, into a diasporic population who maintained horizontal relationships with compatriot communities in various countries as well as with those in the homeland.

Freedom (*Azadi*, 1979) is an example of the compilation genre, filmed by anonymous cinematographers on Super 8 film and blown up to 16mm format, which VVIR broadcast several times. This is not an analytical or historical film; rather, it is a synaesthetic film given to emotional presentation of raw sounds and visions of revolutionary events from the Muslim factions' viewpoint. It has a "you are there" rough and tactile quality, with its well-integrated slogans, chants, songs, and dramatic images that symbolize both the dear cost and the joyful celebration of the revolution: A bullet hole in an empty boot lying in the street next to a pool of blood, people with bloody palms raised in the air, scores of young boys dancing on a captured tank, mutilated bodies, cemeteries so full of graves and so short of gravediggers that ordinary people are forced to dig the graves of their own loved ones, a civilian speeding by in a Mercedes-Benz with his torso sticking out of the sedan's window and jubilantly waving his arm that is holding a rifle. However, this film, which made a great deal out of clerical contributions to the revolution and of Islamic martyrdom, is technically amateurish: many of its shots are out of focus, and the dialog is at times cut off in mid-sentence by careless editing or technical problems. These amateur aesthetics add to the film's urgency, authenticity, and haptic synaesthesia.

Faramarz Baseri's *The Epic of the Quran* (*Hamaseh-ye Qoran*, 1980), made for MCIG and Dramatic Arts College, is a sixty-minute film about the revolutionary events, including the fiery destructions of Shahr-e Farang and Radio City Cinemas, that culminated in Ayatollah Khomeini's return. Asghar Bichareh produced, directed, and wrote the hundred-minute, 16mm feature documentary *Living Document* (*Sanad-e Zendeh*, 1979), which focuses on historical developments from the rise of Reza Shah, who established the Pahlavi dynasty, to the victory of the revolution and the plebiscite that established the Islamic Republic of Iran (IRI). Both films heavily rely on footage shot during the revolution, with the latter also containing archival footage. For *Bahman 22* (*Bistodovvom-e Bahman*, 1980?), Alireza Davudnezhad compiled photographs of the revolution, combining them with interviews with the parents of "martyrs." Ahmad Mowlavi produced and filmed *Iran, Iran, Iran* (1978?), a thirty-eight-minute film that contains rare footage of dramatic scenes of soldiers shooting at civilians running away, funeral marches, the sad and weeping faces of mourners of the revolution's martyrs, women and children participating in the revolution, colorful slogans held up and sung by demonstrators, the Shah's exit from the country and the populace's jubilation, lines of people awaiting Khomeini's return from exile, ending with his visit to the holy city of Qom accompanied by the chorus of "Iran, Iran, Iran."

Of the compilation films that traveled abroad as sources of news and as means of mobilization of Iranians in diaspora, several are worthy of note. *Days of Uprising in Tehran* (*Ruzha-ye Qiam dar Tehran*, 1979), a twenty-five-minute Persian-language film screened at UCLA in 1980 without any credits, presents the raw sounds and images of the events leading to the Shah's ouster and the triumphant return of the exiled Ayatollah Khomeini to Iran (the UCLA flier in figure 15 truncates the film's title to *Days of the Uprising*). It contains lengthy sequences of marchers carrying pictures of those killed, and of armed battles between insurgents and the Shah's forces in the street and on rooftops. It also includes rare footage of men and women carrying arms and fighting inside the notorious Evin Prison, a meeting of PMOI members, a meeting of PFOI members, and classes in the use of weaponry (fig. 15). Mehdi Shakiba's short *Happy Memories* (*Khaterat-e Khosh*, 1979), shown at the University of Southern California in 1980, is the director's undergraduate thesis

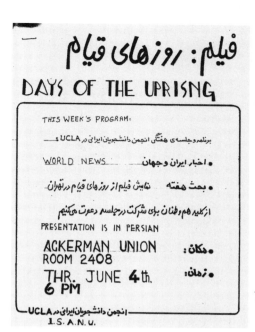

15 Flyer for the screening of *Days of the Uprising* at UCLA, circa 1980, sponsored by the UCLA branch of the Iranian Student Association (National Union). Collection of the author.

for Tehran University's School of Dramatic Arts. The film's narration is from the viewpoint of a man reminiscing about the Shah's ouster. It begins with large newspaper headlines about the Shah's departure into exile and the public jubilation at the news. It then chronicles the events leading up to Khomeini's return (including footage of him and his entourage in the plane) by focusing on demonstrations, exhibits of the Shah's "crimes," and various labor strikes. Of particular importance is the coverage of the strike of NIRT personnel, NIRT's role in the revolution, the appointment of its new director, the Khomeini confidant Sadegh Ghotbzadeh, and the preparation for the first postrevolution broadcasts. Shakiba, who was a NIRT cameraman, filmed some of his footage with a camera he had smuggled out. Davud Rustai's short film *We Are Men of War* (*Ma Mard-e Jangim*, 1979), made for the Cooperative Society of People's Art, focuses on the story of a boy who goes to a street peddler and rents a toy gun to shoot at a poster bearing the pictures of President Carter and the Shah, symbolically blinding them both. The film also contains footage of demonstrators wearing white shrouds of martyrdom outside the former U.S. embassy; street vendors selling books, magazines, and instruction manuals on weapons; and newspapers bearing headlines about the arrival of U.S.S. *Kitty Hawk* in the Persian Gulf.

The UCLA-trained leftist filmmaker Mohammad Sadrzadeh recorded footage of the unfolding revolution in his fifty-four-minute film *The Battle of Iranian People* (*Nabard-e Khalq-e Iran*, 1979), which he turned in to his employer VVIR, when Sadegh Ghotbzadeh headed the broadcast networks. According to Sadrzadeh, television authorities saw the film and praised it, but they asked for some changes. "I disagreed with them," states Sadrzadeh, and he replied to them: "I am turning over the film to you as it is edited; you know what to do with it" (quoted in Jafari Lahijani 2008:vol. 1:283–84). The television network never aired the complete film; instead, it aired it in edited sections, apparently because it contained sequences on Prime Minister Mohammad Mosaddeq and the revolutionary poet Khosrow Golsorkhi. The new film was retitled *Battle of Iran* (*Nabard-e Iran*), removing the leftist connotation of "the people" from the title, as was also done in the film. Ironically, this new film, whose authorship Sadrzadeh denies, was edited by his former UCLA classmate and then current fellow VVIR colleague, Reza Bakhtminu. In an interview, an American soundman, Susumo Tokomo, who worked with the filmmaker Bigan Saliani on a documentary about the revolution, told me that Sadrzadeh's footage was perhaps the most dramatic and "epical" of the early compilation films, since, unlike the others, much of Sadrzadeh's film was taken not from a high angle or from a distance, but in the midst of the action and at eye level, while he was running with the camera or facing soldiers with drawn weapons pointing at him (Naficy 1979g). The Iranian soundman Mahmud Samakbashi, who worked with Sadrzadeh, also says this of Sadrzadeh's personality and modus operandi: "He was a daredevil (*bikaleh*), he was fearless and would get the job done. He did not belong to any organization or group. He worked independently" (quoted in Jafari Lahijani 2008:vol. 1:254). In these features, Sadrzadeh's approach and footage resembled those of Shirdel. While filming at the intersection of Enqelab and Felestin Avenues, Sadrzadeh was shot by security agents. Though badly wounded, "I escaped limping, camera in hand. I did not want the film to fall into the agents' hands," he stated. He was bleeding profusely. People came to his aid and took him in a taxi to the Pahlavi Hospital, where the surgeons wanted to amputate his leg; he refused, and instead received fifty-five stitches. When released from the hospital, he immediately returned to filming in the streets, but since he could not walk, he perched on a van, which drove him around. The most moving footage is of the day the revolution toppled the regime, 11 February 1979, when Sadrzadeh stood face to face with the tanks in the streets and filmed them, or when he was on the phone telling his pregnant wife why he was late coming home and a bullet pierced the handset he was holding.

Sadrzadeh believes that his footage, which was distributed to Western news media, starting with Britain's Independent Television's TV *Eye* program, helped bring "a wave of supportive world public opinion for the revolution" (quoted in Jafari Lahijani 2008:vol. 1:284). He filmed the revolutionary events for four years, from 1977 to 1980, using a variety of 16mm and Super 8 cameras, often filming clandestinely to avoid official detection and harassment. The result was some fifty rolls of 400-foot 16mm film (about nine hours). Filmsaz Studio developed and printed his footage overnight, with him present and without charging him. Unusual among documentarists, Sadrzadeh owned the negatives himself and stored them in his own home and, later, during his fifteen-year stint working at the BBC, he stored most of them in the BBC vault for safekeeping (ibid.:293).

Hasan Tehrani made *Revolution as Narrated by Photographs* (*Enqelab beh Ravayat-e Tasvir,* 1979), a nineteen-minute film in which he compiled a collection not of film footage but of still pictures that the renowned Iranian-French photographer Abbas Attar (who goes by only his first name) had taken of the emergence of the revolution. Hosain Rajaiyan, another UCLA-trained feature filmmaker, who was living in Los Angeles at the time, compiled thousands of feet of the revolutionary protests by filming American newscasts directly from his home's television set. His intention was to make a documentary about the revolution. As he told me in interviews, while compiling these diverse news clips he realized that each segment, filmed on a different occasion and by a different network, began to assume a meaning beyond its original circumstance. His film idea "began to find its own path," giving meaning to the life of a filmmaker in exile, whose country was falling apart without him (Naficy 1979b, 1978). What would have made his film unique, had he finished it, were the sources of his footage, primarily foreign television newscasts. For many exiles, the television set became a fetish object because of its power both to invoke and to tame the homeland's traumas (Naficy 1993). During the revolution, many exiles had the set on and tuned to a news station at all times.

Masud Jafari Jozani and Majid Jafari Shirazi's compilation film *Toward Freedom* (*Beh Su-ye Azadi,* 1978–79) used a comparative editing scheme to contrast the poverty of the population at large with the opulence and arrogance of the Shah and the upper classes (footage of the latter was taken from films that were liberated from the Iranian embassy in Washington). Among the film's historically valuable footage is that of the televised military tribunal of Khosrow Golsorkhi and Keramat Daneshian, of tanks arriving in Tehran streets, of their destruction by Molotov cocktails, of the takeover of the U.S. embassy, and of the transformation of the Israeli embassy into the Palestinian embassy, which included Yasir Arafat's speech. Both filmmakers had been living in the United States, where Jozani had received a film-production degree from San Francisco State University, had done some filming for the local PBS station, and had filmed wild demonstrations at the White House, when Iranian students protested the Shah's visit to the United States, in the late 1970s. The demonstrators were tear-gassed, famously causing President Carter and the Shah to wipe tears from their own eyes. With the formation of the military government in Iran and the appointment of General Azhari as prime minister, both Shirazi and Jozani returned to Iran to join the uprising, where the latter used his status as a stringer for NBC News to film the revolutionary events. He soon returned to the United States to edit the Iranian footage he had brought with him (Tahaminejad 2000:127–28).

Mahmud Jafarian's fifty-minute film *What Was the Goal?* (*Hadaf Cheh Bud?*, 1978–79) also uses a comparative structure that pits Muslims against the Shah's autocratic, wasteful, Westernized regime. For example, the film begins with archival footage of the opulent 2,500th anniversary celebrations of the establishment of the Persian Empire and the Shah's famous promise to Cyrus the Great, who established the Achaemenian Empire: "Cyrus, sleep easy for we are awake." The film mobilizes compiled images of the people's revolution against the Shah from a Muslim point of view, covering most of the pivotal events, demonstrations, shootouts, destructions, and colorfully written and sung slogans that led to his downfall. This comparative structure continues throughout, the people's resentment and opposition is set against the background lavishness of the Shah's way of life, his palaces, royal planes, and ceremonies in which he crowned himself and the Empress Farah (these latter scenes are run in reverse, showing him removing the crowns).

Road to Victory (*Rah-e Azadi*, 1979) was a four-part, 156-minute compilation film that Hamid Hirbod, Nassib Nassibi, Hosain Taheridoust, Reza Aqili, Farideh Shafai, Reza Bakhtminu, and Mahasti Badii directed for VVIR. As expected from the genre, the sources of the footage used in this film was diverse, the most unusual source being the Super 8 footage that VVIR's "call for footage" had elicited from the public. The film also tapped into Torabi's film *For Freedom* and Shahdust's film *The Pulse of History*, as well as into Western newscasts of the revolution. Finally, it contained original footage of revolutionary activities, demonstrations, shootouts, and destruction. The provenance of the footage used came under fire, most notably by Hosain Torabi. In a letter to Hadad Adel, the Revolutionary Council's representative at VVIR, Torabi complained bitterly that while his film, *For Freedom*, had not been screened publicly inside Iran and had been praised abroad, it was now being cannibalized without permission or credit to make a new film, *Road to Victory*, which was being broadcast on the national channels, not in full form, but in mutilated segments. He ended his letter by asking, "Is it fair and just to trample so brazenly on the intellectual rights of a group of filmmakers in the government of fairness and justice such as that of Islamic Republic of Iran?" (quoted in Jafari Lahijani 2008:vol. 1:368). This charge of plagiarism, too, points to one of the pitfalls of the compilation genre, which necessitates ethics of the highest order in using and crediting the works of others.

Hirbod produced, directed, and edited another film on the revolution for VVIR, this one on its manifestation in the province of Kerman. Called *Iran in Revolution* (*Iran dar Enqelab*, 1980), this film was to be one episode of a multipart television documentary series examining the revolutionary struggles in the country's then thirteen provinces. Due to administrative problems, however, the other episodes were not filmed. That Hirbod began the series with the film on Kerman was both natural and practical: natural, because this was his hometown, whose history, people, and culture he knew well; practical, because Kerman had been one of quietest cities during the revolution, garnering less footage, which made it easier to produce a film about it (Jafari Lahijani 2008:vol. 1:395). One of the film's primary focuses is the massacre of peaceful protesters by the Shah's soldiers in Kerman's Jame' Mosque on 16 October 1978 (24 Mehr 1357), which the film dissects by means of interviews with eyewitnesses. Although Hirbod was unable to make further films about the revolutionary struggles in the provinces, several other filmmakers succeeded. Baqer Khosravi's *I Come from War-Torn Nahavand* (*Man az Nahavand-e Jangzadeh Miayam*, 1978–79?), focuses on the emergence during the Shah era of the Abuzar Group, a Muslim student group critical of the government's lack of morality and lack of attention to developing the Nahavand area, which turned to armed struggle. Among their actions were the torching of Taj (Crown) Cinema in the city of Nahavand and the killing of a policeman, which led to their arrest. Six members were subsequently executed. Sirus Qahremani's ninety-minute film *The Role of Gilan in the Movement* (*Naqsh-e Gilan dar Jonbesh*, 1978–79) deals with revolutionary actions in the northern cities of Rasht, Lahijan, and Fuman. Mehdi Sabbaghzadeh directed, filmed, and edited *Mashhad's Events* (*Vaqay'eh Mashhad*, 1978), which centers on the bloody events that took place in the winter of 1978 in the holy city of Mashhad. Sabbaghzadeh, who was head of Cinema-ye Azad's Mashhad branch, filmed with a Super 8 camera that he always carried with him scenes such as the burning of Shahr-e Farang (Peep Show) Cinema, the occupation of a top hotel, and the torching of the Pepsi-

Cola bottling plant—all symbols of the "decadent" Pahlavi regime (Jafari La-hijani 2008:vol. 1:400–401).

Among the most accomplished documentarian of the revolution was Ho-sain Torabi who made the 116-minute historical documentary *For Freedom* (*Bara-ye Azadi*, 1978–79) for MCIG, with an English voice-over by a veteran Sufi journalist living in Iran, Terry Graham. *For Freedom* documents chron-ologically the key events of the seven-month period of the anti-Shah upris-ing, which gave way to the Islamic Revolution (August 1978/Mordad 1357–April 1979/Farvardin 1358). The narrative arc of this chronology is the battle of the people against the state, specifically the Shah, encapsulating the long-standing story of politics in Iran. Many cinematographers worked on it, form-ing a tight group.[25] The film begins with historically valuable footage of the public mourning for the "martyrs" of the Rex Cinema fire and continues with footage of revolutionary events and the participation of political groups: blood-ied handprints and anti-Shah graffiti on the walls; a large English-language banner carried by throngs of demonstrators reading "Down with Imperial-ism, Communism, Zionism, Racism"; Tehran's wrecked high-class movie houses, some with intact billboards of scantily clad movie stars; the Shah's in-terview, at the Tehran airport, about being tired and needing rest abroad, and his tearful demeanor as he is about to depart the country for permanent exile; jubilation in the streets at his departure, marked by massive newspaper head-lines of "Shah Raft" (Shah's Gone); an interview with Prime Minister Shapur Bakhtiar, who welcomes Ayatollah Khomeini back to Iran, but not to take over the government; street battles with soldiers; rows of hundreds of naked male bodies lying in the morgue covered with blocks of melting ice; Khomeini's ar-rival from exile to a tumultuous welcome at Azadi Square and massive news-paper headlines of "Imam Amad" (Imam's Here); Khomeini's first speech at Behest-e Zahra Cemetery, in which, referring to Bakhtiar's government, he famously announced, "I will appoint a new government, I will slap this gov-ernment across the mouth"; Khomeini's appointment of Mehdi Bazargan as the new interim prime minister; massive displays of support for the new gov-ernment; popular disarming of the military barracks which unleashes an im-mense number of weapons into the hands of young demonstrators; the attack on the U.S. embassy in Tehran; footage of the Shah's opulent coronation in the 1960s, reversed to show the royal crown being removed from his head and the royal cape from his shoulders; and ending with the footage of long lines of people of all ages, genders, races, persuasions, and ethnoreligiosities voting in a national referendum to replace the Pahlavi dynasty with the Islamic Repub-lic, creating unity out of revolutionary chaos (figs. 16–18).[26]

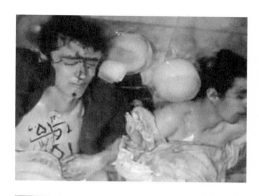

16 The bodies of those killed during the revolution are kept on ice in the Tehran morgue. Frame enlargement from Hosain Torabi's feature documentary *For Freedom*.

17 Bloody handprints on public walls, shop windows, and objects were a common sight. Frame enlargement from Torabi's documentary *For Freedom*.

18 "Imam Amad" (Imam's Here): *Ettela'at*'s famous headline on the day Ayatollah Khomeini returned from exile. It echoed an equally famous headline: "Shah Raft" (Shah's Gone). Frame enlargement from Torabi's documentary *For Freedom*.

The film's visuals are buttressed by sounds of street chanting, of demonstrators shouting slogans, of brief interviews with participants, of gunfire and fighting, of emergency police and medical vehicles' sirens, and of music composed by Shayda Qarachehdaghi. Sometimes the soundscape is used contrapuntally to deconstruct or undermine the visuals. For example, in the solemn scene in which the Shah is being interviewed on his way out of the country, people are heard on the soundtrack chanting, "Would that you traitor Shah would become homeless / Since you ruined our home country," which under-mines the Shah's remaining dignity.[27] *For Freedom* became an ur-film of the revolution, feeding images to many other documentaries. The film provides neither a voice-over narrator nor titles that identify places, people, or events. As a result, it leaves the viewer with too many narrative and historical am-biguities and questions. Nevertheless, it is a unique film of a country in the throes of a social revolution.

Torabi was the first head of the cinematographic affairs of MCIG, but *For Freedom* did not receive a domestic exhibition permit; as he tells it, it was banned in Iran for two decades (Torabi 2000:134), although it was screened in Moscow and New York (Tahaminejad 2000:126–27). After a few months, Torabi resigned from his post, citing bureaucratic wrangling, lack of author-ity, and the indecision of higher-ups, as well as the censoring of his film, which remained off-screen even though it had been shown to the cabinet and the Revolutionary Council and was approved by Prime Minister Bazargan (Ja-fari Lahijani 2008:vol. 1:170–76). The film was finally aired on national tele-vision, in 2003, nearly twenty-five years after its production, with some of the scenes removed.

Another key compilation film about the revolution is Kianush Ayyari's forty-four-minute film *Summer 1979 in Today's Tehran: First Timers*, made for VVIR's First Channel Network. Ayyari's camera roams the streets and side-walks of Tehran in the first few months of the uprising to show how the city has changed. Like a playful flâneur, the camera observes with wry humor the newfound freedom as exercised by first-timers, those who are experienc-ing it for the first time. Streets are lined with venders selling books, publica-tions, posters, music CDs, tapes, and clothing. People are involved in heated discussions in the streets and parks. Of particular interest are the Lalehzar Street theaters; instead of featuring their usual ribald Pahlavi-era shows, they feature prorevolutionary political performances and postrevolutionary fiction movies like Hosain Qasemivand's *Cry of the Freedom* (*Faryad-e Azadi*, 1979) and Amir Shervan's *Mujahid* (*Mojahid*, 1979). This film, which produced a lively portrait of a postrevolutionary Tehran, has never been screened publicly. It is not so much a compilation film as a city symphony film.

Yet another veteran filmmaker who turned to the compilation genre to document the revolution was Barbod Taheri, with his feature-length film *The Crash of '78*, which he filmed with his cameraman, Mahmud Oskui. Since the Iranian compilation genre, like its counterparts elsewhere, tended to deal with historically sensitive events and evaluated and passed judgment on them, compilation films became subject to early efforts at censorship—the first example being Torabi's *For Freedom*. Prorevolution films were soon censored because fast-changing events forced redefinitions of previously accepted history. Taheri's documentary chronicles the uprising against the Pahlavi regime from September 1978 (Shahrivar 1357) to February 1979 (Bahman 1357), when the revolution triumphed, concluding with scenes of people planting and decorating the graves of the revolution's martyrs with the most recognizable revolutionary icon—the tulip—in Behest-e Zahra Cemetery in Tehran (where another revolutionary icon—the "fountain of blood"—was also erected). Like Moshiri and cohorts, Taheri and Oskui filmed Khomeini from the moment his plane arrived, and they followed him through the tumultuous crowds into Behest-e Zahra Cemetery. Taheri recalled the emotions of filming him: "Standing against him in those days was like a small tree against a heavy flood. He would break anything in his path. He didn't compromise. . . . I saw him up close. He walked among those multitudes of people like a knife cutting through a cake" (quoted in Sullivan 2001:166). Taheri filmed some forty hours of the revolution (and thousands of stills), which he edited into his documentary. It was perhaps the first domestic documentary to be commercially screened, and not only in Tehran and major cities, but also in rural cinemas. Once popular, the film was banned, in 1984, because it dealt with topics that the authorities no longer wanted discussed. Taheri, who had produced and filmed Baizai's first feature film, *Downpour*, told me in an interview the reason he was given for banning *The Crash of '78*: "There are moments in the life of a nation when people no longer need to know the truth of what has actually happened" (Naficy 1985b). He was told that to obtain a new exhibition permit, he would have to remove documentary footage of actual events whose official interpretation had now changed. This included the footage of the widespread revolutionary participation of secular and leftist groups and of unveiled women, the attacks the Shah's armed forces made against demonstrators, and even a clip of a Khomeini speech in Behest-e Zahra Cemetery, in which he condemned the Shah for making cemeteries "prosperous." The new government wanted to erase evidence that leftists, secularists, and modern women had contributed to the revolution, a revolution that was now credited solely to the Muslim forces, signaled by its popular labeling as the "Islamic Revolution." The government also wanted to curb anti-army sentiments, as it now needed the armed forces for the war with Iraq, and it also needed fresh recruits. Khomeini's speech had to be removed because the Islamic Republic in its short existence had itself made the cemeteries prosperous, giving the lie to his speech. "Only with their particular version of the revolution could they say that women without scarves were antirevolutionary. But I had evidence to the contrary. They were in my film as part of the revolution," he stated (quoted in Sullivan 2001:167).

The rewriting of history entered documentary cinema almost immediately after the historical events. Taheri's film was banned and he was blacklisted, able to work only under the table and using an alias. Complaining to me that "Islamic censorship" had gripped cinema "like an octopus," Taheri chose life in exile, leaving the country in mid-1985 for Los Angeles. Born in 1942 in Abadan, Iran, he died in 2010 in a hospital in San Jose, California, from heart and kidney failure (Naficy 1985b).[28]

The eight-year war with Iraq produced its own share of compilation films. The death of Ayatollah Ruhollah Khomeini, in 1989, after the ceasefire, produced a moving and historically important example. Made by Majid Majidi, Javad Shamaghdari, Naser Sorudi, Ataollah Salmanian, and Abbas Naseri, *Sunshine and Love* (*Aftab va Eshq*, 1989) compiled poignant images of ordinary people's outpouring of love, emotion, and devotion for the deceased leader into an eighty-minute elegy. It has been rarely publicly screened (Kalantari 2004:34).

Archiving the Revolution's Footage

During the revolution—between mid-1978 and mid-1979—hundreds of hours of documentary footage was shot in a variety of formats—35mm, 16mm, Super 8, 8mm, and video—by professionals and amateurs, much of it processed inside the country. It is impossible, however, to make an accurate accounting of all the footage or of its whereabouts (Naficy 1979c:462).[29] Fearing police confiscation of the footage, some filmmakers did not risk processing their films inside the country. According to the filmmaker Shahriar Farahvashi some of the footage filmed by Mohammad Sadrzadeh was sent abroad for processing, safekeeping, and later use in compilation films (Naficy 1979f). Ayat Film members Najafi, Anvar, and Hashemitaba took their exposed Super 8 footage of the revolution to London for processing and subsequently edited it into *The Night of Power*. Other filmmakers stored their exposed footage in cool, dry places for later processing by foreign or domestic labs. Some of the processed footage was edited into compilation and historical documentaries, but in many cases it is not known what happened to the leftover rushes. For example, 40 hours of rushes were filmed for Shahdust and Kan'ani's 144-minute film *The Pulse of History*; 9 hours were filmed for Sadrzadeh's 54-minute film *The Battle of Iranian People*; and 40 hours were recorded for Taheri's 90-minute film *The Crash of '78*. It is not known where, or in what condition, the rushes and the negatives of these films might be archived. Some were never edited and now languish in personal or institutional archives, such as thirty hours of unedited 16mm footage that Hasan Qolizadeh had filmed and given to VVIR. Some were edited into films that were never seen, as with the footage that a group consisting of Ahmad Shah Hosaini, Mohammad Reza Bakhtminu, and Mohammad Tahaminejad filmed of the conflagration of Tehran movie houses; this footage was apparently used in the film *That Year Was the Year of the Horse (Ansal, Sal-e Asb Bud)*, directed by Hashemi and Reza Mirlohi, which has never been seen and, due to the death of both directors, has been impossible to track down (Jafari Lahijani 2008: vol. 2:636). In addition to the cameramen of government film and media organizations, such as VVIR and MCIG, various partisan political groups, such as PMOI and PFOI, and activist ethnic groups, such as the Kurds, recorded footage of the revolution from their own points of view and of their own activities, some of which was turned into films, but it is not known where and how these films are archived.

On the first anniversary of the revolution, VVIR sent out a call to all the people who had filmed the revolution to deliver their films to the network for broadcast and archiving. Apparently, people responded in droves by turning their original reversal 16mm and 8mm films to the network, some of which were edited and used in the anniversary programs, but, again, it is not known where and how they are archived. The network has repeated such calls for citizen footage to celebrate other special occasions as well, with similar results.

In addition to these uncertainties, television and film archives in Iran have been highly politicized, affecting what is kept, damaged, or destroyed and what is made accessible or withdrawn from public access. Changing times and politics have affected the contents of the archives, subjecting them to retrospective purification. Taheri's claim that his film was banned because the war with Iraq necessitated a revised view of history, one which elided how the Shah's armed forces worked to suppress the revolution, is corroborated in another way by the documentary filmmaker Mohammad Tehrani.[30] As he told me in an interview in summer 1979, when he was conducting research for his film in Iran, Tehrani received permission from Sadegh Ghotbzadeh, director general of VVIR, to access the television network's extensive documentary and news film archive. After viewing hours of footage, he noticed that shots of the armed forces attacking demonstrators were missing. Tehrani speculated that these had been removed to conceal the fact that the armed forces had been involved in suppressing the revolution (Naficy 1979e).

According to the dissident writer Gholamhosain Saedi, on Ghotbzadeh's orders, images of unveiled women were cut from prerevolution documentaries, as were images of the intellectuals and academics involved in the revolution. Instead, Party of God Islamists were recruited to organize phony demonstrations, which were filmed and presented as documentary footage (Saedi 1984a:17). Thus, not only were the television archives damaged, but also primary audiovisual historical materials were altered, manipulated, and effaced permanently, affecting the accuracy of future historical works, including compilation films.

Film archives and libraries were subjected to these manipulations as well as to spontaneous acts of "purification." In the heat of the revolution, many archives and libraries were ransacked and their contents—fiction films, documentaries, and news films—were burned, the ostensible purpose being to remove the Shah's culture of corruption and idolatry. However, some officials were also motivated by the desire to destroy incriminating evidence of their own complicity with the fallen regime in news footage (such as bowing and kissing the Shah's hand at official events). Some paid to have such footage removed from local film or television archives.

Fiction movies were also purified. Ali Abbasi, a well-known producer of Pahlavi-era commercial movies, including Naderi's *Tangsir*, describes movingly the psychological toll of this: "I regret that they burned this film like my other movies. If some day someone tells me that the negatives of this movie weren't burned, it will be the best news to me. Some things have deep roots inside you; they are valuable, like your mother. From 1984 when they burned my movies to today, I still suffer from desperation and depression."[31]

The black burn marks on the pavement outside film studios, film labs, and television stations provided material evidence of these wanton acts. As Mohammad Hasan Khoshnevis, director of the National Film Archive of Iran (NFAI), told me in an interview, many historically valuable news films, documentaries, and fiction films of the Pahlavi era were forever lost. Eventually NFAI obtained a directive from Mohammad Khatami, then minister of Culture and Islamic Guidance, to send the remaining "suspect" footage to the film archive in Tehran for safekeeping (Naficy 1998a). The conditions under which the revolutionary and postrevolutionary footage were collected and archived is worthy of further investigation.

Oppositional, Sectarian, and Underground Documentaries

Another new development was the emergence of nongovernmental nation-wide exhibition and production networks managed by radical opposition groups, instrumental in the uprising and the revolution, which had quickly become the new government's prime victims and enemies. These opposi-tional media units existed thanks to the short-lived relative openness of the "spring of freedom" and to the chaos of immediate postrevolution circum-stances. Within a year, with consolidation of the Islamist government, these groups were forced underground, from where they continued, for a while, to produce and show films and videos. Many members subsequently escaped the country into exile, where they either distributed existing Iranian under-ground oppositional media or produced more in diaspora. These production and exhibition networks were alternative "small media" venues, like the pre-revolution audiocassette networks opposing the Shah, set up to counter the "big media" that were monopolized by the Islamist regime. This new film and video network of small countermedia opposed the monopolistic tendencies of the Islamic Republic's state-run broadcast media.

People's Fadaiyan Organization of Iran (PFOI)

PFOI's media unit opted for film instead of video and thus needed film prints to feed its exhibition network in schools and colleges. This was expensive to maintain, and the organization was run as a commercial enterprise. The choice of medium was dictated perhaps by the fact that a filmmaker, Reza Allamehzadeh, headed the unit, and unlike PMOI members, PFOI members were diverse in their beliefs. As Peyman Vahabzadeh notes in his study of the evolution of the guerilla organization, "The seemingly ideologically mono-lithic Fadaiyan were indeed internally diverse and heterogeneous in all re-spects" (2010:246). Diversity brought on division, such that before PFOI's eradication by the Islamic Republic regime in the mid-1980s, the Fadaiyan had split into at least seven splinter groups (ibid.:76). Such divisions and divi-siveness may have been conducive to individual filmmaking efforts, but they worked against the more cohesive requirements of television (not so much video), which in those days needed studios and cumbersome recording, edit-ing, and transmission facilities and larger institutional personnel.

As Allamehzadeh described it to me in an interview, the PFOI's program-ming consisted of reedited and dubbed documentaries from Vietnam, the Soviet Union, and Eastern Europe, as well as domestic documentaries made by Fadaiyan members or sympathizers. Allamehzadeh himself directed one such documentary, *Speak Up Turkmen* (*Harf Bezan Torkaman*, 1979–80), a sixty-minute film about what he describes in his curriculum vita as "the war between Turkmen tribe and Islamic government." PFOI was not only popular among students, workers, and urban dwellers, but also among Kurds and Turkmen, inflaming government attacks on these groups. *Speak Up Turkmen* concerns a peasant cooperative in north Iran organized by a Fadaiyan "martyr" named Tumaj. Fifty prints of the film were circulated nationally. It was in discussing this film that Mohammad Ali Najafi, in charge of cinema at MCIG, first used the term "underground cinema" (*sinema-ye zirzamini*). He correctly predicted that an underground cinema would emerge from undue intolerance.[32] Soon after releasing *Speak Up Turkmen*, Allamehzadeh directed *The Wise Little Black Fish* (*Mahi-ye Siah-e Kuchulu-ye Dana*, 1980), about the Marxist writer Samad Behrangi. Finally, Allamehzadeh made *Stream and Moisture* (*Shat va Sharji*, 1980), a documentary on the war with Iraq, commissioned by VVIR and filmed in Abadan during the first months of the war; the film was never shown. PFOI films such as *Speak Up Turkmen* were generally shown in mosques, colleges, universities, and other educational institutions throughout the country. However, an official MCIG censor, Mehdi Argani, who according to Allamehzadeh and others was blind, banned *The Wise Little Black Fish* (Naficy 1988b).

Another PFOI product was *Death to Imperialism* (*Marg Bar Amperialism*, 1979), a film depicting the Theater Workshop's production of a polemical play of the same name, written by the Marxist poet and playwright Said Soltanpur and staged in the streets of Tehran using a mobile trailer. All the principal actors in the play, representing leaders of Western "imperialist" nations (Britain, the United States, the Soviet Union, and Israel) and the Shah, wore giant papier-mâché heads. The performances drew enthusiastic crowds. Called the "inventor" of "workers theater," Soltanpur wrote a Shah-era pamphlet, on the "arts of resistance," that attacked both that era's theater-supporting institutions and well-known Iranian and European modernist theater directors— Davud Rashidi, Feraidun Rahnema, Peter Brooke, Antonin Artaud, and Jerzy Grotowski—as corrupt and in the service of the official culture (Soltanpur 1970).[33] Soon after the pamphlet's publication, he spent some time in the Pahlavi prisons (after which he participated in the famed Ten Nights of Poetry). He was adamantly opposed to the rule of the mullahs, who harassed him, and used his plays and poetry to supplement his political activism (he ran as a PFOI candidate for the Majles). In April 1981, the security forces arrested him during his wedding; two months later, apparently having failed to obtain his recantation, they executed him by firing squad, along with thirty-six other antigovernment activists.

Mohammad Sadrzadeh made *What Happened in Gonbad-e Qabus?* (*Dar Gonbad-e Qabus Cheh Gozasht?*, 1978) for VVIR, which dealt with the armed struggle between the PFOI forces that were attempting to take military possession of the city of Gonbad-e Qabus, a predominantly Turkmen city, and the IRI forces that were trying to dislodge them. Sadrzadeh states that on entering the city he and his crew found it "deserted and full of corpses left from recent battles. People were telling us that since there was no security to safely remove the bodies, some of them had been devoured by wild dogs" (quoted in Jafari Lahijani 2008:vol. 1:438). They filmed a few days of the fighting in the city and interviewed Abbas Amir Entezam, Bazargan government spokesman and deputy prime minister, about the fighting. *What Happened in Gonbad-e Qabus?* was not a pro-PFOI film, but it was about the PFOI and thus was aired by VVIR.

The open operation of oppositional video and film networks gradually came to a halt when, in 1980, the government launched its "Islamic cultural revolution" campaign, which closed down all universities to "purify" their staff, faculty, students, curricula, and textbooks. Dissident groups lost their main exhibition venues and audiences: university halls and students. This was part of the larger project of Islamicization of knowledge and culture. By mid-1981, when the government began to violently suppress all opponents, including the PMOI, which had taken up armed struggle against the regime, no aboveground oppositional film practice remained. Many filmmakers stayed, but many also left the country, with the media-use differences between PFOI and PMOI resurfacing in exile. Of PFOI filmmakers and sympathizers, Allamehzadeh fled to the Netherlands, Abbas Samakar to Germany, and Barbod Taheri to the United States. These and other filmmakers made films about the convoluted modern history of Iran, the revolution and its disastrous aftermaths, the difficult lives of Iranians in exile, and their transformative journeys, as individuals or as collectives of leftists. Some of them also worked for exile television programs and channels, including Taheri, who also tried, unsuccessfully, in the early 1980s to return to Iranian Kurdistan by way of Iraqi Kurdistan to make films. Allamehzadeh's film *Speak Up Turkmen* was circulated abroad, in Europe and the United States, by PFOI branches on various occasions. To celebrate Labor Day (1 May) in 1984, it was screened in Gothenburg, Sweden, where PFOI slogans were "Death to the Islamic Republic Regime" and "Long Live the Democratic People's Republic." PFOI supporters screened it in Vienna, Austria, before "many progressive Iranian and Aus-

بزرگداشت شهدای خلق

از خون جوانان وطن لاله دمید

"مرگ بر امپریالیسم" فیلمی از
فدایی شهید سعید سلطانپور

برنامه : مقاله - سخنرانی - نمایش فیلم (آخرین اثر سعید سلطانپور)

زمان : یکشنبه پنجم سپتامبر - ساعت ۷ بعدازظهر

مکان : دیکسون هال یو - سی - ال - ا
دوره به ۲ دلر

دانشجویان پیشرو - هواداران راه فدائی

19 Flyer announcing the UCLA
screening of the film of Said
Soltanpur's street play, *Death
to Imperialism*, circa 1980. The
flyer is titled "Commemorating
People's Martyrs: Tulips
Have Grown from the Blood
of the Homeland's Martyrs."
Progressive Students,
supporters of the Fadai
path, sponsored the event.
Collection of the author.

trian forces."[34] Likewise, on the anniversary of the playwright Soltanpur's
execution (23 May 1984), the film was screened at the University of Southern California, Los Angeles, along with poetry reading and declamation. A
year later, in February 1985, the student supporters of PFOI screened it again
at USC, this time to celebrate the anniversary of the PFOI's armed rebellion
against the Siahkal gendarmerie station in 1971 (fig. 19).

PFOI split into the Majority Faction and the Minority Faction. Through its
front organization, the Society of Iranian Students in Southern California, the
Majority Faction screened many movies, the bulk of which were documentaries dealing with revolutionary topics, particularly those involving Iran and
other third-world countries. The films screened included Pooya's *Bloody Friday*, shown in the House of Iran; *Days of the Uprising* (*Ruzha-ye Qiam*), shown
at UCLA; *Scenes from Iran's Revolution* (*Sahnehhai az Enqelab-e Iran*), at UCLA;
Nicaragua, One Year after Revolution (*Nicaragua, Yek Sal Ba'd az Enqelab*), at
UCLA; *The Role of Multinational Corporations*, at UCLA; *The Last Grave of Dimbaza*, at UCLA; *We are the Palestinian People*, at UCLA; CISPES *Videotape about El
Salvador*, at UCLA; CIA *Operations* (*Amaliat-e Sia*), at UCLA; *Angola*, at UCLA; and

Lenin's Life (Zendegi-ye Lenin), at UCLA.[35] Through its own front student unit, the Organization of Iranian Students in Southern California, PFOI's Minority Faction also screened films, but at a much slower pace than its nemesis, and many of them dealt with non-Iranian revolutionaries, such as a film called *The Palestinians.* Because of the defeat and the routing of the left by the Islamist government, the disintegration of the Soviet Union and Eastern bloc communist regimes, and the factionalism among Iranian exiles, a dispirited and disorganized Left did not coalesce into a cohesive party, organization, or movement. As a result, POFI's film-based effort at home and abroad gradually declined and disappeared. Only individual filmmakers remained to make films.

People's Mojahedin Organization of Iran (PMOI)

In contradistinction to PFOI, PMOI opted for video and television, by means of which it showed its own products to its supporters throughout Iran free of charge. Unlike PFOI's film unit, whose programming consisted of a mix of PFOI productions and foreign films, PMOI's programming was produced almost entirely in-house. This consisted of lightly edited documentary footage of events, political actions, rallies, speeches, and interviews given by PMOI leaders, without official program titles or production credits (their titles generally consisted of a descriptive phrase). A hermetic, top-down video system circulated PMOI-approved propaganda and information to the cadres, inculcating the organization's authoritarian ideology and systems. In exile, this task was given to the PMOI television.

Among the tapes containing footage of rallies, demonstrations, and military maneuvers were *Demonstration of the Muslim Mothers (Tazahorat-e Madaran-e Mosalman,* 1979?), *The Extensive Maneuver of the People's Mojahedin Armed Forces (Manovr-e Gostardeh-ye Qova-ye Mojahed-e Khalq,* 1985), and *Attack on the Misaq Society (Hamleh beh Anjoman-e Misaq,* 1980). Tapes of speeches and interviews included *Interview with Families of Khoshdel and Zolanvar (Mosahebeh ba Khanevadeh-ha-ye Khoshdel va Zolanvar,* 1979), *Masud Rajavi's Speech (Sokhanrani-ye Masud Rajavi,* 1979), *Speeches of Brothers Masud Rajavi and Musa Khiabani (Sokhanrani-ye Baradaran Masud Rajavi va Musa Khiabani,* 1980), and *Ashura: Philosophy of Freedom (Ashura: Falsaeh-ye Azadi,* 1980).

Unlike PFOI, PMOI regrouped and consolidated in exile. Its leaders, including Masud Rajavi, escaped Iran in July 1981 in a daring flight to Europe, taking along with them the first postrevolution president, Abolhasan Banisadr, who had fallen out of favor with his mentor, Ayatollah Khomeini (he would soon part ways with PMOI as well). PMOI established its political headquarters in Paris and its military headquarters in Saddam Hussein's Iraq, which was at war with Iran. From their Camp Ashraf base in the enemy country, PMOI forces repeatedly attacked Iranian forces and villages. This undermined their legitimacy as a democratic and nationalist alternative to the Islamist regime. International and regional geopolitics, which Ervand Abrahamian details in his book on the Mojahedin (1989), gradually forced the organization to move its political headquarters to Iraq in 1986. The ceasefire in the war, two years later, which prevented PMOI from attacking Iran from Iraqi soil, further isolated it, turning it into an inbred, authoritarian, and cultist organization headed by the charismatic leaders Masud Rajavi and Maryam Rajavi. Despite the organization's smart and diligent public-relations campaigns, throughout the 1980s, 1990s, and 2000s the United States and major European countries continued to place PMOI on their official list of "terrorist" organizations (with periodic relaxation and tightening of that classification as an expedient way to keep PMOI functioning well enough to serve as a possible weapon against the Islamic Republic). Nevertheless, PMOI established a political front organization, the National Council of Resistance of Iran, and political branches in many key cities abroad, particularly through its subsidiary front sympathizers' organizations, such as the Muslim Students' Association of the United States and Canada (Anjoman-e Daneshjuian-e Mosalman-e Emrika va Kanada), which organized regular lectures, sold PMOI's publications, and screened in colleges, universities, and churches many of the Mojahedin's videos (fig. 20). To earn money for the organization, some of these regional branches set up shops (such as bakeries and groceries), where they also sold, among their regular products, Mojahedin literature and periodicals. PMOI also created two television programs, one for broadcasting in Iraq, the other for broadcast in the West, including the United States. Of all the opposition groups, the PMOI was the most effective in its use of media abroad, particularly television.

The documentary *A Sun in Darkness* (*Khorshidi dar Zolmat*, 1982?) focuses on the history of PMOI's opposition to both the Shah and the Khomeini regimes, featuring footage of many of its leaders, executed or killed in action. It recounts the various reasons for the Mojahedin's split from the Islamist government, with whom they had originally collaborated, stating in its rhetorical voice-over narration, typical of oppositional films, that "Khomeini came forward first with the politics of deceit and then with the politics of suppression. He hid every one of his crimes under the cover of fighting imperialism." The film documents various PMOI actions against the Islamist government,

20 Flyer for a screening at UCLA, on 16 November 1986, of a film about the funeral and burial ceremony of ten Mojahed "martyrs" whose blood was spilled in Suleimaniyeh by the "criminal Talebani [Kurdish] group." Muslim Students' Association of the United States, a supporter of PMOI, sponsored the screening. Collection of the author.

including its urban guerrilla warfare, the most dramatic act being the massive bombing that destroyed the Jomhuri-e Eslami Party building and the prime minister's office in Tehran, killing seventy-two people, some of them top government officials, including Chief Justice Ayatollah Mohammad Beheshti, President Mohammad Ali Rejai, and Prime Minister Mohammad Javad Bahonar. *A Sun in Darkness* dramatically recounts the bombing: it announces the date (7 Tir 1360/28 June 1981), shows a clock whose second-hand dial is approaching 9 P.M., announces that fifteen seconds remain until the moment of detonation, shows the dark streets outside, and then the sudden, devastating explosion. All this is followed by graphic scenes of the next day's armed hit-and-run street battles, in which PMOI fighters shoot from rooftops and from behind cars at security and police forces. Another PMOI documentary, *With the People's Suffering* (*Ba Dardha-ye Mardom*, 1983), focuses on the paramedical assistance the Mojahedin provided in the areas held by the Kurdish resistance in western Iran.

A third film, *A Voice from the Summits* (*Sedai az Qollehha*, 1984), is a rare ninety-minute, Super 8 documentary about the installation of a powerful new

هفته حماسه موسی و اشرف

ویدئو سخنرانی **برادر مجاهد مهدی ابریشمچی**
عضو دفتر سیاسی سازمان مجاهدین خلق ایران
گزارش گونه‌ای در مورد موقعیت فعلی مقاومت نوین مردم ایران در جمع
عده‌ای از اعضاء انجمنهای دانشجویان مسلمان خارج از کشور

صدائی از قله‌ها بهمراه

فیلمی مستند از نقل و انتقال و
نصب دستگاه فرستنده بزرگ رادیو مجاهد

این صدای مجاهدین خلق ایران است
صدای مجاهد صدای خروش خلق
صدای نسل انقلابی مجاهد
صدای انقلاب کبیر ایران است

21 Flyer for the PMOI supporters'
screening of two films in the
United States to commemorate the
"epical" deaths of the PMOI leaders
Musa Khiabani and Ashraf Rabii
at the hands of security forces in
February 1982: first, a video called
*Speech by Mojahed Brother, Mehdi
Abrishamchi* about the "new resistance
of Iranian people"; second, *A Voice
from the Summits*, a film about
PMOI's radio station in Iranian
Kurdistan. Collection of the author.

antenna and studio for the Voice of Mojahed Radio (Radio Seda-ye Mojahed),
which the film calls the voice of Iran's "great revolution" (*enqelab-e Kabir*), in
the mountains of Iranian Kurdistan. It shows in remarkable detail program
production under conditions of armed struggle, and it contains interviews
with various professionals working for the radio station. It situates the radio
as a means to an end by tying the story of the radio station to the story of the
antigovernment resistance in Iranian Kurdistan. Armed Kurdish *peshmerga*
soldiers are seen guarding the station in temperatures that fall to twenty degrees below zero, and the Mojahedin fighters are seen in the field listening to
the station's broadcast on their portable radios (fig. 21).[36]

These documentaries were few and their screenings, however wide, could
not be sustained for long. PMOI screened other videos for its members,
sympathizers, and lay people abroad. These contained footage of its leaders' speeches, sermons, military maneuvers staged in Iraq, military actions
against the Islamic Republic forces in western Iran, and PMOI's various political conventions, ceremonies, confessions, and testimonials. These were influenced by massive ideological shifts that engulfed the organization peri-
odically. Their long and convoluted titles, using the coded language of the
Mojahedin, point to the ideological work of the videos. For example, *The New
Year Ceremonies in Presence of the New Leadership of the Organization and the*

نمایش ویدئوی دومین سخنرانی

برادر مجاهد مهدی ابریشمچی، عضو دفتر سیاسی سازمان مجاهدین خلق ایران، درجمع گروهی ازهواداران سازمان دراریزیس درباره

انقلاب ایدئولوژیک درون مجاهدین خلق ایران

معرفی رهبری نوین انقلاب دمکرانیک نوین مردم ایران

مسعود و مریم رجوی

محورهای سخنرانی :

• رهبری عقیدتی و جایگاه آن در انقلابات اجتماعی
• رهبری ایدئولوژیک سازمان مجاهدین خلق ایران (مسعود و مریم رجوی)، ویژگیها و عملکردان
• آفرینش نوع نوینی از رابطه بین رهبری انقلاب و مردم
• معرفی رهبری انقلاب درمرحله کنونی، ضرورت پیشرفت انقلاب و تحقق قیام در جهت سرنگونی رژیم ضد بشری خمینی
• پاسخ به سوالات

بانضمام نمایش ویدئوی مانورگسترده قوای مجاهد خلق

زمان : یکشنبه ۱۷ آذر۶۴ (۸ دسامبر۸۵) ، ساعت ٤ بعدازظهر

مکان : لس آنجلس ، دانشگاه U.S.C. ، Bovard Auditorium

انجمن دانشجویان مسلمان ـ آمریکا (هواداران سازمان مجاهدین خلق ایران)

22 Flyer for a Mojahedin event at USC, on 8 December 1985, consisting of a videotaped speech, by the PMOI leader Mehdi Abrishamchi, about the organization's "ideological revolution," which entailed a new marriage plan introduced by the leadership, as well as a video of a large military maneuver by PMOI forces in Iraq. Collection of the author.

New Democratic Revolution of Heroic Iranian Masses, Maryam and Masud Rajavi (*Marasem-e Tahvil-e Sal-e Jadid dar Hozur-e Rahbar-ye Novin-e Sazman va Enqelab-e Demokratik-e Novin-e Khalq-e Qahreman-e Iran, Masud va Maryam Rajavi*, 1985), shows the celebration of Noruz (the Iranian New Year) by PMOI leaders and many uniformed male and female cadres segregated by gender. Both the gathering and the video celebrate more than the New Year, however. They celebrate and justify through long-winded speeches—the tape is four hours long—a major "ideological revolution" in the organization, as well as a "personnel revolution" in the Mojahedin, involving Maryam Azodanlu's divorce from her husband, Mehdi Abrishamchi, a high-ranking PMOI leader, in order to marry Masud Rajavi, her co-leader of the Mojahedin. She soon became the "Elected President" of the opposition, working side by side with her husband, who remained the PMOI's supreme leader. Following the grand traditions of authoritarian parties, this divorce cum marriage was presented with pomp and circumstance as having been necessitated by PMOI's organizational and ideological exigencies—the collective good—not by the personal desires or mutual love of the two participants. The video was screened on 9 June 1985 in at least four Los Angeles locations simultaneously, including at UCLA and at Palms Junior High School. In December of the same year the PMOI's front organization screened it again at the University of Southern California, along with other films (fig. 22). The footage of the maneuvers and military actions were also shown in PMOI's regular meetings, but it found its rightful place in the Mojahedin's television programs and in what I have called their "militia music videos" (Naficy 2002a).

These were, in essence, company training videos that promoted the sponsoring entity, PMOI. Masoud Banisadr, a high-ranking member who defected from the Mojahedin in 1996, described movingly the screening of the aforementioned New Year's video for the Mojahedin members and its cathartic effect on them. Toward the end of the long tape, Abrishamchi stands up to endorse the marriage of his superior, Rajavi, to his former wife, Maryam, whom he had divorced for that purpose, and to sanction the new ideological shift of the organization, which this divorce represented: enforcing divorce among PMOI members. It was based on the idea that by divorcing each other, members could devote themselves more fully to the organization. This ideology of the dissolution of the individual into the collective was similar to that practiced by the Islamic Republic, particularly during the war years. Abrishamchi continued: "We must all pass through this furnace and melt away our filthy parts. . . . Then we can find ideological brightness. Then all will become true members of the Mojahedin." Banisadr reports that, during the video screening, "Everyone wept as he [Abrishamchi] spoke" (2004:217). In addition, the screening of the videos of Mojahedin's military operations, or those showing their public-health services among Kurdish Democratic Party rebels fighting the Iranian government, strengthened the PMOI's members who were exiled in Britain: "We were proud to see them working under such difficult conditions, helping ordinary people, even performing operations and relieving long-standing problems" (ibid.:198).

Some of the videos of ceremonies, sermons, speeches, confessions, and testimonials had other, peculiar internal uses among the Mojahedin in Iraq. According to Banisadr, every ideological shift within the organization—and there were many—necessitated marathon indoctrination sessions, with PMOI members required to watch, in private viewings, as many as thirty hours of videotape about the current ideological shift, to write their responses to the shift, and to participate in brutal and grueling marathon public sessions in which they confessed to their own "crimes" and shortcomings, being then ruthlessly berated by their comrades and reconfirming their unquestioning loyalty to the leadership.

Early in 2003, the United States and its allies attacked Iraq and removed Saddam Hussein from power. When American troops pulled up outside the Mojahedin's vast headquarters (Camp Ashraf) shortly after the fall of Baghdad, PMOI members offered no resistance and later agreed to disarm (Masud Rajavi soon "disappeared"). Behzad Alishahi, who had spent more than fifteen years at the camp working as a TV presenter, reported that he and colleagues at the TV station were ordered by PMOI commanders to "destroy film and other evidence of close ties to Saddam Hussein." Such archival destruction aimed at rewriting history is reminiscent of similar acts by the Islamist zealots immediately after the revolution inside Iran. The destruction was not thorough or systemic, however, for when the French police stormed the PMOI's Auvers-sur-Oise compound near Paris and arrested Maryam Rajavi, who was carting away $9 million in cash and documents detailing bank accounts, in France, the United States, and elsewhere, that held tens of millions of dollars, they also found videos of Masud Rajavi meeting Saddam Hussein and ninety-nine satellite-positioning devices programmed with coordinates for Iran. In the meantime, the Mojahedin satellite TV station pumped out "adulatory propaganda for Ms. Rajavi and her missing husband, Massoud" (Higgins and Solomon 2006).

In addition to film and video production, broadcasting, and screenings, PMOI created a veritable industry and cultural spectacle in the 1980s out of its cadres who had been tortured in the Islamic Republic prisons and who, on their release, had either left the country legally or escaped. PMOI printed their pictures and the details of the atrocities committed against them in thick albums, which its members showed to horrified passersby in many American city shopping centers and airports, such as in Los Angeles and New York, or printed such matters in the organization's various magazines and publications. In these years, PMOI attempted to establish its revolutionary credentials by publicly recounting—and, in truth, shamefully boasting about—the large number of its supporters who had willingly died for its goals and in its cause. In 1985 it circulated a massive 181-page, large-format illustrated book listing in detail the manner of death of 12,028 "martyrs" who had belonged to opposition organizations and factions and were killed in battles against the Islamist government (Mojahedin-e Khalq-e Iran 1985). Of these, 9,069 belonged to the Mojahedin. The stories of their deaths were a litany of IRI cruelty and barbarism: 1,333 killed in fighting, 6,262 executed by firing squad, 210 executed by hanging, 305 tortured to death, 14 burned to death, 17 dragged to death, 21 assassinated, 907 not specified (Abrahamian 1989:226). Based on these tortured and decimated bodies—in 1990 PMOI claimed the incredibly high number of 90,000 dead, a figure that was upped to 120,000 by 2006—PMOI nominated itself as the "sole" tenable challenger to the Islamic Republic regime.[37] In the race to martyrdom it had won hands down.

Taking a page from the culture of spectacle of its adversaries, during the 1980s PMOI put on public demonstrations and street theaters in major American and European cities, enacting scenes of imprisonment and torture on sidewalks. Once, in Westwood Village, near the UCLA campus, PMOI cadres recreated prison cells and torture chambers before crowds of surprised and affected onlookers. They depicted prisoners being interrogated and tortured to death, and mock executions were reenacted, while Mojahedin supporters worked the spectators with their thick albums of photographs of tortured, scarred, and maimed bodies. The discourse on torture and martyrdom produced by the Mojahedin was designed not only to promote solidarity within the organization, but also to arouse public and political sympathy in the West, gain media attention, and generate financial contributions.[38]

In the United States, PMOI torture victims gave public talks in tours of colleges and churches, during which they showed before awed and hushed spectators the signs that torture had left on their bodies or the limbs it had removed from them. The Muslim Students' Association of the United States circulated tapes of some of these appearances. One was released as *Epic Resistances in Khomeini's Prisons from the Lips of Tortured Mojahedin Members, Hajar Mansuri, Behzad Naziri, and Robabeh Bodaghi* (1987?), circulated to seven tour sites in American cities (fig. 23).[39] This same tape, along with other PMOI videos, was shown by *Vision of Freedom (Sima-ye Azadi)*, PMOI's weekly television show in the United States and Europe, and by its counterpart in Iraq, *Vision of Resistance (Sima-ye Moqavemat)*.

Unlike leftist opposition groups, which were splintered and diverse, and the monarchist opposition groups, which competed with and undercut each other, PMOI was a united autocracy, for the consolidation of which centralized television and radio broadcasts were more suitable than individualized films. *Vision of Resistance*, a half-hour program broadcast from the Mojahedin's base in Iraq on Saddam Hussein–era Iraqi television, could be watched in many regions of western Iran, thus introducing an alternative voice into an Iranian mediascape monopolized by the government (Kempster 1987). Branches of the Muslim Students' Association of the United States screened tapes of this program on college campuses in the United States, including at UCLA and USC, in Los Angeles (fig. 24). The *Vision of Freedom* television program in the United States was subjected to the U.S. State Department ban in the late 1980s, because the department had designated the Mojahedin—under its various aliases, including its political arm, the National Council of Resistance—a "terrorist" group and because it had violated some of the terms of its contract

23 Flyer for a U.S. tour by three PMOI members, Hajar Mansuri, Behzad Naziri, and Robabeh Bodaghi, who claimed to have been tortured by the Islamic Republic. Collection of the author.

24 Flyer for PMOI's *Vision of Resistance* television program, whose tapes were shown at USC on Sunday afternoons in 1987. Collection of the author.

with the transmitting station, KSCI-TV, in Los Angeles. However, in a series of fascinating legal and other deceptive maneuvers, it managed to stay on the air for quite some time (see Naficy 1993:74–75).

PMOI and the National Council of Resistance also utilized their television programs and the Internet to air videos recorded clandestinely inside Iran and smuggled out of the country. These show the Iranian government's draconian and inhumane treatment of its prisoners. One such video, aired in May 2005, shows the public hanging of three young men in broad daylight.[40] Another, a fifteen-minute video that Mojahedin posted on the Internet, shows the stoning to death of four men who had committed moral crimes (rape, adultery) and military offenses. After the verdict is read, a man is lashed hard for minutes to the chants of "God is great, God is great." Then crowds of men drag the four convicted men into an open field. They are alive but tightly wrapped inside white sacks. With much ado, the crowd places these shrouded men into individual holes in the ground, burying them to their waists, all the while arguing with each other about the correct manner of doing the job. Clearly this is a primitive, makeshift operation. Then the men proceed to noisily stone the victims after a man identified as Ali Razini, the head of Judicial Organization of the Military Forces, casts the first stone. As the stoning by scores of young men shouting "Allaho Akbar, Allaho Akbar" continues in an atmosphere that mixes cruel frenzy with youthful levity, at least one victim appears to manage to loosen himself and to crawl several inches out of his hole and out of his bag. The film was apparently shot clandestinely at a police barracks in Tehran in 1992 and smuggled out of the country in 1998. The Mojahedin's website warned, "The images in this video are NOT EASY TO WATCH. They are NOT suitable for children or people with heart conditions." It spelled out the main reason for providing such videos: "As unfortunate as it is, this brutal and inhumane action is part of the reality in Iran under the rule of the mullahs and we are presenting it here to further expose the atrocities committed by them."[41] Such exposé is the reverse side of the Islamist regime's practice of exposing PMOI's atrocities by airing movies about "grouplets," which began immediately after the organization broke with the regime.

In the 2000s, the Internet became a major means of global dissemination for the PMOI. Particularly glossy was *Sima-ye Azadi: Televizion-e Melli-ye Iran*, which morphed from a mere television program into an Internet portal carrying PMOI videos, documentaries, television shows, music videos, and news that propagated the organization's aims and means.[42] The Mojahedin operate another website and a YouTube channel, which contain a treasure trove of pro-PMOI films and videos.[43]

In the early 1980s, the Muslim Students' Association of the United States was active in organizing regular screenings of revolutionary and counter-hegemonic movies, documentaries, and fiction films made by Iranians or others.[44] After a while, the society seemed to have changed allegiance, as it began showing anti-PMOI films and pro–Islamic government films. The secretive operations of the opposition groups and the complicated politics of the Iranian government and exiles make difficult the tracking of the splits and alliances, which occurred frequently. Another Muslim group supporting the politics of the Islamic Republic, the Muslim Research and Art Group, also screened many movies—mostly made in Iran by various government organs—in Southern California universities during regular events that included lectures, Quran readings, and discussion.[45]

The Mojahedin videos, publications, musical concerts, television and radio programs and channels, websites, and street theaters were designed not only to improve PMOI's public relations and to consolidate its identity, but also to counter the media that the Islamic Republic's culture industry regularly churned out against the organization, which it routinely labels as "the hypocrites." It was also aimed at removing the label of "terrorist organization" bestowed on it by major Western governments. In the late 2000s, the Mojahedin bolstered these public media efforts at changing the terrorist designation of PMOI with a sophisticated campaign in Europe and the United States aimed at winning over lawyers, politicians, and lawmakers. These efforts paid off. In December 2006, the EU Court of Justice ruled that the PMOI should be removed from the European Union's terrorist list, "partly on the grounds that the reasons for its inclusion were 'unclear.'" In January 2008, the EU compiled and delisted PMOI.[46] After this victory the organization's campaign in the United States intensified winning over some prominent politicians, congressmen, and senators, who justified the delisting on the dubious ground that the organization was fighting a common enemy, IRI, for a democratic Iran.

This was a public diplomacy war that PMOI fought in the fields of culture and ideology to offset defeat in military fields, which had driven it into foreign exile and collaboration with the enemy. In this front, it achieved some of its goals, at least with foreign governments, but not with the bulk of Iranians either in exile or at home for these remained highly suspicious of the organization's democratic credentials, current ideology and structure, and future plans.

Kurdish Resistance Groups

Immediately after the revolution, the Islamic Republic adopted a relatively egalitarian stance toward Iranian national and ethnic minorities—Azeri, Persian, Kurd, Baluch, Arab, Bakhtiari, Gilaki, and Turkmen—allowing minoritarian cultural and linguistic education, political representation, and media expressions. Indeed, the new constitution acknowledged the multiethnic, multilingual, multireligious, and multicultural aspects of the Iranian society, while maintaining Shiism as the country's official religion and Persian as the national language. This was driven by the emancipatory, anticolonial, and antimonarchic dimensions of the revolution and by the demands of the awakened ethnic and national minorities for fair treatment and representation. However, with the consolidation of the guardianship of the jurist and the Shiite theocracy, Persian and Shiite dominance were once again reinstated as the central tenets of Iranian national identity. With that, the "highly romanticized rhetoric regarding racial and ethnic equality all but disappeared into thin air" (Asgharzadeh 2007:109). In the meantime, various ethnoreligiosities and nationalities engaged in self-representation by means of the media of film, television, video, the press, and the Internet.

Among Iranian national minorities, the Kurds, who are mostly Sunni and share language and culture with Kurds in neighboring countries—Turkey, Iraq, and Syria—were most active in self-representation immediately after the revolution. Kurdish groups made documentaries about their national aspirations, about various military battles and skirmishes with government forces over their claims for autonomy in western Iran in the 1980s, and about the executions and martyrdom of their members. Many of these films were shown abroad, on college campuses, high schools, and churches. Among these were *Altercations in Mahabad* (*Dargiriha-ye Mahabad*, 1980?), *Battle of Sanandaj* (*Jang-e Sanandaj*, 1980), *Ceremony of Arming Women Peshmergas* (*Marasem-e Mossalah Shodan-e Zanan-e Pishmargeh*, 1983), and *The Lives and Struggles of Komele Peshmergas* (*Zendegi va Mobarezeh-ye Pishmargan-e Komele*, 1983).[47] Like the PMOI videos, these films generally did not list any production credits, partly for security reasons and partly due to their amateur or collective productions (fig. 25). The names of their directors and producers are unknown (although *Battle of Sanandaj* is probably the controversial Sadrzadeh movie discussed earlier). Because Kurdish groups controlled parts of Iranian Kurdistan and Azarbaijan in the early 1980s, the Kurdish rebels and some of their sympathizers, such as PMOI, were able to set up not only radio stations (Voice of Kurdistan, Voice of Mojahed), but also film screenings inside Iran in those areas. According to the Kurdish leader Abdolrahman Qasemlu, these screenings had "much positive effects" (1984:42).

In *Ceremony of Arming Women Peshmergas* women soldiers who had attained the honor of becoming *peshmerga* received their bandoliers, which they proudly put on, and their rifles, which they sling over their shoulders. This forty-five-minute film carries an English voice-over, revealing a desire for audiences beyond Kurdish and Iranian populations. It calls the women fighters "the tigers of Kurdistan mountains." A young fighter gives a lecture about

25 Flyer for a "night of coalition with the movement of Kurdish People's resistance" at UCLA in the early 1980s, which consisted of speeches (including one by Hasan Nahid, whose two brothers, Ehsan and Shahriar, had been executed by firing squad, as captured in a famous photo), slide show, chorale, declamation, and films. The two films screened "for the first time" were *Battle of Sanandaj* and *Altercations in Mahabad*. The Iranian Student Organization in Southern California, which supported PFOI, sponsored the event. Collection of the author.

the changing social roles of women, who she says now engage in all aspects of life, and about the bravery of women fighters, which has "cast fear in the hearts" of government soldiers. Men and women sing the communist international anthem and resolutely thrust their fists into the air. Historically significant, the film also contains interviews with the first female *peshmergas* about their training and duties, and with women on the streets who declare that more women must become soldiers.

The Lives and Struggles of Komele Peshmergas provides an insider eyewitness account of the Komele Party members fighting government forces. The camera documents the battle from the rebel point of view. The cadres shoot at government helicopters and crawl across the fields, guns in hand; a camera pan reveals tanks and heavy machinery destroyed by the rebels. A Pasdar (a revolutionary guard) arrested by the Komele in the town of Saqqez states that the Komele has treated him well and that it is a "revolutionary" party that is "defending Iranian toilers." The good life that Komele provides for the Kurds under its control is a focus, as are women *peshmerga* soldiers, who dance in uniform with male soldiers. Showing armed civilians and mixed-gender dancing were banned in the Islamic Republic, but the government was not fully in control of the Kurdish region in the early 1980s.

The emphasis in Kurdish films on the *peshmerga* fighters was to capitalize on the legendary bravery of these fighters in Kurdish history and to note how many had died. The general secretary of the Democratic Party of Iranian Kurdistan, Abdolrahman Qasemlu (later assassinated), reported in an official publication in 1984 that during 1980–82, some 735 *peshmergas* had been "martyred" and 554 were wounded in clashes with government forces; however, he boasted that in the same period the Kurdish fighters had killed a disproportionately high number of government soldiers, 18,820. He claimed that these figures demonstrated the truth of the "warning" of his party that the "*peshmergas* will turn Kurdistan into the graveyard for the enemies of the Kurdish people" (Qasemlu 1984:43).

Because of the Kurds' agitation for greater autonomy and cultural, ethnic, and religious identity, they were violently suppressed. The Kurdish language was barred from schools, and Kurdish literature was constrained. The confluence of geopolitics led to an increased transnationalization of Kurdish identity. Pan-Kurdish film festivals contributed to this, particularly in an increasingly multicultural Europe, to which many Kurds relocated. The Kurdish Film Festival was founded in London, and the Douarnez Film Festival in Brittany, France, devoted an entire section to films made by Kurdish filmmakers of various nationalities and by others about the Kurds.[48] In December 2009, the hitherto unthinkable happened: the first Kurdish film festival was held inside Turkey, in Diyarbakir, featuring films previously not screened there. These were by young Kurdish directors from Iraq, Iran, Turkey, and the United States, and their primary focus was the young generation of Kurds in diaspora.

Radio and television broadcasting had an earlier and wider impact than films in fanning the flames of pan-Kurdish nationalism, due to the fragmentation and dispersion of the Kurds. They linked Kurds of different nations not only in the Middle East but also in European diaspora. If print journalism was responsible for creating imaginary nations within nations, broadcast journalism served that function among the Kurds across nations, helping create a nation without a state. The impact of satellite television was wide. Within the Kurdish areas of Iraq, five Kurdish satellite channels were inaugurated in the 2000s, and they could be received throughout the Middle East. One satellite channel, ROJ TV (formerly MED TV), for example, "played an instrumental role in mobilizing" the Kurdish discontent in northwest Iran in August 2005, while Kurdsat Channel, based in Sulaimaniyeh, Iraq, reported on the thousands of Iranian troops that had been deployed to quell the protest (Fathi 2005). Also, according to the Kurdish media scholar Amir Hassanpour, the Komele, whose radio station was active in Iran for years, and the Communist Party of Iran-Komele in 2006 launched satellite television stations of their own, which quickly acquired "vast audiences in the Middle East and Europe" (Hassanpour 2005a). These broadcast media were significant forces in creating and sustaining a pan-Kurdish national identity in diaspora as a "nonstate nation." As one resident of Mahabad in Iranian Kurdistan told Hassanpour, "No one watches Iranian TV. Everyone watches the Kurdish channels, and Med-TV is one of them" (Naficy 2005a). However, it is important not to overestimate the impact of the transnational satellite television and not to underestimate the continued power of the nation-states, which use nationalism and secularism (in Turkey) and nationalism and religion (in Iran) to manipulate and mobilize opposition to the Kurds and to other minority nationalities. Despite the supposedly globalized world, borders matter and nation-states, which control and patrol them, do as well. However, with the formation of the Kurdistan Regional Government in northern Iraq, in 1992, after the imposition of the no-fly zone on Saddam Hussein by British and U.S. forces, and with Hussein's defeat and demise, in 2003, an autonomous Kurdish nation, a pan-Kurdish TV, and a pan-Kurdish national cinema became a reality.

During the Pahlavi regimes, Persian-language Iranian fiction movies subtitled or dubbed into Kurdish were shown in Iranian Kurdistan (Hassanpour 1996). Iranian Kurds had not produced films in Kurdish, so the aforementioned postrevolution documentaries constitute the first steps toward Kurdish cinema. Tayfur Patai, a Kurd born in Sanandaj who graduated from Tehran University's School of Fine Arts, contributed significantly. He made several films in Persian for NIRT, which aired one of them, a twenty-minute 16mm film in Persian called *Return* (*Geranewe*, 1970). However, Patai's next two films, both forty-five minutes in length and in Persian, were banned: *Who Will Carry His Own Ashes to the Mountains?* (*Cheh Kasi Khakestar-e Khish beh Kuhestan Mibarad?*, 1971) and *Water* (*Aw*, 1971). He was arrested and tried in 1973, along with Daneshian, Golsorkhi, Allamehzadeh, and others, in a televised military trial, which condemned him to death for involvement in a plot to kidnap the royal family.[49] Fortunately, he was not executed; the revolution freed him. Soon after, he made *Pain* (*Azar*, 1979), aired by VVIR's regional station in Sanandaj in Iranian Kurdistan. His next two projects, both forty-five minutes and shot in 8mm format, were underground films in Kurdish. *The*

Light of the Candles (*Rûnakî emekan*, 1983) screened in liberated areas of Iranian Kurdistan and during ceremonies of the Kurdish Democratic Party of Iran in diaspora, while *The Proud Summits of Kurdistan* (*Çiya Serberzekanî Kurdistan / Qollehha-ye Sarfaraz-e Kordestan*, 1983) was screened by the exile film festival in Saarbrücken, Germany, and in Los Angeles. In this film, which was produced by the Kurdistan Democratic Party of Iran, Patai documents attacks on Kurdish towns: billowing smoke can be seen rising from damaged towns like Sanandaj and Naqadeh, whose displaced Kurdish people live in tents, open fields, or mountain caves. *Peshmerga* guerrillas—male and female—guard the fields and mountains, over which hover attacking helicopters. The film ends with a gravestone bearing these words: "Democracy for Iran, autonomy for Kurdistan." The Democratic Party of Kurdistan branches in Europe and the United States screened this film around discussions of the Iranian government and Kurdish statehood. As one of the Kurdish presenters, who wished to remain anonymous, told me, "These films are meant to publicize what the government is doing to Kurdish people who want autonomy, and wish to document the bravery of the rebels."

Patai left Iran for exile in Sweden; his subsequent films were shown in European festivals. Among them were *Camp* (*Hewar*, 1984), 30 minutes; *Bread and Freedom* (*Nan va Azadi*, 1984), 104 minutes; and *Pack of Wolves* (*Gele Gurg*, 1990), 35mm, 80 minutes, all of which are in Kurdish. *Pack of Wolves*, a professional production of diaspora Kurds headed by Patai, was shown in twelve cities in Sweden, which has a sizable Kurdish diaspora.[50] It was made in one of the Central Asian states because it was less expensive, but the film crew was robbed and attacked. Patai thus called it *"Pack of Wolves*, a film the wolves ate!"

Both the Pahlavi and the Islamic Republic regimes generally suppressed Kurdish-language theatrical movies until 1985, when the latter allowed movies not only to be dubbed into Kurdish, but also to be filmed in Kurdish and with Kurdish themes. Assimilationist states, like Iran, tend to discourage minority-language theatrical movies, because they fear that these movies might empower nationalist, cessationist, and autonomy-seeking movements. "It is not surprising, therefore, that the first Kurdish dubbed films, as in the case with broadcasting, find their origins in political imperatives, rather than in government support of a minority language or culture" (Hassanpour 1992:344).

Nevertheless, by 2000 a non-state Kurdish cinema consciousness and even an actual non-state Kurdish fiction cinema were emerging thanks to the aforementioned documentaries and the works of innovative fiction directors such as Bahman Ghobadi from Iran and others from Turkey and elsewhere, who employed Kurdish characters, stories, landscapes, language, and music in fiction movies.

Jewish and Baha'i Films

Among ethnoreligious minorities, the Jews and Baha'is were legally prosecuted and violently persecuted more than others, the former because of mutual hostility between Iran and Israel, the latter because it was declared a heretical religion—Baha'ism is an offshoot of Shiism born in Iran in the mid-1800s. Massive emigration of adherents of these two religions began. Iranian Jews, constituting the largest Jewish population in the Middle East outside Israel, and Baha'is do not appear to have made many documentaries inside Iran about their plight. Both populations were discriminated against and vilified, but the Baha'is were specially targeted and were deprived of almost all of their human and citizen rights, including the rights to employment, higher education, and election to public office. However, Muslim filmmakers made feature movies involving Jewish characters and communities, including Masud Kimiai's thriller *Lead* (*Sorb*, 1988), about the way the Zionist Jews in Iran after the Second World War reputedly fomented panic among fellow Jews to promote emigration to the newly created state of Israel. In 1979 the Ministry of Culture and Higher Education made a very brief film (2.38 minutes), *Jews in the Course of the Glorious Iranian Revolution* (*Kalimian dar Jarayan-e Enqelab-e Shokuhmand-e Iran*), about the Jewish demonstrations against the Pahlavi regime and their meetings with Ayatollahs Taleqani (in Tehran) and Khomeini (in Paris). Shot on 35mm film, all images were from photographs of the revolution (Jafari Lahijani 2008:vol. 1:433–34).

Much later, Ramin Farahani made a one-hour documentary, *Jews of Iran* (*Yahudian-e Iran*, 2005). Filmed in 2001, it covers the lives of the Jews in Tehran, Isfahan, and Shiraz, noting that the Jewish population of the country, which stood at 100,000 before the revolution, had dwindled to less than 20,000, due to persecution and emigration to Europe, the United States, and Israel. Interviews with teachers, doctors, patients, artists, musicians, athletes, and students show a wide range of views and a catalog of ill treatment under the Islamic Republic: one smart student is determined to leave the country, even though she will miss her country, because her classmates humiliate her by calling her "polluted" (*najes*) and "dirty." Whereas before the revolution most of Tehran's music shops and instrument sellers and tuners were Jews, only one lonely Jewish man now remains in the business. While weeping, an old Jewish patient intones, "I am an outsider and without a friend in the world." Due to emigration and decreasing population, Jewish synagogues and hospitals are depopulated, forcing the congregations of several synagogues to be combined into one. Dwindling population has also created a critical shortage of partners for the young Jews who seek spouses. Thirteen Jews are charged with espionage and jailed in Shiraz, to be exonerated only after many years. Foreign policy plays a role not only in Iranian official policy and conduct but also in the politics and conduct of individuals: a Muslim student says she opposes the Iranian Jews because of Israel's policies against Iran. At the same time that the film provides such a catalog of discontent, however, it documents the long history of the Jews in Iran (claiming they founded what became Isfahan in memory of Jerusalem over 2,500 years ago) and the Jewish contributions to Iranian culture and arts. In addition, the film points to certain moments of reconciliation even in today's Iran: at a music concert a Jewish leader declares, "We are Iranian first, then Jewish," and it shows an intimate friendship between two women athletes, one Muslim, the other Jewish, whose hip-hop–loving sons have also been friends since childhood.

If the Baha'is did not make any documentaries inside Iran, they made, or participated in making, documentary films and television programs in exile. Aided by an active network of coreligionists outside Iran, these tended to document and express the pain, persecution, and the terrible loss of life and property that the Baha'is suffered under the Islamic regime. *Baha'i: Iran's Secret Pogrom* (1980), a film by Knut Kucharski for CTV Television, Toronto, Canada, examines the persecution of Baha'is in the religion's birthplace, Iran, using interviews with relatives of those executed, along with their photographs and films of the desecration of Baha'i holy sites. In *The Baha'is of Iran: A Report on the Persecution of a Religious Minority* (1982), the program host Roxanne Terrel interviews members of the U.S. Baha'i National Assembly and others at a memorial in Los Angeles in honor of executed Baha'is in Iran. The program contains shots of the Baha'i shrine in Shiraz. *A Cry from the Heart* (1982) contains footage of the U.S. House Subcommittee on Human Rights and International Organizations hearings about the Islamic Republic's persecution of the Baha'is. Some of the twenty-six-part television series *The Spiritual Revolution* (1981), produced by the Baha'i Center in Wilmette, Illinois, and aired on local television channels in the United States, including on KSCI-TV in Los Angeles, dealt with similar issues. Rozita Riazati produced and Kasra Naji reported *Baha'is in Iran (Baha'iha dar Iran*, 2010) for BBC Persian, a twenty-seven-minute film about the history of the mistreatment of Baha'is in Iran and the lives of the Baha'is in Haifa, Israel, the site of the world administrative headquarters of the faith—one of the reasons the Islamic regime charges the Baha'is with espionage for Israel. *Human Rights in Iran and the Plight of the Baha'is* (2010) is a multipart video containing the proceedings of a night of speeches and performances at Columbia University, New York City, by various human-rights activists and performers, including Rudi Bakhtiar, Roxana Saberi, Shohreh Aghdashloo, and Houshang Touzie. The event was in protest of state-sanctioned terrorism against the Baha'is inside Iran and the wholesale imprisonment and secret trial of seven Baha'i leaders charged with spying for Israel.[51]

Music videos, too, dramatized the plight of the Baha'is. Particularly noteworthy is the six-minute video *Mona with the Children*, sung in English by the Canadian pop singer Doug Cameron, backed by Dan Seals, of Seals and Crofts, and the Cree Indian–Canadian singer Buffy Saint-Marie. It recreates the last days of Mona Mahmudnizhad, a sixteen-year-old Baha'i girl in Shiraz, in fall 1982. She is teaching a class of preschool children when revolutionary guards enter to take her away. They blindfold her, imprison her, torture her, and eventually hang her, in June 1983, when she refuses to recant her religion. Broadcast on Iranian exile television in the United States in the 1980s, the video's recreation is graphic in its passionate details, and it ends when, at the gallows, Mona defiantly takes down her veil, kisses the noose, and places it around her own neck. Many people, including Cameron, Seals, and Saint-Marie, gather to sing the song's refrain and to grieve and place wreaths on Mahmudnizhad's grave.[52]

With time and consolidation of the Islamist regime, the human-rights violations of ethnic and religious minorities worsened. In 2010 the International Federation for Human Rights and the Iranian League for the Defense of Human Rights made public a report, "The Hidden Face of Iran," which documented "the severe discrimination faced by ethnic communities and religious minorities in every domain/area" and concluded with this damning statement.

> The Islamic Republic of Iran is based on a theocratic theory that is very narrowly interpreted to favour a small group among the Shi'a Muslims and in particular one group of the Shi'a clergy. This theory serves to discriminate against other Shi'a and Sunni Muslims as well as believers of other religions and non-believers. The IRI system and structure of government is extremely discriminatory and excludes not only the non-Shi'a Muslims and other believers on religious grounds, but also ethnic

peoples on ground of their origin. Further, the IRI denies the right to believe in or practice a religion or belief of one's choice and the right of ethnic groups to receive education, to write and publish freely in their own mother tongue and to celebrate their cultural events. Discrimination based on ethnicity and religion is widespread in Iran, both in law and in practice, in the political, social, cultural and economic fields. The regime responds to peaceful demands for the respect of the rights of minorities and abolition of discrimination by further repression and terror: violence, arbitrary arrests, torture, summary trials and executions.[53]

Women's Films

Despite the highly visible social presence of women during the revolution and their strong screen presence in the documentaries about it, the initial postrevolution documentary cinema was entirely dominated by male directors. There is no record of camerawomen making a film about the early revolutionary events that was publicly screened, although it is possible that television camerawomen filmed footage or that women filmed home movies of the revolution. The only definite and reliable account of women publicly filming immediately after the revolution comes from Mehrnaz Saeed-Vafa and from foreigners.

Kate Millet, the outspoken American peace activist and a lesbian feminist artist, provides a memorable account that, much like Shirdel's, conveys the excitement, chaos, and freedom of filming then. She and a friend, Sophie Keir, had been invited to Iran by the Committee for Artistic and Intellectual Freedom of Iran, a Trotskyite group splintered from the Confederation of Iranian Students (National Union), which opposed the Shah, to travel to Iran to lecture, observe, document, and support the Iranian struggle for liberation and equality, particularly by women. The two carried both still and motion-picture cameras with them. A day after the veil was reinstated by the Islamic Republic, they participated in the giant women's demonstration in Tehran University in opposition to it. Here is Millet's account.

> Sophie goes above to shoot film. I am in the sea of women. We are packed so tight it is hard to stand, still harder to sit down when the speakers begin. And the claustrophobia never comes. Nor the fear of being lost here, nor even the fear of being shot; the chants, the surge of upraised arms, the power of the crowd sustains me entirely. They are women, how safe one feels with women. . . . The Ayatollah [Khomeini]

clinging in ubiquitous photos to the wall, and his minions, the tough young men with guns, behind them the robes of clergy, bureaucrats, the laws, the lies, the edicts—we are a greater force. Greater than I have ever felt in America in our demonstrations. Even the mammoth demos of the peace movement, we are a wild force with unknown power, fresh tapped, springing, yet careful, controlled for all its passion. And the chants are passion itself. *Azadi, Azadi, Azadi* [Freedom, Freedom, Freedom]. . . .

Sophie joins me again, the movie camera high over her head, our fear of its being broken; its weight by now is great. And finally out of film. Militia helped her through the crowds, she says, probably thought she was a reporter. We de-escalate to still film, little cameras, both of us shooting. A light floods the speakers, some Italians shooting sixteen-millimeter film with a big movie camera, sound sync. We envy them a second. . . . There is but one roll of black-and-white movie stock left in our knapsack, today's ration, we'll save it for later. Meanwhile we have lots of thirty-five-millimeter and each a still camera to shoot with, shooting like maniacs, loading for each other, Sophie often loading for both of us since I take longer; but loading and shooting continuously, the frenzy of the chants making us high, the fierceness, the valor of the women shouting down Islàmic prejudice, the mullahs' repression. Beginning the revolution again. This is how it must have been during the uprising, this the fury, the fearlessness. And the guns surrounding us, an army undecided, never protective but at this moment neutral or almost, their own notions of what we are put aside, yet the finger still holds the trigger. (Millet 1982:139–40)

It was during this day that women who protested against the imposition of the veil were called "antirevolutionary monarchists" and "idolaters" (*taquti*), taunted with the famous slogan "Either cover on the head, or a blow to the head," and in some cases physically attacked. The time for decision had arrived. Roya Hakakian, an Iranian-American journalist, who was then a teenager, recalled the stark choice that the situation posed for women the next day: "As I listened to the news and the rumors, shame began to chase away the pride I'd felt upon watching them [women protesters] the day before. The decision before every woman, as it was painted, was between the love of country and the love of self. Being a patriotic teenager, I willingly added a scarf to my fashionable T-shirt and jeans by the week's end" (2005). With this, women were shoehorned into joining the segregated, unequal, and collective category of "woman," one step back in their march toward recognition as distinct modern individuals. It would take years for the anonymity, homogeneity, and uniformity of the veil to be attenuated by individuality and personality.

Tired of their "meddling," the authorities soon expelled Millet and Keir from the country; the women appear not to have completed their film. In the meantime, the March 8 Committee, a coalition of Iranian feminists and four members of France's Psychanalyse et Politique who were in Iran at the time, produced a twelve-minute documentary of the women's march in Tehran on International Women's Day, 8 March 1979. Titled *Iran's Women's Liberation Movement Begins* (*Shoru-e Jonbesh-e Azadi-ye Zanan-e Iran / Mouvement de Libération des Femmes Iraniennes—Année Zero*, 1979), the film shows tens of thousands of women, mostly without veils, marching in the streets and in Freedom Square, waving their fists in the air, displaying placards, and shouting slogans, among them "We did not make a revolution to go backward" and "Freedom, neither Western, nor Eastern, but Universal," the latter a reworking of the Islamists' favorite slogan then prevalent, "Neither Western, nor Eastern, but Islamic Republic." The film, with Persian and French voice-over narration, includes interviews with participants, including one with a chador-wearing mother who says she has six daughters but does not want them to be forced into the veil, pressing the idea of personal rights. Kate Millet is also interviewed, as are female nurses who presciently assert that the time to fight for gender equality and freedom of expression and assembly is now, not after the constitution is written—which is the dominant position. Some 15,000 women also gather outside the headquarters of the Voice and Vision of the Islamic Republic to protest the fact that Sadegh Ghotbzadeh was allowing Islamists to monopolize the airwaves. Shot with a shaky, 16mm, hand-held camera, the film imparts the immediacy, intensity, and spontaneity of the revolution and the seriousness of the issues that brought so many women together, providing a historical document of the last major demonstration in which women were allowed to be unveiled in public.[54] It is possible that this film contains some of the footage that Millet and Keir had filmed.

In their sixty-minute documentary *Headscarf as a System/Does Hair Drive People Crazy?* (*Pftuch als System/Machen Haare verrückt?*, 2004), Shina Erlewein, Fatiyeh Naghibzadeh, Bettina Hohaus, and Meral El dealt with a broad range of women's issues, including the 1979 demonstrations excerpted from *Iran's Women's Liberation Movement Begins*, interviews with Iranian women in Germany describing the politics of the hijab, and footage of the controversial Iran Conference in Berlin, organized by the Heinrich-Böll Foundation in April 2000, which played into the cultural invasion discourse inside Iran. Soon, women inside Iran, too, began making documentaries, fiction movies, art films, and animated films.

The monarchist factions were less involved in making films against the Iranian regime; they were decimated and dispirited by their exile to foreign lands and following the humiliating serial exile and homelessness of the last Pahlavi king and his untimely death, at sixty, in Egypt in July 1980, from complications related to non-Hodgkin lymphoma. Many monarchists were members of ethnoreligious minorities persecuted in the Islamic Republic, and they had been trained in pop music, advertising, broadcasting, commercial film, and other entertainment fields. Their massive congregation in Los Angeles turned the city into the capital of exilic pop culture and music, a veritable "Persian Motown." They also produced television programs and other media, which deftly combined politics with popular entertainment, dystopic iconography, and nostalgic narratives to form a syncretic cultural formation that nurtured them while they caught their breath and licked their wounds (Naficy 1993:chap. 5; Naficy 2002a).

Biographical Documentaries

The upheavals of the revolution and its aftermath affected individual lives tremendously, making them more interesting as film subjects. It also brought home an important aspect of Iranian modernity: the role of individuals as architects not only of their own lives but also of their society. While historical and compilation documentaries focused primarily on the social and historical forces in shaping history, biographical documentaries emphasized the role of individuals as a force in history. This section deals only with the biographical films made during and immediately after the revolution, most of which were pro-regime and pro-Islam. Some of the major thinkers whose works and lives had inspired resistance and opposition to the Shah, and ultimately contributed to the revolution, had died during his reign, but no film had been made about them at that time. With the new freedoms, even chaos, of the revolutionary times, these "great men" became proper subjects of films (indeed, they were all men). In their choice of subject matter, these films underscored the great men theory of history at the same time that they reflected the male-dominated reality of the Iranian politics. In addition, some of the living great men and architects of the revolution were aged, and they needed to be celebrated and eulogized on film. Finally, there were those who had become "martyrs" in the cause of the revolution and thus necessitated filmic elegies.

Among the films made about the great men whose works and thoughts had influenced the emergence of the anti-Shah revolution were the following. Zahra Mozhdehbakhsh produced and directed a twenty-nine-minute film for VVIR, *Crystal Ball: Jalal Al-e Ahmad* (*Jam-e Jahanbin: Jalal Al-e Ahmad*, 1980), which focused on the writer Al-e Ahmad, whose influential critical analysis of Westernization and Western intellectuals in the 1960s, his turn from communism to Islam, and his suspicious death made him an inspiration for both leftist and Islamist critics of the Pahlavi regime. Reza Allamehzadeh directed *The Wise Little Black Fish* (*Mahi-ye Siah-e Kuchulu-ye Dana*, 1980), a forty-five-minute film for CIDCYA on the life and times of Samad Behrangi, the famous Marxist Pahlavi-era schoolteacher and author whose children's book, *The Little Black Fish*, had become Fadaiyan's "unofficial manifesto" and had "attracted more militants to the Fadai movement" than any of the organization's manifestos or Marxist texts (Vahabzadeh 2010:134). The film visits Behrangi's birthplace, Tabriz, and other relevant sites, and interviews his mother, his brother, and writers who knew him, including Gholamhosain Saedi and Nasim Khaksar.

The most influential of the prerevolution Islamic thinkers who died before the revolution was Ali Shariati, about whom Puran Safari made the thirteen-minute *Martyred Witness: Memory of Dr. Ali Shariati, May He Remain in Our Thoughts* (*Shahid-e Shahed: Yad-e Zendehyad Doktor Ali Shariati*, 1979). Made for VVIR, the film reviews Shariati's life and work through his taped speeches and interviews with his father, spouse, child, and friends describing his life and times, accompanied by films and photographs of him. VVIR produced another film about Shariati, *For a Man Who Reached the Sun* (*Bara-ye Mardi keh beh Khorshid Resid*, 1979?). An anonymous director made this thirty-eight-minute film at VVIR's branch in Mashhad, Shariati's hometown. It contains rare 8mm films and recordings of his speeches, including the footage of his Hajj pilgrimage in Mecca and his funeral in London. Another VVIR film on the topic is *Emigration of Dr. Shariati* (*Hejrat-e Doktor Shariati*, 1979), a thirteen-minute film devoted chiefly to Ayatollah Taleqani's memories of Shariati.

Of the nationalist figures of the 1950s whose lives, thoughts, and actions resonated during the revolution and were turned into films, the following are notable. Hosain Torabi wrote and directed, for MCIG, the thirty-two-minute film *Remembering a National Leader* (*Yadi az yek Rahbar-e Melli*, 1979), in which he chronicled the tumultuous life of the renowned Prime Minister Mohammad Mosaddeq, whose impact on Iranian politics spanned the Qajar and the First and Second Pahlavi periods. Mohammad Tahaminejad wrote and directed *Remembering Doctor Fatemi* (*Yadi az Doktor Fatemi*, 1980), in which the sister of the Mosaddeq-era foreign minister Fatemi and others who knew him graphically recall the minister's efforts on behalf of Iran's independence and his fatal knifing by the famous pro-Shah tough-guy Shaban the Brainless. The film, made for VVIR, contains family photographs and Fatemi's letters smuggled out of prison. *Commemorating Navvab Safavi* (*Bozorgdasht-e Navvab Safavi*, 1979), filmed by Kashanchi for VVIR, contains interviews by Fatemeh Navvab Safavi about the life, Islamic beliefs, and terrorist actions of her father, Mojtaba, who as a founder of Fadaiyan-e Eslam was involved in assassinating "corrupt" Pahlavi officials in the 1950s, for which he was executed. Vartan Antasian produced and directed *World Champion Takhti* (*Jahan Pahlevan Takhti*, 1979), a forty-five-minute film for VVIR about the extremely popular wrestler Gholamreza Takhti, who rose from very modest beginnings to international fame—he won gold and silver medals in the Olympics—and to national respect as a champion of the downtrodden, a perception magnified when he died in his room in Tehran's Atlantic Hotel, in 1967, in suspicious circumstances, which the government interpreted as suicide and Takhti's supporters interpreted as government-engineered murder. Hasan Torabi made for MCIG *Bazargan from Premiership to Resignation* (*Bazargan az Nokhostvaziri ta Este'fa*, 1979), a seventy-minute film about Mehdi Bazargan, a respected nationalist Muslim intellectual who ran the Iranian oil industry after Mosaddeq had nationalized it in the 1950s and who later became the first postrevolution prime minister. His term ended when he and his cabinet resigned in protest against the taking of Americans hostage in their Tehran embassy on 4 November 1979.

Hosain Fadaifard's twenty-one-minute film for VVIR, *Commemorating General Qaraney* (*Bozorgdasht-e Timsar Qaraney*, 1980), chronicles the political life of General Mohammad Vali Qaraney through interviews with his wife and colleagues. Qaraney rose against the Shah and maintained relations with oppositional clerics in the 1950s and 1960s, for which he was imprisoned several times. One day after the revolution succeeded, Ayatollah Khomeini appointed him to head the new national armed forces and to reorganize it; a little over a month later, a member of Forqan group assassinated him.

Several leading clerics of the twentieth century were submitted to biographical treatments. *Exalted Martyr* (*Aqa-ye Shahid*, 1979?), made for VVIR by an anonymous director, is a sixty-two-minute film about the life, political activism, and "martyrdom" of Ayatollah Seyyed Hasan Moddares, who was a staunch supporter of the constitutional movement in the early twentieth century and who later opposed Reza Shah, for which he was murdered in his prison cell in 1937. Faraidun Andalib made for vvir the twenty-nine-minute film *Commemorating Ayatollah Seyyed Abolqasem Kashani* (*Bozorg-dasht-e Ayatollah Seyyed Abolqasem Kashani*, 1980), about the political life of the Mosaddeq-era clerical leader, who as the speaker of the Majles supported nationalization of the Iranian oil; however, Kashani soon abandoned Mosaddeq over his secularizing reforms and supported the coup against him. The film was made in honor of Kashani's eighteenth anniversary.

Ayatollah Mahmud Taleqani, one of the most influential and respected leaders of the Islamic Revolution was treated in several films. Farhad Lesani produced and directed for vvir *Ayatollah Taleqani: 9 September 1979* (*Ayatollah Taleqani: 18 Shahrivar 1358*, 1979?), a thirty-four-minute film that begins with a picture of the ayatollah's birth certificate, which details his personal and familial origins, and ends with his grave in the Behest-e Zahra Cemetery after a massive funeral march in Tehran's streets (the date in the title is his date of death). In between, the film chronicles his clerical education and his public political life against the Pahlavi Shahs by means of photographs, films, and interviews. Ali Asghar Oqabi also directed a film about Ayatollah Taleqani for vvir, *Remembering Ayatollah Taleqani* (*Yadvareh-ye Ayatollah Taleqani*, 1980), which was aired on the anniversary of his death. vvir sponsored and aired two other political biographies of Ayatollah Taleqani: An anonymous director made the seventy-five-minute film *Father Taleqani* (*Pedar Taleqani*, 1979), which features an interview with the ayatollah's daughter, who discusses his thoughts and actions. Parviz Nabavi directed *Father* (*Pedar*, 1979), a twenty-seven-minute film that contains interviews with the ayatollah, his speeches, and an interview with his wife, Azam Taleqani. Ruhollah Emami and Parviz Amir Afshar codirected for mcig *The Path of God* (*Rah-e Khoda*, 1979), a sixteen-minute film on the political life of the ayatollah. Despite its short duration, it is a dense chronicle of his life, beginning with a touching scene of his room, where his lonely personal effects signify a sense of national abandonment and loss after his death.

These revolution-era biographical films are part of the "official cinema" of the Islamic Republic for several reasons. For one thing, they were made in a two-year span of time, during great upheaval, when the country and the new regime needed to be anchored ideologically. Reviving, remembering, commemorating, and rehabilitating past and present heroes who had contributed to the revolution helped address this need. All the films are about the people who contributed to the Islamic Revolution and to the creation of the IRI. For another, the official state-run film and television bodies—Voice and Vision of the Islamic Republic and the Ministry of Culture and Islamic Guidance—made almost all of them. That the makers of several of the films are anonymous emphasizes even more the official and institutional stamp of the state on these works. Finally, VVIR aired a majority—perhaps all—of these films nationwide, helping to synchronize the nation ideologically. After the fever of revolution subsided, there appeared biographical films about other types of outstanding individuals—writers, filmmakers, actors, artists, musicians, and other politicians and revolutionaries.

CONSOLIDATING A NEW

"ISLAMICATE" CINEMA AND

FILM CULTURE

Periods of major social turmoil and transition seem to produce some of the most innovative cineastes and cinematic movements. The formalist Soviet films of Eisenstein and Vertov followed the Russian Revolution; the British realist documentaries immediately preceded and followed the Second World War; the Italian neorealists emerged during and immediately after the Second World War; and the Polish "black films" emerged during the "spring thaw" of de-Stalinization in the mid-1950s. Concurrent with the worldwide social turmoils of decolonization, of anti–Vietnam War activism, and of the counterculture movements of the 1960s and 1970s, too, several innovative film movements surfaced, including "cinema novo" in Brazil, "new wave" cinema in France and Iran, "cinema vérité" in the United States, France, and Canada, and "third cinema" in Latin America and elsewhere. Thus, there was good cause to expect that the 1979 revolution in Iran, popularly known as the Islamic Revolution, and its preconditions and aftermath would produce a new cinema. This turned out to be an Islamicate cinema and film culture. In this chapter, I chart the emergence of this cinema and film culture and the undergirding film industry formations during four distinct political phases: the Islamicization and war years under Ayatollah Khomeini (1980–88); the reconstruction era under President Ali Akbar Hashemi Rafsanjani (1989–97); the reform era under President Mohammad Khatami (1997–2005); and the retrenchment era under President Mahmoud Ahmadinejad (2005–10). I emphasize the first three phases.

State Consolidation and Reemergence of Cinema

The Islamist hardliners gradually took charge of all major institutions and with their continuation of the Iraq-Iran War, the resolution of the American "hostage crisis" in their favor, the passage of a new constitution that institutionalized an Islamic government, and the routing of all major organized oppositions, they consolidated their grip on the country. The resulting theocracy consisted of two parallel, unequal, and irreconcilable formations. One was the semi-democratic formal state government based on Western republican models, consisting of an elected president whose cabinet members running the country's formal economy, culture, and industries had to be confirmed by, and be accountable to, a nationally elected parliament (Majles). The other was the theocratic command structure of *velayat-e faqih* (guardianship of the jurisprudent), consisting of a supreme leader (first, Ayatollah Ruhollah Khomeini, then, later, Ayatollah Ali Khamenei), who controlled the various religiously dominated bodies staffed by unelected members, such as the expediency council, the guardian council, and the supreme national security council, as well as the judiciary, the armed forces, and the broadcast media.

This structure, which vested greater power in unelected religious officials, produced not only a "clientelist state," in which competing autonomous groups fought over personal bonds with the state (Alamdari 2005), but also an authoritarian "rentier state" that, like its monarchical predecessor, was propped up by the wealth generated from renting its natural resources of oil and gas, freeing it somewhat from needing to tax its citizen or to be accountable to them (Najmabadi 1987). However, it was not an entirely homogeneous, monolithic, or totalitarian state. Rather, this structure favored the reemergence of another "rickety society" or "pick-ax society" (Katouzian 2009) whose competing power centers and evolving frameworks ensured a lively opposition within the malleable and increasingly militarized ruling apparatuses. The dynamism of the postrevolution cinema was a result of this structural complexity and its interplay of forces, discourses, dispositions, formations, institutions, maneuvers, tactics, and techniques, recounted here.

During and after the Constitutional Revolution, various factions—among them, religious moderates, religious modernists, secular modernists, and absolute monarchists—vied with each other to insinuate, or to resist the insinuation of, democracy and modernity into the Iranian public sphere.[1] Similarly, after the consolidation of the Islamic Republic the interplay of forces and discourses of modernity and democracy was motivated by various formations, among them, Islamic conservatives (Islamists), Islamic reformists, and secular modernists (Kamrava 2008). As Farzin Vahdat notes, "Iran's century-and-a-half experience with modernity should be understood in terms of a dialectical process involving aspects of modernity conducive to emancipation, on the one hand, and those more conducive to domination, on the other. In this process, different elements of modernity often vied with each other, leading to different phases in the development of the new civilization in Iran. Furthermore, at different times different aspects of modernity were developed and elaborated upon by different social groups" (2002:xii). In both the Pahlavi and the Islamic Republic periods, filmmakers allied themselves with one or another of these social formations and discourses of emancipation and domination to gain ascendancy and self-expression. That is why the transformation from Pahlavi to Islamicate cinema was not rapid or unidirectional, but was impacted by major cultural and ideological shifts, contestations, negotiations, and transformations. In cinematic terms, using the words of Mohammad Beheshti, the first director of the Farabi Cinema Foundation, "Transformation in the context of cinema" had to occur with a "'dissolve,' not a 'cut.'"[2]

The structural reorganization of entertainment and broadcast industries under the Islamic Republic resulted in a system that resembled the Pahlavi version, as both were authoritarian regimes using both a command economy and private enterprise in which the state's share grew (Arjomand 1988:173). The processes of Islamicization and national integration continued with new institutions of development and ideological inculcation and coercion—the Reconstruction Crusade, the Foundation of the Dispossessed, the Islamic Revolutionary Guards Corps, and the Basij Militia Force—as well as the suppression of all ethnic separatist or autonomous and democratic movements. The broadcast media and film industry were important in imagining the new Islamicate national identity. Differences, however, helped both to bring about an Islamicate cinema—not an Islamic cinema—and to institutionalize modernity in the country and in the industry.

Negotiating the Early Obstacles to Cinema's Re-emergence

Purification measures were only one set of reasons—though important—for why the re-emergence of a new cinema had to be a slow dissolve. Islamicization was not pro forma; many other factors contributed to creating a fluid and contentious atmosphere. Many obstacles appeared early; some were negotiated quickly; some persisted for years. One nonnegotiable problem was the financial damage inflicted on the industry during the revolution. Recovering the destroyed movie houses was a Herculean task. Within a year and half after the revolution—during the transition period—none were rebuilt in the provinces, and only one in Tehran returned to operation. The courts confiscated many of the cinemas, which became publicly owned. The giant Foundation of the Dispossessed (Boniad-e Mostazafan, FOD) took possession of them. Among them were the cinemas in which the Pahlavi Foundation had investments. By mid-1983 FOD had become the largest owner, operating some 137 cinemas in sixteen provinces—approximately half of all cinemas in the country. Producers and importers did not fare much better. An estimated two thousand prints of feature movies valued at four million tomans at the time were burned. The loss to film importers was estimated to be twelve million tomans. Disastrous for domestic producers was the fact that many of the forty Iranian features in the works prior to the revolution could not be shown because of the emergence of Islamicate values, and others had to be reworked at great cost.[3] The destruction of movie houses rendered film production an economically foolish activity. This paved the way for imports.

A vacuum in authority meant the inexperienced Islamist regime was under siege even as it was still working out the institutions necessary for running a complex economy and society. Centers of power competed for ascendancy, including in cinema. The Pahlavi period's Progressive Film Cooperative (PFC) was revived in the first two months of the revolution, holding meetings in Bahman Farmanara's Iran Biograph Film offices, which many new-wave filmmakers attended, including Reza Allamehzadeh, Hushang Baharlu, Hajir Dariush, Bahman Farmanara, Ali Hatami, Abbas Kiarostami, Masud Kimiai, Dariush Mehrjui, and Kamran Shirdel. A new syndicate for film industry artists and technical personnel was also formed, which PFC members joined (Allamehzadeh 1991:17). Members of the Islamist-oriented Ayat Film Company soon joined both the PFC and the syndicate, setting the stage for ideological war. The Council for Cultural Planning and Policy Making was formed to plan the transformation of all cultural spheres within the new Ministry of Culture and Higher Education (MCHE), which had assumed many of the functions of former Ministry of Culture and Art and consisted of some twenty subcommittees, one of which was devoted to cinema. Personal feuds and ideological differences soon surfaced between secularists and Islamists, with the latter becoming ascendant within MCHE. The ministry's power in matters cinematic was quite circumspect, for while it ruled on which movies were to be exhibited in Tehran, the revolutionary committees were making separate decisions in the provinces. The ministry claimed that it did not censor and that provincial committees engaged in film censorship on their own. Even in Tehran, the ministry's power to regulate cinemas was limited. It shut down ten movie houses in February 1980, but it had to do so on the grounds of unsanitary and unsafe conditions.[4]

Institutional rivalries were rampant, seen in improvised and shifting strategies. In early 1980, MCHE and FOD were in such hot competition that the ministry shut down all the country's movie houses in an attempt to thwart the foundation's meddling, only to have the order rescinded a week later, after Sadeq Tabatabai, a relative of Ayatollah Khomeini, was appointed to investigate the film industry's transition problems, including the rivalry between MCHE and FOD. All along, however, the foundation disregarded the ministry's order and continued to operate its cinemas.[5] The ministry and the foundation had their differences. For example, the foundation disagreed with the ministry's proposal to have Iranian importers of foreign movies also produce films, for it feared that such importers would be secular, pro-West individuals; instead, the foundation wanted only "committed and pious" agents sent abroad to select foreign movies. The ministry had apparently proposed to review and censor local films only after their production, while the foundation insisted that prior to production all film treatments and screenplays be submitted to a group of "committed and revolutionary Muslims" for review. It also insisted on reviewing completed films after their production.

FOD had its own share of problems with commercial exhibitors, as it repossessed many movie houses for one reason or another and thus angered cinema owners. For example, Mohsen Mazaheri, the manager of the deluxe Shahr-e Farang Cinema, published a letter to Ayatollah Khomeini, in *Ayandegan* newspaper, promising to fight his theater's repossession to the end.[6] The rivalries between FOD and various ministries and commercial production companies concerned access to financial capital as well as to cultural-ideological capital.

FOD and many postrevolutionary organizations represented the emergence of a new sector in the Iranian political economy: the paragovernmental sector, which reinforced mainstream Islamist ideology without public oversight or accountability (Saeidi 2004). Soon after the war, the Islamic Revolutionary Guard Corps (IRGC) joined this paragovernmental sector, adding a paramilitary dimension to Iranian civilian and cultural formations, with grave consequences for further militarization of culture and media.

Big-time importers of foreign movies competed intensely with small-time producers and exhibitors of domestic movies. The government had banned the importation of certain foreign movies, but it failed for quite some time to come up with a coherent plan to support domestic productions. In the meantime, many foreign movies from the Pahlavi era were still around—many repossessed by FOD—and were being screened, with or without license. In fact, these movies were doing a brisk business, while more stringently censored domestic movies withered. An old Norman Wisdom comedy, almost worthless before the revolution, was now being sold for over $250,000, while a domestic movie could hardly get a screening. Additionally, the Eastern bloc embassies flooded the screens with their "propaganda" movies under very agreeable conditions.

The eroded prestige of cinema was another impediment to cinema's resurgence. Film's stigma justified for those involved the purifications described, the takeover of the movie houses by FOD, and the new regulations. With cinema having been purified and regulated, another impediment surfaced: film business personnel were largely non-Muslim or secular, and there were no models of what a film with "Islamicate values" would look like, or what an Islamicate film "genre" would consist of. *Soroush*, the official publication of the Voice and Vision of the Islamic Republic (VVIR) condemned as "calendar films" the early postrevolution movies, which failed to exhibit Islamicate values beyond their current-events subjects. The shortcoming was not just in Iran. Media from other Muslim countries were also considered to be either non-Islamic or "against Islamic values and criteria."[7] It took some time before Islamically inclined filmmakers created an Islamicate aesthetic.

The internal withdrawal and purification and the external exile of scores of film professionals created a vacuum. Many infrastructural support people and technicians were around, but the new regime lacked high-level and mid-level personnel. A *Mahnameh-ye Sinemai-ye Film* study of film-production personnel reported that between 1983 and mid-1986, the percentage of Pahlavi-era directors employed decreased from 55 percent to 7 percent; while those of cinematographers decreased from 75 percent to 14 percent, screenplay writers from 42 percent to zero, and lead male and female actors from 64 percent to 21 percent.[8] Rivalry, bickering, power plays, incompetence, and interference by those whose mission was not yet well defined wasted valuable time and resources. The result was confusion of authority and policy, leading to industry stagnation. Finally, during the transition phase, the new Islamist government seemed to concentrate more on iconoclastic destruction of the vestiges of the Pahlavi regime than on building new institutions, particularly cultural ones.

This lack of concern with building a new cinema was evident in the first five-year budget plan, in which cinema did not appear.[9]

It was under these circumstances that in January 1980, in an open letter to the minister of Culture and Higher Education, the Society of Cinema Owners could chide the government for its inaction, announcing that if the government "*approved the necessity of the existence of cinema,*" then the private sector, with government assistance, could put the film industry on the track of "the revolution and the people" within five years. The letter concluded by reminding the minister that unplanned "spontaneous reform" in cinema is not possible.[10]

Progressive filmmakers shared these concerns and in 1981, in an open letter, took the government to task. They charged that two years after the "holy and anti-dependence revolution of Iranian people" the revolutionary spirit had not been integrated into the film industry; instead, as in the Shah's time a kind of dependency had been fostered. The writers, among whom were the new-wave directors Baizai, Mehrjui, Shirdel, Kiarostami, and Naderi, urged the government to apply the constitution "organically and comprehensively," or Iranian cinema would become a caricature of Eastern bloc government control. The "solution to the problem [would] result in the elimination of the problem"—that is, cinema.[11] The solution that evolved gradually was the Islamicization of the film industry.

Emergence of Islamicate Filmmakers: Ayat Film Studio and the Islamic Art and Thought Center

If the Shah ensured his control of the culture industry partly by appointing royal relatives and loyal confidantes to head the key ideological state apparatuses, cronyism based on Islamicate values and kinship provided cultural control to the Islamist state.[12] The Ayat Film Studio provides an appropriate example. Although considered to be one of the first postrevolutionary film studios, it was actually formed prior to the revolution, apparently in response to a call by Ali Shariati, who urged Muslim youths to turn to the arts for expressing their socially conscious beliefs and anti-Pahlavi sentiments. Shariati was no stranger to dramatic arts, having attended movies frequently and staged a play at the University of Mashhad in 1971. His own lectures were captivating performances.[13]

Mohammad Ali Najafi, born in 1945 in Isfahan to a religious family, met Shariati in 1968; Shariati, along with Ayatollahs Behesti and Motahhari, encouraged Najafi to seek film and theater as a "social and religious duty." Backed by Shariati, Najafi organized a performing-arts group within Hosseiniyeh Ershad, which put on religiously inflected political plays. Fakhreddin Anvar and Mostafa Hashemitaba were members, and Shariati helped with the text of the plays, such as *Sarbedaran*, and taught Islamology to the students. Savak shut down *Sarbedaran* and eventually the Hosseiniyeh Seminary, in November 1972. Discouraged from theater, the group turned to film. Najafi soon directed his first feature film, *By Dawn* (*Valfajr*, 1974), inspired by Shariati's analysis of quietist Shiism vs. rebellious Shiism.

The origin of Ayat Film goes back not only to these inchoate theatrical and cinematic activities, but also to Samarqand Company, an architecture and construction firm in Tehran, run by a young Shariati protégé, Hassan Aladpush, whom Shariati frequently visited in the 1970s. During these visits Mir Hosain Musavi, a young architect, admirer of Shariati, and attendee at the Hosainiyeh Ershad, was also sometimes present. Savak raided the company and arrested all the partners. It soon released some of them, including Musavi, but it did not release Abdolali Bazargan and Aladpush. The latter, a member of PMOI who became a Marxist member of PMOI when the group split, was killed in action against the Shah.[14] Ayat Film was formed in 1977 with assistance from the Islamic Society of Engineers, of which Mohammad Beheshti, Hashemitaba, and Abdolali Bazargan were members. Majid Jafari Lahijani states that Ayatollahs Beheshti and Motahhari encouraged this filmic formation and leaned on wealthy bazaar merchants, such as Hosain Mehdian and Mahmud Manian, to finance it (2008:vol. 1:323). However, in an interview with me, the filmmaker Barbod Taheri, who knew the backstory of Ayat Film's formation, claimed that IRI's interim prime minister, Mehdi Bazargan, and his brother, Abdolali, members of Hosseiniyeh Seminary, were instrumental in facilitating the initial financing of the company through contacts among the bazaar merchants (Naficy 1988a).

Ayat Film was significant not only because of its deep connection with Shariati and senior clerics who provided the ideological and financial backing for the revolution, but also because at the time that most opposition groups were advocating armed struggle, it was engaging in politically informed performing arts. Its earliest productions were short films on Super 8 format. One film, made in 1977, commemorated Shariati's death by focusing on the empty hall of the now closed Hosseiniyeh Seminary, its dusty seats, and the unattended microphone and water glass that he had once presumably used. Shariati's loss was palpable in these images. Mostafa Hashemitaba produced and Hojatollah Saifi filmed several short documentaries about the hard lives of people on the margins of society. Ayat Film also produced many slide-tape presentations, each containing fifty to seventy slides and an audiocassette, which were widely distributed (50,000 packages). At first, the topics they dealt with were primarily religious and Islamic, but as revolutionary ardor gained momentum, images of revolutionary leaders, "martyrs," and anti-Shah political actions increased along with taped speeches by Shariati and Ayatollahs Khomeini and Motahhari (Jafari Lahijani 2008:vol. 1:324). These slide-tape and filmstrip packages could be thought of as a low-cost, new form of illustrated lecture, a veritable illustrated sermon (rowzeh), and they were apparently effective.

Soon, the company began making what it thought would be professional films. It produced two feature-length films, both directed by Najafi. *Athar's Syllabus* (*Jong-e Athar*, 1978), a fiction film about a socially conscious teacher who loses his life helping his students, was made when the Shah was still in power. As a result, when the film was first shown in a private screening at Iran Film Studio to film industry people, "They were amazed that a group was engaged in filmmaking whose members were religious who, for example, prayed or wore the hejab on the set" (Jafari Lahijani 2008:vol. 1:325). One of these was Farmanara, whose company, Iran Biograph, agreed to distribute the film after the filmmakers modified it to bring up its quality. Savak interrogated Hashemitaba and Saifi, but questioned them less about their filmmaking than about Ayat Film's connections with leftist and Islamist guerilla groups who were engaged in armed struggle. Savak was missing the point, of who was its most effective adversary—guerilla fighters or artists and filmmakers.

The second Ayat Film feature was *The Night of Power* (*Lailat al-Qadr*, 1980), a documentary about the anti-Shah revolution, which included not only graphic footage of revolutionary upheavals—a helicopter firing at crowds, demonstrators throwing Molotov cocktails, an interview with a torture victim—but also a history of modern Iran from a pro-Khomeini point of view. Rather pedantic and amateurish, the film used watercolor paintings, historical stills, and film footage to depict Iran after the First World War, Reza Shah's reign, Mohammad Reza Shah's reign (with an emphasis on his image as a playboy), and the positive role of Fadaiyan-e Eslam and the leading clerics opposing the Pahlavi regime. The film claimed that the Shah's Westernized excesses, "naked" girls, and dancing had spurred the revolution.

With the success of the revolution, Ayat Film for all intents and purposes ceased operation, a process finalized when Hashemitaba packed all of the company's films and footage and turned them over to MCIG. The impact of the company, however, far exceeded its limited film productions, for its politically committed (moto'ahhed) and religiously committed (motodayyen) members fanned out in the 1980s to take key positions within the government and in the film and allied industries, creating a powerful web of affiliation. Fakhreddin Anvar, a co-scriptwriter for *The Night of Power*, became deputy minister in the Ministry of Culture and Islamic Guidance (MCIG) and later took up high positions within VVIR; Najafi, the film's director, was appointed director general of cinematic affairs within MCIG and continued to direct films; and Mostafa Hashemitaba, the film's producer, was appointed to a high position in Khomeini's Propaganda Office and for a while was minister of industry. Other members of Ayat Film achieved even higher government positions: Mir Hosain Musavi, an architect married to an outspoken Islamic feminist writer and artist, Zahra Rahnavard, became prime minister in 1981, and Mohammad Beheshti, a nephew of Ayatollah Mohammad Beheshti, became the director of the powerful Farabi Cinema Foundation, which played a pivotal role in postrevolutionary cinema.[15]

Initially, Ayat Film personnel were among the few Islamists who could be trusted by the government, because of their background in both arts and "correct" Islamicate values. Their resultant positions allowed them to influence from early on the Islamicization and modernization of cinema. Their impact was augmented by their longevity in office: the first decade of the Islamic regime was theirs. When one considers that the first major postrevolutionary director general of VVIR was Sadegh Ghotbzadeh, the close ally of Ayatollah Khomeini, that his successor was Mohammad Hashemi Rafsanjani, the brother of the powerful speaker of the Majles Ali Akbar Hashemi Rafsanjani, who in due course would become Iran's president, the convoluted but real impact of Islamic cronyism and nepotism becomes clear.

Some Ayat Film veterans and other Islamically trusted film personnel, such as Najafi, Mohammad Ali Hashemi, and Masud Kimiai, formed the nucleus of the Council of Film and Cinema at the Ministry of Culture and Higher Education in May 1980. They took the first official crack at a new vision of cinema by proposing to partly nationalize the film industry, following the model of some Asian and African countries.[16] Najafi, then supervisor of MCHE's Office of Development and Exhibition (Edareh-ye Tarvij va Namayesh), announced measures to encourage domestic production by tying movie imports to film production inside Iran, by banning karate movies, and by creating a cooperative form of filmmaking in which all participants would benefit financially from their films' profits.[17] In the early 1980s, the MCHE was reorganized, leaving the film industry reform to MCIG, which continues to this day.

Another important new entity was the Islamic Thought and Art Center (Howzeh-ye Andisheh va Honar-e Eslami, IATC) of the Islamic Propaganda Organization, a semi-public, paragovernmental, Islamic institution independent of MCIG. Headed for nearly two decades by a moderate cleric, Hojjatollah Mohammad Ali Zam, the organization became, according to *Film International* magazine, "the largest private/government cultural institution."[18] Founded in 1979 by a group of Islamically committed artists—including two ardent film fans from the Mosque of Javad al-A'emmeh, in Tehran, who would become famous film directors, Mohsen Makhmalbaf and Majid Majidi—IATC produced chiefly war movies and "official" films in the early years of the war with Iraq (Tahaminejad 2001:78). It produced most of Makhmalbaf's first-phase movies, presenting the viewpoints of committed Muslim characters, with Islamicate iconographies, narratives, rhetoric, and values. The IATC director himself was the producer of Makhmalbaf's films, which included *Nasuh's Repentance* (*Towbeh-ye Nasuh*, 1983), *Seeking Protection* (*Esteazeh*, 1983), *Two Sightless Eyes* (*Do Cheshm-e Bisu*, 1983), and *Boycott* (*Baykot*, 1985). Manuchehr Haqqaniparast turned a Makhmalbaf screenplay into the IATC's first movie, *Justification* (*Towjih*, 1982). Ebrahim Hatamikia also produced two of his early Islamicate movies, *Sentry* (*Didehban* 1988) and *Immigrant* (*Mohajer*, 1989), for the IATC (figs. 26–27).

To produce these movies, Zam set up production companies and even, in a novel and controversial move, established an oil refinery whose profits went to film production. Like Makhmalbaf, who evolved from an Islamicate filmmaker to a critic of the Islamist regime, and Hatamikia, who gradually moved away from strictly Islamicate subjects and aesthetics, Zam also gravitated toward bolder treatments and moved the IATC in that direction. Some productions, such as Davud Mirbaqeri's *The Snowman* (*Adam Barfi*, 1998), Mohammad Reza Honarmand's *The Wrong Man* (*Mard-e Avazi*, 1999), Behrouz Afkhami's *Hemlock* (*Showkaran*, 2000), and Feraidun Jairani's *Fire and Water* (*Ab va Atash*, 2001), became very controversial, and occasionally cinemas showing them were assailed by Islamist mobs. (In 2000, Afkhami was elected as a member of the Majles on a semi-reformist platform.) Although a popular figure, Zam was dismissed from his post at IATC in early 2002.

Ayat Film, IATC, and other organizations brought to cinema a new cadre of Islamically committed film people. At the same time, many Pahlavi-period new-wave filmmakers were "rehabilitated," serving to revitalize cinema. Very few commercial cinema directors and actors were revived, and only much later. Iraj Qaderi was among the commercial cinema directors and actors who were allowed to return—but to directing, not acting. Several women

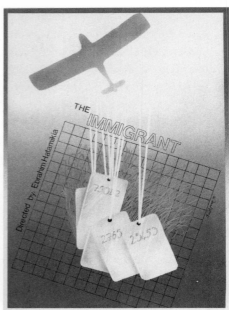

26–27 Posters for two early productions of the Islamic Thought and Art Center of the Islamic Propaganda Organization: Mohsen Makhmalbaf's *Boycott* and Ebrahim Hatamikia's *Immigrant*. Collection of the author.

actors with strong moral and acting reputations were able to gain permission to work, among them Parvaneh Masumi, Jamileh Shaikhi, and Fakhri Khorvash.

Production was redefined to introduce division and the stratification of labor, necessary for modernizing and industrializing cinema. Farabi Cinema Foundation introduced a new pivotal position, "production manager," whose job was coordination of various production elements. In addition, it divided the generally single position of cinematographer into two, creating a "director of cinematography," who was in charge of the look of the film, including lighting, and a "cinematographer," who was the camera operator. These and other improvements in the production process, which were instituted with Farabi Cinema Foundation's first production, *Stramonium* (*Tatureh*, 1984), directed by Kumars Purahmad, were partially responsible for the professional look of the Iranian postrevolutionary cinema.

State Structures Governing Cinema and Film Industry

After the transition period, major social and cinematic restructuring continued to both Islamicate (Islamicize) cinema and to modernize and industrialize it. The country continued to transform the village-based agricultural economy and small industrial workshops into an industrialized economy. Millions displaced by revolution and war flocked to cities without the safety net of traditional social networks, and a volatile population of disaffected youths became the subjects of future movies and politics. But the postrevolution economy was hampered by internal mismanagement and by a slew of sanctions and boycotts against Iran by Western powers in response to Islamic Republic policies, including its support and practice of international terrorism, its opposition to the Israel-Palestine peace process, its human-rights violations at home, particularly those involving minorities, women, and intellectuals, and its pursuit of nuclear energy and alleged nuclear weapons programs. These slowed the movement of film into a self-sustaining industrialized mode. Nevertheless, thanks to the intrusion of a centralizing state and the emergence of key players and paragovernmental foundations (*bonyads*), the film industry's rationalization, professionalization, and industrialization continued.

The Ministry of Culture and Islamic Guidance and the Farabi Cinema Foundation

The organization centrally concerned with cinema was the Ministry of Culture and Islamic Guidance, headed by a midlevel reformist cleric, Hojjatoleslam Mohammad Khatami. His decade of liberal support for the arts created the conditions that led to the assertion of a new postrevolutionary national cinema.[19] As the political scientist Sussan Siavoshi noted, in the latter half of the 1980s cultural policies were primarily formulated by the "modern left" faction under Khatami's leadership (1997:510). His sprawling ministry contained many subdivisions dealing with visual arts, crafts, cinema, performing arts, book publishing, music, culture, research, press relations, censorship, and tourism. All of the bodies concerned with film industry and cinema were concentrated in its General Department of Cinematic and Audiovisual Affairs, led by a deputy minister. In addition, the Farabi Cinema Foundation (FCF), created in 1983 as an independent institution but still attached to MCIG, served to implement the cinematic policies of the ministry. According to Alireza Shojanoori, FCF's first head of international relations, the foundation started small and humbly, with only three people and two chairs: "We were amateurs and fans of movies; an amateur society makes amateur films" (Naficy 2001a). FCF became a dynamic and formidable organization that helped professionalize the film industry at home and promote its products abroad.

Over the years, MCIG couched its involvements with cinema and the motion picture industry under three chief rubrics. As Mohammad Beheshti, FCF's longtime director general, told me in an interview, "We have a three-pronged policy toward cinema: To support (*hemayat*), to supervise (*nezarat*), and to guide (*hedayat*) cinema" (Naficy 1991b). The MCIG's important booklet *The Cinematic Policies and Procedures of the Islamic Republic of Iran*, issued near the end of the century of cinema, also repeated these policies as foundational to its operations (Ministry of Culture and Islamic Guidance 1999:1). In essence, "supporting" and "guiding" meant bolstering the production of Islamicate films, while "supervising" entailed discouraging and censoring of other types of productions. MCIG's General Department of Production and Support offered technical facilities and support to the movies; the General Department of Development and Audiovisual Collaboration facilitated upgrading of existing, and construction of new, movie houses; FCF assisted the movie producers and filmmakers with financing, raw stock, cinematography and editing equipment and facilities, and with promotion of the movies abroad; the Center for Development of Documentary and Experimental Cinema channeled support to its relevant production sectors; Young People's Cinema Society helped the young filmmakers with their amateur and short films; and the General Department of Research and Film Relations and the National Film Archives assisted with film research, publications, archiving, and preservation of the movies.[20] Exporting Iranian movies was declared a "strategic goal" to bolster the country both economically and ideologically, and several institutions were charged with its facilitation: FCF worked to export and promote professional and features movies abroad; the Center for Development of Documentary and Experimental Cinema did so for documentary and short films; and the Young People's Cinema Society did so for young people's films.

FCF provided other important services to raise the standard of cinema. It awarded cash prizes to A-list directors, producers, and screenwriters, and it offered raw stock and film facilities as a loan to A-grade directors whose films were either innovative in theme, anticipated to bring more than 400,000 spectators into the cinemas, or followed Ayatollah Khomeini's definition of "committed art." It also aided with renovation of old movie houses and construction of new ones (Ministry of Culture and Islamic Guidance 1999:12–

13). However, FCF's own involvement in producing movies did not bear early fruit. Productions such as Manuchehr Asgarinasab's *Beyond the Fog* (*Ansu-ye Meh*, 1985), written by the FCF director Beheshti, and Masud Jafari Jozani's *Cold Roads* (*Jaddehha-ye Sard*, 1985) were not successful in offering models of Islamicate cinema. Overall, like Khatami's long tenure as minister of Culture and Islamic Guidance, the decade-long tenure as FCF director of Mohammad Beheshti, a former Ayat Film member, provided both continuity and cumulative expertise.

The supervisory and guidance policies, on the other hand, involved, as Beheshti told me, "guiding the attention" of the various people involved in film industry "to the ideals and to the constructive functions of cinema in uplifting the culture at large" (Naficy 1991b). These declared functions of culture and cinema under the Islamic Republic were similar to the efforts during the first Pahlavi period to shape public opinion by means of the Public Opinion Guidance Organization and the efforts during the second Pahlavi period to create a pro-Pahlavi culture of spectacle through various cultural and performing arts organizations and festivals. The similarities point to the authoritarian structures of the three regimes, which tended to support cinema and culture instrumentally. Under the Islamic Republic, agencies were also directed to improve the ideological and professional qualities of the movies so as to "deepen the religious, national, and ideological values" and to help "attain a cinema of which we are proud and by which we are honored" (Ministry of Culture and Islamic Guidance 1999:2). The MCIG's General Department of Supervision and Evaluation was charged with the laws and regulations governing the industry, including film review, film censorship, and issuance of production, exhibition, import, and export licenses. While MCIG was in charge of overall film censorship in the country, two other film-producing institutions, unaffiliated with MCIG, had their own censoring apparatuses for the films they made independently—VVIR and the IATC. To be sure, these institutions followed Islamicate values; however, they had different missions and ideologies, and different reporting structures. VVIR reported to the Supreme Leader, while MCIG reported to the president. These parallel structures of censorship and authority ensured a certain amount of space for variation and contestation amid the general tendency toward centralization and authoritarianism.[21]

Despite these centralizing tendencies, the industry was diverse; more production centers surfaced in Islamic Iran than existed in Pahlavi Iran and they were not all concentrated in Tehran—a new development. The following (adapted from Talebinezhad 1987:6–11), lists each sector's production centers, some of which had branches in the provinces.

Public (Governmental) Sector

— Office of Film, Photo and Slide Production (a division of MCIG)
— Farabi Cinema Foundation (MCIG)
— Center for Developing Experimental and Semi-amateur Films (MCIG)
— Islamic Center for Film Instruction (MCIG)
— Young Cinema Society (MCIG)
— Center for Intellectual Development of Children and Young Adults
— Voice and Vision of Islamic Republic (TV networks' various film divisions)
— Ministry of Reconstruction Crusade
— University Crusade
— War Propaganda Command
— Islamic Revolutionary Guard Corps' Cultural Unit
— Revolutionary Committees' Film Section
— Traffic Organization
— Iran Air

Semi-Public (Paragovernmental) Sector

— Islamic Propaganda Organization
— Islamic Thought and Art Group
— Foundation of the Dispossessed

Private (Commercial) Sector

— Film cooperatives
— Independent producers
— Commercial production companies
— Commercial film studios
— Commercial film distributors
— Commercial film exhibitors

By 1987 the public-sector institutions were producing only one-third of all the movies, but governmental funding and licensing meant its impact on the film industry exceeded the statistics.[22] Nevertheless, the commercial, private sector continued to expand. By the twentieth century's end, some sixty commercial companies were active (Devictor 2002:69). Many film cooperatives also sprang up, producing feature films. By 1999, ninety-two film production and distribution companies and thirty-two film labs and studios were operating in Tehran alone.[23] The multiplicity of production centers and production sectors presumably bolstered competition.

Foundation of the Dispossessed and Islamic Revolutionary Guard Corps

Formed immediately after the revolution, the paragovernmental Foundation of the Dispossessed took possession of the assets of many of the public and private entities, including those of the Pahlavi Foundation.[24] The largest conglomerate in Iran by the mid-1980s, it controlled 15 percent of all the industries in the country and owned an estimated $10 billion worth of land.[25] Its holdings embraced some six hundred companies and factories (including movie houses), several five-star hotels, hundreds of agribusinesses and mechanized farms, and many private properties, dwellings, and real estate at home and abroad. FOD's ownership of the movie houses was pegged at 137 in 1983, or 50 percent of the total nationwide. Of these, 107 were acquired through confiscation, and 20 to 30 were burned cinemas that had been repossessed.[26] Within two years, FOD owned 80 percent of the nation's movie houses (Ehteshami 1995:86).

In time, as the Islamic Revolutionary Guard Corps (IRGC) grew into one of the most powerful and diversified military, security, and commercial enterprises in the country, it took over the Foundation of the Dispossessed, deepening its penetration of the cultural and ideological fields, as well as militarizing them. In addition, it took over the Basij Militia Force in 2007 and, as a Rand Corporation study showed, under the presidency of Mahmoud Ahmadinejad it increased its hold on the national politics, for not only the president but also "much of the cabinet, many members of parliament, and a range of other provincial and local administrators hail[ed] from the ranks of IRGC" (Wehrey et al. 2009:xi). This included the appointment of directors general of the powerful state broadcasting monopoly, VVIR, from among former IRGC officers and commanders, such as Ali Larijani and Ezzatollah Zarghami, and of the minister of Culture and Islamic Guidance, such as Mohammad Hosain Safar-Harandi. In this way, IRGC moved closer to becoming an effective "counterauthority" to the Supreme Leader, with profound consequences for militarizing the country's cultural, cinematic, and media industries (ibid.:xvi).[27]

In the meantime, FOD had a major effect on the production and exhibition of movies, not all of it positive. Its exhibition business lost money, since attendance dropped by 300,000 in just one year, from 2,600,000 in 1981, and the number of cinemas it owned declined precipitously, to eighty, by mid-1987.[28] The manager of FOD's cultural department, Mohsen Tabatabai, blamed this on a shortage of film imports with appropriate Islamicate values. The foundation thus began assisting Islamic filmmakers to make "model" movies inspired by Islamicate stories. In addition, the foundation's relation with other movie industry sectors was not smooth.

Most of the early foundation movies were "journalistic," such as Amir Qavidel's *Shower of Blood* (*Khunbaresh*, 1980), about three soldiers who in the throes of the uprising against the Shah desert their units to join the ranks of the rebels. Savak kills one soldier, while the other two are arrested. This was perhaps the first fictional movie that recreated a real event—both the defection of the three soldiers and the massacre of civilians by the police on Bloody Friday (8 September 1978)—and it was made in the context of its time, during the unfolding revolution, preserving some of its sights and sounds. Two soldiers, Ali Ghafuri and Qasem Dehqan Sangestani, as well as others who had participated in those events, played themselves in the movie, often in the actual locations.[29] For example, soldiers, families of the protagonists, and their neighbors played themselves. Even those who were in jail were freed temporarily to play their parts and then were returned to prison. As a result the film has a documentary quality to it (it was based on a news article by Rasul Sadrameli), and at the same time, because Qavidel was assistant to the master crime thriller film director Samuel Khachikian, it benefits from shot composition and editing that are characteristic of action movies. Remarkably, six hundred 16mm film prints of *Shower of Blood* were struck and distributed nationally through FOD's network for exhibition in mosques (Jafari Larijani 2008:vol. 1:610). The film was also screened in Efriqa (Africa) Cinema and other movie houses that FOD owned. This shows the extensiveness of FOD's national network and its deep pocket, for it would have been very expensive to reproduce so many prints, particularly in that immediate postrevolution period, when film supply and chemicals were in short supply. Other FOD productions were Mehdi Sabbaghzadeh's *Dossier* (*Parvandeh*, 1983), about

28 Production still for Khosrow Sinai's *The Monster Within*. Sinai is on the far left, and the director of photography, Esmail Emami, is behind the camera.

the revenge of a worker unjustly accused of murdering a feudal landlord and jailed for fifteen years; Khosrow Sinai's *The Monster Within* (*Hayula-ye Darun*, 1984), on a former Savak torturer's struggle with his own conscience; and Yadollah Samadi's *The Bus* (*Otobus*, 1985), co-produced with Urumiyeh's Ayat Film, about a typical Haidari-Nemati village feud (similar to the Hatfield-McCoy feud), couched as a struggle between modernity (*tajjadod*) and anti-modernity (*tahhajor*). None of these early works were outstanding, perhaps because of censorship. Sinai's film waited two years for an exhibition permit, and the producer cut forty-five minutes without consulting with him (Baqerzadeh 1987:343) (fig. 28).

Higher quality movies followed. Dariush Farhang's *The Spell* (*Telesm*, 1986), a gothic tale of Qajar-era newlyweds whose carriage breaks down, forcing them to take refuge in a haunted mansion, is one of the few horror films made in Iran (Farhang had written *The Bus*'s screenplay). Hasan Hedayat's *Message of the Jungle* (*Paik-e Jangal*, 1982) told the story of the rebel Mirza Kuchak Khan-e Jangali's fight against the Qajar government through one of his fighters. Rakhshan Banietemad's *Off the Limits* (*Kharej az Mahdudeh*, 1988), supported by the foundation's Khorasan branch, was a social comedy about a couple whose house is accidentally omitted from city-planning maps and therefore is off limits to police and legal protection. Mohsen Makhmalbaf's *The Cyclist* (*Beysikelran*, 1988), about the plight of an Afghan refugee in Iran who engages in a desperate bicycle race to raise money for his wife's medical bills, was an early text on the two million refugees who had fled Soviet-occupied Afghanistan, and instigated a genre of 1990s Afghani movies (figs. 29–30). FOD also produced Makhmalbaf's seminal film, *Marriage of the Blessed* (*Arusi-ye Khuban*, 1988), which marked his public break with Islamicate cinema.

To adjust to the financial realities of production and exhibition, to increase the reach of its films, and to build new theaters in poorer urban areas the foundation announced in May 1988 that it would divest forty more of its movie houses to raise funds to export "Islamic films" for exhibition to Iranians in diaspora. Not much came of these plans. By the 1990s, FOD turned over its cinemas to IATC of the Islamic Propaganda Organization.

Ministry of Reconstruction Crusade

The Reconstruction Crusade (Jehad-e Sazandegi), established by Khomeini in 1979, became a full-fledged ministry contributing not only to rural development but also to Islamicate cinema. Its original aim was to "repair the ruins"

29–30 Posters for two Foundation of the Dispossessed
movies: Rakhshan Banietemad's *Off the Limits* and Mohsen
Makhmalbaf's *The Cyclist*. Collection of the author.

caused by the Shah and to build up rural areas.[30] Early on the Ministry of Reconstruction Crusade (MRC) made and distributed appropriate films, slides, videotapes, posters, and audiocassettes through its vast nationwide network. Thanks to Ayatollah Khomeini's exhortation to publicize the accomplishments of the Islamic regime in order to fend off "the spirit of despair," the MRC published reports of its accomplishments.[31]

At first, these accomplishments were meager, particularly within individual localities, but since MRC had numerous branches nationwide its impact was wide and cumulative. According to MRC's statistics, in 1980 in Eastern Azerbaijan it showed twelve movies and produced four hundred fifty slides and eight rolls of film about agriculture.[32] In the same year, in the city of Rey, it screened many Iranian feature movies. Among Pahlavi-era new-wave films were Naderi's *Tangsir* and *Harmonica* and Mehrjui's *The Cow*; among postrevolution films was Alireza Davudnezhad's *Pahlavi's Justice* (*Adl-e Pahlavi*, 1981), made for VVIR.[33] The latter used the comparative, binary narrative structure common in Iranian fiction and documentaries to compare the pomp and luxury of the 2,500th anniversary celebrations of the Persian Empire in 1971 and the palaces and yachts of the Pahlavis with the poverty-stricken lives of common folk, in this way condemning the former. In and around the southern town of Kazerun, MRC showed to twenty small, media-naïve villages the following seven movies: *Harmonica, Pahlavi's Justice, Path of God (Rah-e Khoda), Parachutist (Chatrbaz), The Tortoise and the Hare (Mosabe-qeh-ye Lakposht va Khargush), Palestinian Self-Sacrificers (Janbazan-e Felestin)*, and Pontecorvo's *Battle of Algiers*—a mixture of domestic and foreign as well as fictional, nonfictional, and cartoon movies.[34] Nationwide, in the first nineteen months of its operation, MRC held 9,739 film and slide programs, put on 1,911 exhibits, and distributed 2,850,000 posters and publications.[35] Its productivity grew, as in 1983 it held 31,024 theater, film, and video shows, and distributed 74,789 audiocassettes and 2,912,062 posters and photographs nationwide (Markaz-e Amar-e Iran 1984:723).

In addition to exhibiting films, MRC made documentaries about its activities and social problems besetting the nation under the new regime. Many of MRC's films were made at VVIR, which established a Television Reconstruction Crusade Unit in Tehran and in the networks branches in the provinces. Seyyed Mohammad Beheshti headed this unit for several years before moving on to head the Farabi Cinema Foundation. Among the films made under its rubric at VVIR's Mashhad branch was *Cesspool (Gandab,* 1980), a twenty-one-minute film attributed to Nader Javan Khoshdel (?), which focused on the crusade's revitalization of Khorasan villages. In particular it dealt with the lack of sanitary water in a small village near Mashhad, which forced the thirty-seven resident families to drink polluted standing water. The film ends with Khomeini's declaration of the importance of the reconstruction crusade. This was one of the films screened for Iranian exiles.[36]

The veteran cameraman Manuchehr Moshiri began working for the MRC unit in Tehran around summer 1979. Moshiri, who had primarily been a cinematographer prior to the revolution, found the atmosphere at the unit so sincere and edifying that he presented an idea about a film series, which he would direct. He explained, "After the revolution inspired by the transformations in the society I became highly empowered and motivated to become a filmmaker. The Reconstruction Crusade Unit gave me this opportunity. I presented the outline of a few documentaries and began my work. In truth, it is thanks to the revolution that I became a documentarian" (Jafari Lahijani 2008:vol. 2:573). Among the films that Moshiri produced and directed were *Qorveh* (1979), about the efforts that MRC volunteers in the Kurdish village named in the film's title undertook to improve the villagers' quality of life;

Our Story Is Over . . . (*Qesseh-ye Ma Tamam Shod* . . . , 1979), which also deals with deprivation in the Qorveh; and *Narrating the Pain* (*Hadis-e Dard*, 1979), which focuses on the poverty and difficult lives of residents of Jask, a Persian Gulf city. Moshiri also made two films on the city of Damghan, in northern Iran: *Agriculture in Damghan* (*Keshavarzi dar Damghan*, 1980) and *Crusaders' Activities in the City of Damghan* (*Fa'aliatha-ye Jahadgaran dar Shahrestan-e Damghan*, 1980).

MRC's reach was actually wider than the earlier statistics indicate, since many of its films were screened on nationwide television, in mosques, and in movie houses operated by the FOD. VVIR's First Channel aired the crusade's films after the nightly newscasts, and FOD screened them in its network of movie houses before features. This nationwide distribution had its roots in the mobile film units of the British Council and the United States Information Service's Point Four programs of the 1940s and 1950s.[37] While the Pahlavi-era programs emphasized Western-style modernization, technological transfer, and monarchy, the crusade's film effort relied on indigenous, nativistic, and Islamic solutions. The former was a film-based system, but the latter, although it did use film, gradually relied mostly on video. The screening of MRC's documentaries before feature movies in commercial cinemas is reminiscent of the *Akhbar* newsreels during the Pahlavi period.

According to Moshiri, MRC films aired by VVIR left a strong impression on audiences immediately after the revolution, when the spirit of collective good was in the forefront. For example, his *Narrating the Pain* caused a flurry of phone calls and contact with VVIR and MRC from people who, touched by its powerful imagery and story, offered to travel to the Persian Gulf town of Jask and help. Apparently many students did just that, working on health and development projects (Jafari Lahijani 2008:vol. 2:577).

Center for the Intellectual Development of Children and Young Adults

The Center for the Intellectual Development of Children and Young Adults (CIDCYA) was one of two prominent Pahlavi-era public film organizations that kept their names after the revolution. Established in 1965 by Empress Farah Pahlavi, it was reorganized in 1979 as a government-supported company whose board seated four ministers (of Education, Higher Education, Culture and Islamic Guidance, and Finance) and the directors general of VVIR and the Plan and Budget Organization (Mahmoudi 2004a:15).[38] Its mission became the development of young people's artistic talents on the basis of the

31 Poster for the Center for the Intellectual Development of Children and Young Adults' production of Amir Naderi's *The Runner*. The poster's jumbled letters refer to the film's celebrated sequence in which one of the film's characters recited the alphabet by the stormy sea. Collection of the author.

"Islamic educational system and values." It continued to run libraries and support filmmaking for youth, to collect and archive children's movies, and to organize an annual children's film festival, first held in Khorasan in 1983, a year in which CIDCYA put out twenty-three films.[39] By 2000, CIDCYA had 465 cultural centers nationwide—an increase of over 100 centers in three years (Markaz-e Amar-e Iran 2001:602). CIDCYA also produced films of key auteur filmmakers: Amir Naderi's *The Runner* (*Davandeh*, 1985), Baizai's *Bashu, the Little Stranger* (*Bashu, Gharibeh-ye Kuchak*, 1985), Kiarostami's *Where Is the Friend's House?* (*Khaneh-ye Dust Kojast?*, 1988), and Majidi's *Children of Heaven* (*Bachehha-ye Aseman*, 1997), all seminal films (fig. 31).

Iranian Young People's Cinema Society

The second organization was Iranian Young People's Cinema Society (IYPCS), formed in 1974, whose activities stopped with the revolution, but restarted in 1985, under MCIG. By 2005, the society had opened fifty-four centers nation-wide, training some 90,000 youths in photography and filmmaking, and organizing a variety of local and national film festivals. While in its early years society members made 8mm, Super 8, and VHS videos, since 2005 they have been making films on Betacam, 16mm, and 35mm formats, resulting in an impressive 920 shorts, garnering some eighty international awards. The festivals it organized included those devoted to shorts, Quranic films, heritage documentaries, and culture and industry films.[40]

Documentary and Experimental Film Center

The Documentary and Experimental Film Center (DEFC), a division of MCIG, touts itself as "the main center for production, distribution and promotion of fiction, documentary, animation and experimental films in the Middle East."[41] The Center produces some twenty-five feature and three hundred short films per year, including award-winning films like Mohsen Amir Yousefi's *Bitter Dream* (*Khab-e Talkh*, 2004) and Ali Mohammad Ghasemi's *Writing on the Earth* (2004). Given that the total annual output of the film industry is around fifty features and 2,500 professional and amateur short films, DEFC is considered a major producer. And it is expanding to foreign markets. It now co-produces documentaries and features with foreign film and television companies, and markets Iranian films to foreign film festivals, film markets, television channels, theaters, universities, institutes, and organizations interested in Iranian cinema. In 2006, DEFC inaugurated Cinema Vérité, an important annual international documentary film festival in Tehran.

Professional Structures Governing the Film Industry

The film industry needed modernization and industrialization not only of its production, distribution, and exhibition infrastructures, but also of its professional structures. Civil institutions were redesigned to recognize and protect the movie industry's various professions, to preserve the industry's products, and to promote the study, criticism, and propagation of the industry and its products.

National Film Archive of Iran

The National Film Archive of Iran (NFAI), which was rooted in Farrokh Gaffary's pioneering efforts to create a National Cinémathèque in 1949, and which had ebbed and flowed under his leadership during the Pahlavi period, was reinvigorated in 1984 under the leadership of Mohammad Hasan

Khoshnevis and continues to thrive. As Khoshnevis noted in his introduction to the NFAI publication *Newsletter of the National Film Archive of Iran (Nameh-ye Filmkhaneh-ye Melli-ye Iran)*, the state of the archive after the revolution was dismal.

> Thousands of big and small reels of film were scattered around the building of the Undersecretary for the Cinematographic Affairs of the Ministry of Culture and Islamic Guidance, without any identification or cataloguing, under piles of trash, cobwebs, animal dung mixed with garbage from other ministry's divisions, and most important of all, hidden from sight by a mountain of ignorance and carelessness. We had to search for film in basements, storage rooms, offices, toilets, and every nook and cranny. We discovered reels of films unexpectedly anywhere we looked, films that had been kept for tens of years in rusted film cans, or even without cans in canvas bags and cardboard boxes, as though left there either to be forgotten or to be rid of them. (Khosnevis 1989:6–7)

For years the archive's staff had kept cans of film in their offices, where uncontrolled dust, heat, moisture, and, worst of all, cigarette smoke had infiltrated everywhere, damaging negatives and other film and video materials. Much needed to be done, from identifying and cataloging thousands of reels of film, to repairing damage, to separating the archive spaces from offices and creating proper climate-controlled facilities for preservation, restoration, and archiving of films. Facilities for research and viewing of archive materials were also established. In 1991, NFAI reopened its Cinémathèque, where, under the film scholar Abbas Baharlu (a.k.a. Gholam Haidari), weekly screenings of classic films, mostly foreign, were undertaken. This delighted film aficionados. Each season, the Cinémathèque devoted its programming to one national cinema or film genre, including Iranian documentaries.

NFAI's publication program included quarterly Persian and English periodicals (*Nameh-ye Filmkhaneh-ye Melli-ye Iran* and *National Film Archive of Iran Bulletin*) as well as translations and original publications on the history of Iranian cinema. Abbas Baharlu himself was a prolific author of filmographies and film histories of Iran.[42] Following the 1993 Legal Deposit Act, a copy of each new domestic feature is to be deposited with NFAI, which is responsible for purchasing the cultural rights and for paying for the deposited copy and its ancillary materials (a film print, a trailer, twenty posters, and twenty stills). As NFAI's director of international relations, Fereydoun Khameneipour, reported, by 1996, the archive claimed 2,907 feature films, 4,167 shorts, posters for 1,835 titles, and stills for 880 films (1997:12).[43] By the end of the twentieth century, the archive held over 80 percent of all the feature movies made in Iran between 1930 and 2000 (Baharlu 2000:200).

House of Cinema

Another important step was taken with the establishment, in 1989, of House of Cinema (Khaneh-ye Sinema, HOC), an industry-wide alliance of motion picture guilds created to represent and protect all film industry professionals. Over two dozen unions and societies are members of the house, many of them new. In addition to coordinating the activities of these trade societies and unions, HOC assesses and proposes new laws and regulations to promote and protect the film industry, and it contributes to the members' health insurance, social security, and housing funds. In 1998, there were approximately 3,000 members.[44] Moreover, HOC represents and defends film industry personnel before the government, and it engages in public discourses on behalf of the unions on major issues: it condemned the forced closure of reformist periodicals, the arrest of their editors, and the paramilitary's harassment of filmmakers (such as Ahmadreza Darvish) and arrests of filmmakers (such as Tahmineh Milani) (Safarian 2004b:121–32). It issued an international call in July 2006 condemning Israel's air and ground attacks on Palestine and Lebanon following Hammas and Hezbollah attacks on Israel. It called on the world's filmmakers to "record facts and realities in human history now!"

Finally, HOC manages the Screenplay Bank, an organization that registers all Iranian and foreign screenplays submitted, and protects the rights of registrants. It publishes a monthly list of the registered screenplays on its website.[45] HOC's operating budget comes from a 2 percent tax levied on movie houses. However, as a civil society institution mediating between state and industry, HOC does not just protect and represent the industry to the state, but also serves to facilitate the exertion of the state's control over the industry.

Museum of Cinema

In 1997, a totally new institution, the Museum of Cinema (Muzeh-ye Sinema, MOC), was officially established as a clearinghouse for documents, memorabilia, films, and equipment from the history of cinema in Iran. In 2002, the museum moved into Bagh Ferdows, an enchanting renovated mansion, dating back to the 1830s, that is surrounded by beautiful gardens and trees. The museum houses fifty thousand items: photographs, screenplays, posters, books, documents, periodicals, movies, costumes, wigs, theater seats, and film equipment. It screens films nightly in comfort and quiet—unusual for Iranian moviegoers.

Film Festivals

Film festivals are important in introducing new movies and filmmakers, elevating domestic film culture, and increasing marketing and exchange relations with the world. Founded in February 1982 to commemorate the second anniversary of the revolution, Fajr (Dawn) International Film Festival in Tehran became the showpiece of all Iranian festivals. The criteria for a film's inclusion in the festival were commitment to human beings, defense of the poor, support for the liberation of the weak, and conformity with the Islamic Republic's values. Some of the movies that did not conform to the last criterion were reedited with the acquiescence of the makers.[46] The festival screened revolutionary movies from Cuba, neorealist films from Italy, postrevolutionary films from Iran, and movies about Native Americans and African Americans (including the only public screening of Baizai's *Death of Yazdegerd*). In the years to come, like everything else in Iran, Fajr, which began as a collaboration between MCIG and FOD, lost some of its revolutionary ardor and became a respectable flagship festival, showing domestic and international movies and annually hosting foreign guests who came to sample the movies and to make deals for the import, export, and production of movies in Iran.

Vahdat (Unity) Film Festival, devoted to amateur Super 8 and 8mm movies and videos, started in 1983 in Tabriz. As expected, the first festival faced many technical problems, but eighty-eight documentaries and fiction movies, made largely by amateurs and sponsored by various government agencies, were screened. The young filmmakers who participated lauded the event because it gave those making films outside Tehran a sense of pride and a place to exchange information and films. Such a festival also allowed the deficiencies of moviemaking in the provinces to come to the attention of others.[47] A second amateur festival, Tolu' (Sunrise) Film Festival, organized by the Society of Young Filmmakers associated with MCIG, was established in 1984 in the city of Hamadan. It screened forty-five 16mm films and ten Super 8 movies. In the 1980s, films shot in the Iran-Iraq War formed a large portion of the programs at these amateur festivals.[48]

One festival was devoted entirely to the war's filmic representation: the Festival of the Imposed War Films.[49] CIDCYA continued with its annual Children Film Festival, and the Iranian Documentary Filmmakers' Society also started a festival of documentary films in Tehran and entered Iranian documentaries in international festivals. The IYPCS organized multiple festivals, and the Documentary and Experimental Film Center started its Cinema Vérité documentary film festival. As before, educational films were screened in their own festival, called the Roshd (Growth) Film Festival. As part of the decentralization efforts of cinema under the Islamic Republic, there was a new development: the creation of thematic, generic, and specialized annual festivals in cities outside Tehran, such as the comedy film festivals in Shahr-e Kord and Abadan; a religious film festival, Cinema Truth, in Yazd; and the International Children and Young Adults Film Festival in Isfahan, which, next to the Fajr Film Festival, is often regarded as the most important national festival.[50] Festivals are a changing phenomenon, as new ones are created to fulfill new needs and demand, and as the existing ones transform and evolve into different ones or simply cease to exist.

Film Periodicals and Publications

Books about cinema, both original and in translation, began to form an active field of the publishing industry. Very few scholarly books had been published about Iranian cinema during the Pahlavi period, but after the revolution a plethora of books came out about individual films, filmmakers, film genres, and the history of Iranian cinema, as did reference books that for the first time standardized and made accessible the basic technical, biographical, and historical information about Iranian cinema and films.

Production of the many new film periodicals, like the production of the films, was subject to government attempts at censorship and the periodicals' efforts to negotiate critical discussions of cinema and the industry (see table 4).[51] However, the partners were not of equal power and there was much improvisation (Farhi 2003). The state had its monopoly on publication licenses for all periodicals nationwide, formulating and enforcing laws governing periodical contents, and controlling manufacturing and importation of printing paper. A major film journal, *Gozaresh-e Film* (*Film Report*), for example, had to wait for several years before either being granted a publication license or being supplied with printing paper.[52] *Mahnameh-ye Sinemai-ye Film* (*Film Monthly*), the most enduring and professional of all film journals, was published for some eight years without a long-term publication license. Each single issue had to be taken to the appropriate board of censors at MCIG to receive an individual license before it could be released for sale. Such a state of affairs did not encourage bold investigative journalism. Yet, as Houshang Golmakani, editor-in-chief of *Mahnameh-ye Sinemai-ye Film*, told me, his periodical flourished, becoming the leading journal, with unprecedented circulation, which reached 70,000 in less than a decade (Naficy 1991a). The government further influenced the periodicals by placing paid advertisements in them, if it agreed with their editorial policy, or by withdrawing them, if it did not.

To remain hegemonic, in Gramsci's terms, the government made certain concessions and compromises. It allowed the relatively unfettered publication of small but influential periodicals devoted to professional and technical concerns. Intellectuals and cineastes, Islamist or secular alike, used these periodicals for their information and also to create an environment in which they could critique the government's cultural policies and actions with some impunity, because it was limited to professional spheres. Many advertising-driven film journals ran pieces critical of government film policies and film industry practices. The various government organs associated with film, cinema, theater, culture, media, and visual arts also contributed to this culture of inquiry and criticism with their own periodicals, such as *Faslnameh-ye Sinemai-ye Farabi* (*Farabi Cinema Quarterly*, published by Farabi Cinema Foundation), *Nameh-ye Filmkhaneh-ye Melli-ye Iran*, *Faslnameh-ye Honar* (*Arts Quarterly*, published by MCIG), *Faslnameh-ye Te'atr* (*Theater Quarterly*, published by Center for Dramatic Arts of MCIG), *Naqd-e Sinema* (*Cinema Criticism*), and *Soroush* (published by VVIR). These government-sponsored organs were less pressed by shortages and censorship than others but tended to toe the government line. Less beholden to readers for their income, they could run longer, more research-based articles.

While several commercial and independent periodicals survived, thrived, and were influential, such as *Mahnameh-ye Sinemai-ye Film*, *Gozaresh-e Film* (*Film Report*), *Sanat-e Sinema* (*Cinema Industry*), *Film va Sinema* (*Film and Cinema*), *Farhang va Sinema* (*Culture and Cinema*), *Film Video*, others folded, including *Daftarha-ye Sinema* (*Cinema Notebooks*), *Payam-e Sinema* (*Message of Cinema*), and *Sinema-ye Novin* (*New Cinema*);[53] *Film International* was the only regular English-language film journal in the country that linked the domestic film industry with the world film industry. Literary periodicals such as *Adineh*, *Aineh-ye Andisheh*, *Donia-ye Sokhan*, *Faslnameh-ye Honar*, *Gardun*, *Goftogu*, *Kayhan Farhangi*, *Kelk*, *Ketab-e Sobh*, *Mofid*, *Zendehrud*, *Mehraveh*, and specialist journals such as *Zanan Ruz* (a women's magazine), *Hadaf* (a sports magazine), *Aks* (a photography magazine), and *Rasaneh* and *Sureh* (both media journals) published frequent features on film, sometimes hard-hitting. Almost all the popular press and mainstream dailies, from right-wing papers such as *Kayhan* and *Ettela'at* to reformist papers such as *Hamshahri*,

32 Cover of *Mahnameh-ye Sinemai-ye Film*, no. 258 (21 Shahrivar 1379/11 September 2000), a special issue celebrating "100 Years of Iranian Cinema 1900–2000." Courtesy of Masud Mehrabi.

33 Cover of *Film International* (spring 2000). Courtesy of Masud Mehrabi.

Tous, and *Khordad* (the latter two banned), also carried regular film review columns and news of the film industry and pop culture. To be sure, the state was, to borrow from George Orwell, more equal than the other parties, because of its power to fund, grant newsprint and ads, censor, or ban periodicals—all of which prerogatives it exercised frequently. However, because of the varied sources of funding, diverse types of journalism, and the government's own commitment through MCIG to support the development of a genuinely national cinema, there was considerable discursive dynamism about cinema among the periodicals and between periodicals publishers and the state, problematizing the received notion of the state's direct and total domination of the film industry (figs. 32–35).

Another key to the continued vitality of the film culture was the increasing number and variety of film journalists. By 2004, 255 film critics had registered with the Society of Writers and Critics of Cinema (Anjoman-e Nevisandegan va Montaqedan-e Sinemai), 232 of whom were full members, with

34 Cover of *Gozaresh-e Film*, no. 92 (Tir 1376/June–July 1997),
published by Karim Zargar and edited by Bahar Irani. President
Mohammad Khatami and the director Abbas Kiarostami are featured.

35 Cover of *Sinema-ye Azad* (Farvardin–Ordibehesht 1377/April–May
1998). Edited by Basir Nassibi, this exile magazine, which opposes
the Islamic Republic, was published in Saarbrücken, Germany.

23 associate members, and 71 registered as film writers or journalists (Mahmoudi 2004b:61–63).

Iranians in diaspora also maintained an active film culture by means of
periodicals. As my previous research showed, in their first decade of massive
exodus, between 1980 and 1992, Iranians in diaspora produced ninety periodicals in Persian in Los Angeles alone—an unprecedented and unexpected
efflorescence in exile. The newspapers and magazines covered real estate,
parapsychology, sports, film, health, literature, children, politics, and subeth-
nic minorities' and women's issues (Naficy 1993:35–38). Many contained regular news about Iranian entertainers in Los Angeles and news about cinema
in Iran and in general. With the international success of Iranian films, diaspora periodicals began to carry more items on Iranian cinema, both critical and laudatory. From intellectual and literary quarterlies (*Kankash, Iran*

TABLE 4 Film periodicals (1979–2003)

Title	Pub. Date	Frequency	Publisher
As-re Honar	1997	Weekly	Reza Esmail Owreh
Bani Film	1994	Daily	Masud Davudi
Baztab	1993*	Daily	Mojtaba Aqai
Bidar	1999	Bimonthly	Mohammad Baqer et al.
Buletan-e Filmkhaneh-ye Melli	1999	Quarterly	Mohammad Hasan Khoshnevis
Daftarha-ye Sinema	1981		
Didgah-e Sinema	1997	Monthly	Anjoman Sinema va Defa' Moqaddas
Doniya-ye Tasvir	1992*	Monthly	Ali Mo'alem
Farhang va Sinema	1990*	Monthly	Parviz Samadimoqaddam
Faslnameh-ye Farabi	1988*	Quarterly	Farabi Cinema Foundation
Film International (English)	1993*	Quarterly	Masud Mehrabi
Filmnegar	2003	Monthly	Mohammad Hasan Pesezg
Film va Honar	1998	Monthly	Majid Beheshti
Film va Sinema	1979		Piror Galestian
Film va Sinema	1992*	Monthly	Mohammad Ali Naqiza-deh Sohi
Gozaresh-e Film	1990*	Biweekly	Karim Zargar
Hasht Ruz-e Hafteh	1992	Weekly	Hamid Mohebbi
Honar-e Hafteh	2002	Weekly	Mehrdad Raiani Makhsus
Honar-e Haftom	1999	Monthly	Mehdi Marjui
Jaiezeh	1999	Monthly	Fatemeh Salmanimoradi
Jebheh-ye Sinema-ye Enqelab	1979	?	?
Ketab-e Film va Sinema	1990	Quarterly	Entesharat-e Kheradmand
Mahnameh-ye Sinemai-e Film	1982*	Monthly	Masud Mehrabi
Mardom va Sinema	1999	Weekly	Farabi Cinema Foundation
Mehrab	1980	Quarterly	Kanun-e Sinemagaran-e Iran
Nameh Filmkhaneh Melli Iran	1989*	Quarterly	NAFI
Nameh-ye Sinema	1999	Monthly	Khaneh-ye Sinema

Editor	Affiliations	No. of Issues (as of 2002)
Reza Esmail Owreh		21
Editorial Board		11
	Anjoman-e Sinema-ye Javanan	
		355
Feraidun Khamenehi et al.	Filmkhaneh-ye Melli-ye Iran	
		6
Mehdi Azimi Mirabadi		2
Ali Mo'alem		
Editorial Board		143
Mahmud Arzhmand et al.	MCIG	49
Behzad Rahimian et al.		37
Mehrdad Farid	MCIG	14
Majid Beheshti		56
Ali Sarhangi et al.		106
Bahar Azadi (Hushang Asadi)		189
Gholam Haidari		18
Sohail Eradatmand		21
Bijan Ashtari		
Fatemeh Salmanimoradi		
?		1
Bahman Dari Akhavi		1
Houshang Golmakani		306
Dariush Nowruzi		6
Hojattollah Saifi		1
Mostfa Eslamiyeh		11
Robert Safarian et al.		10

TABLE 4 *continued*

Title	Pub. Date	Frequency	Publisher
Naqd-e Sinema	1994	Monthly	Howzeh-ye Honari-ye Tabliqat-e Eslami
Nur, Seda, Durbin, Harekat	1997	Monthly	Mohammad Reza Zaeri
Paik-e Sinema	2000	Monthly	Shahnaz Moradikuchi
Payam-e Sinema	1981–1982		
Pilban (animated films)	1992	Monthly	Amir Masud Alamdari
San'at-e Sinema	2002	Monthly	Shahram Jafarinezhad
Sinema	1991	Weekly	Hosain Vakhshuri
Sinema	1989–?	Bimonthly	Faraidun Jairani
Sinema '58	1979		Tehran International Film Festival
Sinema dar Video	1982*	Monthly	Masud Mehrabi
Sinema Haqiqat	2002	Monthly	Mohammad Afarideh
Sinema Jahan	2000	Weekly	Mohammadhadi Karimi
Sinema Te'atr	1993*	Monthly	Hosain Farrokhi
Sinema va Te'atr	1980	Monthly	?
Sinema Video	1994	Weekly/monthly	Abolqasem Talebi
Sinema Yek	1993	Annual	Jashnvareh Jahani-e Tak
Sinema-ye Javan	1996	Monthly	Mohammadhosain Sufi
Sinema-ye No	2001	Weekly/monthly	Farabi Cinema Foundation
Sinema-ye Novin	1990	Quarterly	
Sureh Sinema	1991*	Quarterly	Mohammadali Zam
Tasvir '58, '59, '60, '61	1979–1982	Monthly	Sirus Qahremani
Tasvir-e Ruz	1997	Weekly/biweekly	Mohammad Hadi Karimi
Tasvir-e Sabz	2002	Monthly	Seyyed Hadi Monabati
Video Mahvareh	1993*	Monthly	Rasul Sadatnezhad
Video (later, *Film Video*)	1995	Monthly	Akbar Nabavi

Sources: Table drawn by author, based on author's personal archive, data that the Iran National Library librarian Poori Soltani kindly provided me (see Naficy 2005f and Mahmoudi 2004b).

* Periodicals still in publication.

Editor	Affiliations	No. of Issues (as of 2002)
Naser Hashemzadeh et al.		70
Mohammad Reza Zaeri		3
Bijan Ashtari		
	Kanun-e Sinemagaran Amator	
Ahmad Ka'bi Fallahiyeh		
Shahram Jafarinezhad		15
Ghlamreza Musavi, F. Jairani		560
	National Film Archive	
Bahram Raypur		1
	Markaz Gostaresh Sinemaye	
Mahmud Arzhmand	Mostanad va Tajrebi	
Ghlamreza Musavi		44
H. Farrokhi et al.		61
Editorial Board		1
A. Talebi		
Abbas Saleh Madresehi et al.		2
Ali Akbar Fattah	Anjoman-e Sinema-ye Javanan	
Jalil Akbarisettat		40
Shahruz Juyani		6
Seyyed Mohammad Avini	Islamic Propaganda Org.	4
Editorial Board		11
M. Karimi, Naser Puyesh		78
Mohammad Khazai		
Akbar Nabavi	MCIG	3
Akbar Nabavi		38

Nameh, Daftar-e Honar, Barresi-ye Ketab), to feminist periodicals (*Nimeye Digar, Forugh*), to monthly magazines (*Simorgh, Elm va Jameh'eh, Par*), to weekly newspapers (*Kayhan-e London, Iran Times*), to weekly magazines (*Javanan, Tamasha*), to daily newspapers (*Sobh-e Iran, Asr-e Emruz*), and finally to Internet periodicals (http://www.iranian.com, http://irandokht.com), Iranian cinema became a legitimate and attractive, even indispensable, subject.[54] Several periodicals entirely devoted to cinema were also published, but only for short periods: *Film '94*, edited by Masud Daneshvar, was published in Los Angeles; the Internet magazine *cinemairan.com*, edited by Hosain Khandan, was published in Washington, D.C.; and the quarterly *Sinema-ye Azad*, edited by Basir Nassibi, was published in Saarbrücken, Germany.

Exile periodicals were all against the Islamic Republic but they generally praised postrevolutionary films. Under the despised regime a self-empowering cinema had emerged, appealing to their nationalism and cinephilia. Some hardline exile periodicals, such as *Sinema-ye Azad*, accused art-house filmmakers making films inside Iran of collaborating with the despised government. Interestingly, much of what the commercial weeklies and dailies published in exile about Iranian cinema was based on articles originally printed inside Iran, often without attribution. But when diaspora film writers, including me, returned home for visits, they were interrogated by security agencies, ostensibly because by placing their works with the exile press, they were accused of having lent legitimacy to these publications' anti–Islamic Republic stance—even though the writings often praised Iranian films. Like everything else in exile, film criticism became a highly contested arena.

The types of governmental, commercial, and professional structures discussed so far were needed to support and protect cinema. However, what were also needed for the industry to really take off were supervisory and guidance elements, such as regulations and laws defining, standardizing, and routinizing the procedures for producing and exhibiting both an Islamicate cinema and its alternatives. The result of these new institutional and legal structures was the steady rise in quantity and quality of movies produced by all sectors.

Censorship Laws and Regulations Governing the Film Industry

The concentration of power at MCIG helped reduce the confusions and rivalries of the transition period and enhance the rationalization, industrialization, and modernization of the industry and government's control over it, thereby setting the stage for the emergence of an Islamicate unity out of revolutionary destruction and chaos. One of the first tasks was to define and streamline the regulations governing the industry. Even censorship rules contributed to this process, for they prevented the improvised and ad hoc practices of the artisanal production mode. Three sets of regulations are discussed here: on film production, licensing, and exhibition.

Regulations Governing Film Production

All films designed for public screening must obtain a production license. Initially, this involved a four-phase approval process, described briefly below (Ministry of Culture and Islamic Guidance 1985:appendix 1:34–37).[55]

Phase 1. Reviewing Screenplays

The applicants were to send their screenplays to MCIG's General Department of Supervision and Exhibition for review. The Review Council (Showra-ye Bazbini) considered both content and form. Content was to follow regulations derived from the new constitution, approved by the cabinet (see below). The council made sure that films' form followed the "scientific criteria" of character development; that they were not aimless, unclear, verbose; and that they did not contain slogans, extraneous scenes, or extremely unusual or accidental events. When these content and form criteria were applied in 1980–82 to the 202 submitted screenplays, 151 (or 75 percent) were rejected (Ministry of Culture and Islamic Guidance 1985:appendix 1:35–36). This massive rejection paralleled a similar rejection rate of the prerevolution movies cited elsewhere. Clearly, much change was needed to transform the film culture from Pahlavi to Islamicate cinema.

For some time, there was an additional step in this phase. First a film treatment (synopsis) had to be approved; then the full screenplay was submitted.

Phase 2. Issuing Film Production Licenses

If the screenplay were approved, the producer could submit to MCIG a cast and crew list and a production budget. The list ensured that Pahlavi-period personnel did not return to the industry. This step institutionalized the purification process at a microlevel. On approval of budget and of cast and crew, film production and processing could begin.

For some time, an additional step was instituted in this phase, which involved supervising the filming process. During productions, MCIG monitors were present on the set to make sure that illegal, un-Islamic, or immoral behavior such as "casting couch" shenanigans, presumably rampant during the Pahlavi era, did not return.

Phase 3. Previewing the Dailies or Rough Cuts

To economize on postproduction costs, filmmakers could present their dailies or rough cuts to the council for review to make sure they were on the right track.

Phase 4. Final Review and Issuing Exhibition Licenses

Producers were to submit fully edited final films to the Review Council to obtain exhibition permits. All new movies underwent all these phases. Previously made domestic and foreign movies also underwent this fourth phase to ensure they were appropriate, or were made appropriate through censorship, for postrevolutionary times. The results of these reviews, which banned an overwhelming majority of films, have already been discussed. One result was a thriving black market for approved screenplays: with such a screenplay in hand a filmmaker was eligible to receive raw stock and equipment at the government rate, which was much lower than the market. Interestingly, once approved, a screenplay had to be quickly ushered into production, as approval was in effect only for a brief period. This allowed both the government and filmmakers more flexibility in responding to new social situations, to be more or less open.

Over the years, these approval phases were reduced and liberalized, as the Islamic Republic consolidated itself and as cinema evolved from a despised medium into a prestigious industry. Screenplay approval and viewing of rough cuts were first removed for A-list directors and then for all directors. The film treatment reviews were also discontinued. In judging screenplays and issuing production and exhibition licenses, the Review Council exercised three types of graded management. It ensured *quality management* by grading screenplays and movies from A to D, with A indicating highest quality. The idea was to draw audiences by ensuring high-quality products. To that end, the council made sure that 30 percent of the movies approved for production and exhibition each year were in the A category, 50 percent in the B category, and 20 percent in the C category. The standard for quality grading was the past performance of directors, producers, and screenplay writers. The council also exercised *thematic management*, to ensure a variety of themes for each age group. Here, too, MCIG regulations created a grading system, designating approximately 17 percent of the movies for children, 28 percent for teenagers, 43 percent for adults and families, and 11 percent for special audiences. Finally, the council exercised *human resource management*, to ensure the continuous flow of fresh, new talent into the film industry (Ministry of Culture and Islamic Guidance 1999:4–7).

On 3 July 1982 (12 Tir 1361), the cabinet under the leadership of Prime Minister Mir Hosain Musavi approved two sets of landmark regulations—one governed the issuing of exhibition licenses to movies, videos, and slides, and another governed their public exhibition—and it charged MCIG with their implementation and enforcement. These regulations, which codified much of the Islamicate values and provisions of the new constitution, were instrumental in facilitating the shift from Pahlavi cinema to Islamicate cinema, hence their verbatim presentation here (see Appendix 1).

MCIG regulations stipulated a rating system that allocated movies to appropriate movie houses according to their grades, so that grade A movies were exhibited in grade A movie houses, and grade D movies could not appear in grade A cinemas.[56] In general, grade A movies were allocated to better cinemas during better movie seasons and for longer periods of screening (Ministry of Culture and Islamic Guidance 1999:8–11). By 2000, the government had pulled out of the executive processes of distribution and exhibition, which had caused much criticism about government meddling in business affairs and favoritism. Limiting itself to maintaining a regulatory and censorship functions, MCIG eliminated the Screening Committee and turned over the committee's other functions, such as allocating the movies to cinemas nationwide, entirely to the private sector.[57]

A comparison of the Pahlavi censorship codes with these regulations elucidates much, not only about the state of cinema and the role of cinema in each period, but also about the differences and similarities in the larger politics and ideologies of the Pahlavi and Islamic Republic states.[58] Here I point out only a few of these similarities and differences, leaving further analysis to others. Both sets of regulations insist on protecting the respective regime's pantheon of sacred figures; in one, these were the Shah and royal family; in the other, these were the Supreme Leader (*velayat-e faqih*), Shii imams, and contemporary top jurisprudents (*mojtahed*). In addition, both sets of regulations are highly paternalistic, treating citizens more like children and "subjects" than like modern individuals with autonomy, responsibility, and authority, thus implying that citizens need protection from corruption, particularly that caused by Western pop culture. Both regimes are self-protective, particularly the Pahlavi state, whose regulations appear to be paranoid and banned any movie plot that involved a struggle against ruling powers.

While the Pahlavi regulations did not inscribe its tenets of syncretic Westernization, those of the Islamic Republic consciously formulate the principles of Islamicate values, particularly in the provisions of article 2 of the regulations governing movie exhibition. Surprisingly, the Pahlavi regulations were inward looking, dealing with the protection of the citizens from the inflow of corrupting and revolutionary ideas, while those of the Islamic Republic tend to be both inward and outward looking, wishing not only to protect the citizens from imported ideas, but also to export Iranian movies and the Islamic revolution to other countries.

To control nudity, unacceptable sexuality, and pornography from showing up on public screens, Pahlavi-era regulations defined the boundaries of propriety in relative detail; the Islamic Republic regulations, on the other hand, are totally silent about such matters, as nudity, sexuality, and sexual relations were banned outright in the society and severely punished, obviating the need to include them in these regulations. The representation of women in both regimes is controversial; one regime was criticized for its liberal but sexually commodified and demeaning representations of women, while the other is condemned for its subjugation and sequestration of women. The first inkling that the Islamic Republic might be in need of guidelines about women's hair, make-up, clothing, and acting appears in a note to article 3 of the movie exhibition regulations.[59]

Finally, in neither regime are the written official regulations applied equally, uniformly, or according to the letter or even the spirit of the regulations. Their applications depend on many unofficial factors, evolving with time and with the censorship officials and filmmakers involved. The veteran director Bahram Baizai, who had ample experience with official and unofficial censorship at the hands of both regimes, summarized the contingent and complicated applications of the regulations under the Islamic Republic, in an interview with Shahrokh Golestan.

In the cases of the movies they don't like, they [officials] will make sure that those movies suffer economically and go bankrupt. I have frequently seen that they try to make sure that the cultural films with which they disagree . . . are not distributed well; their exhibition is made limited, or it is scheduled during bad seasons and on inappropriate screens. They make sure they are not exported. If export turns out to be necessary, they will export them, but to discredit them they will make sure that these movies burn out in their initial screenings. Then, they can produce statistics showing that the films were screened but failed. . . . About my own film *Bashu* [*Bashu, the Little Stranger*], which was exported and was also successful, I must state that it was out of circulation and suspended at home. I can say that it was banned for four years. And when it was screened in Tehran, it was in the worst season, in the worst condition, and limited to only one screening. I can say that it was not sent to any prestigious festival and was not entered in any important competition. It was not even screened in any of the appropriate festival sidebars anywhere. (Golestan 1995b:48)

Movie Houses, Audience Demography, and Audience Decline

In the heyday of the uprising, in 1978–79, movies were shown not just in movie houses. Liberated from their usual commercial and official venues, the films were available for spectators to watch in universities, colleges, mosques, gyms, hotels, factories, government offices, hospitals, military barracks, and even in neighborhood open spaces. It was sufficient to obtain a film, a portable projector, and a white wall or a screen; audience attendance was guaranteed. The Tehran Film Center (Kanun-e Film-e Iran), a third revival of Gaffary's film center, reestablished after the revolution, increased its film exhibition program. In fact, it began its operation with Hosain Torabi's *For Freedom* (*Bara-ye Azadi*, 1978–79), a compilation film about the revolution, and it screened films nightly (it ceased operation in 1983). Film societies operated by the cultural attachés of the Soviet Union, France, and Germany were particularly active in screening movies, as were the College of Fine Arts of Tehran University and the College of Cinema and Television. Once the Islamic Republic was established in spring 1979, the more regular film venues began to take over from these places.

As in previous periods, the spectators took advantage of the darkness and the safety in numbers provided by movie houses to voice their opposition to government. For example, Ayatollah Khomeini had once made a speech in which he had colorfully threatened to both "slap America across the face" and "appoint a new government in Iran." Later, when in an Isfahan cinema the electricity went out halfway through the movie due to bombing by the Iraqis, a clever spectator's voice was heard in darkness above the din of spectators, saying, to great applause, "I will slap the projectionist across the face, I will appoint a new projectionist."[60]

Despite gaps and inconsistencies, statistics show that the number of movie houses and moviegoers increased over time. The number of cinemas nationwide grew from 198 to 277 between 1979 and 1984 (with 81 cin-

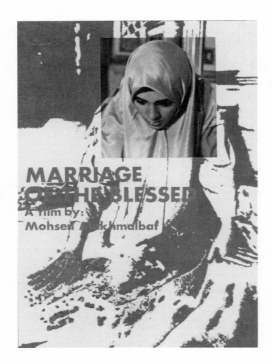

36 Poster for Mohsen Makhmalbaf's *Marriage of the Blessed*, a Foundation of the Dispossessed production. Collection of the author.

emas in Tehran), and the seating capacity in the same period increased from 141,399 to 170,265. Likewise, attendance at Tehran cinemas rose from some 24,000,000 to nearly 28,000,000 between 1984 and 1986 (Markaz-e Amar-e Iran 1984:203; Markaz-e Amar-e Iran 1985a:46; Ministry of Culture and Islamic Guidance 1984:37, 295; Farabi Cinema Foundation 1987:8). Movie house attendance nationwide for 1984 topped 48,000,000 (Haidari 1986:6). To get a fuller idea of movie viewing, one must add the 31,000,000 people who attended MCIG's mobile film units' screenings in 1984 (Markaz-e Amar-e Iran 1985b:207), as well as the many people who also attended the Reconstruction Crusade's film screenings (fig. 36).

Despite growth, however, movie attendance from the 1980s through the 2000s never reached the peak of the Shah's era, even though the Islamic government's curtailment of previously allowed forms of entertainment had made cinemagoing one of the few forms of mass entertainment, and even though the quality and quantity of the movies as well as the population had increased. The main reason was the drastic reduction in movie houses. The reduction of movie houses is starkly evident in the statistics. While the number of nationwide cinemas increased—bringing by 2000 the number of movie houses in Tehran to 86 and in the provinces to 232, making a total of 318 movie houses nationwide (Markaz-e Amar-e Iran 2001:597)—this was still far below the Pahlavi period's total number of 432 movie houses, in the mid-1970s. When one considers that the population of the country had more than doubled from the 1970s to the 2000s, reaching 71,000,000 by 2007, the comparative inadequacy of the number of cinemas becomes more striking.[61]

In the 1980s, youth movie attendance was relatively high, particularly for males. In an audience survey, taken in 1983, of 1,800 Tehran high-school students, 78 percent of the boys and 59 percent of the girls said they went to the movies (Haidari 1986:7). There were many reasons for why spectator interest were not higher, particularly among women: the decreased number of movie houses nationwide, the undesirability of cinema locations, the bad conditions of halls and projection systems, the low quality of many of the movies exhibited, and the demographics of spectators, who were predominantly young, unmarried, unemployed males who ogled and sometimes heckled women. These factors were compounded by the highly aggressive and male-oriented genres and themes of the movies during the war years. Haidari's survey of Tehran students reflected audience preferences for action and war movies in 1983: 45 percent favored "revolutionary" films, 39 percent comedies, 32 percent religious films, 32 percent crime films, and only 10 percent socially relevant films. It is hard to determine whether this survey revealed the actual preferences of youngsters or their opinion about what was available.

Attendance in the 1990s remained shockingly low despite the upsurge in both the quantity and quality of the movies. This is borne out by an analytic article in the monthly *San'at-e Sinema* (*Cinema Industry*), which reported that while Tehran residents on average went to the movies 10.8 times in 1976, they attended cinemas only 0.8 times in 2000 (Sabri-Laqai 2002:16). There were complex reasons for this, many of them related to the economic and political woes of the country due to revolution, political instability, war with Iraq, population explosion, high inflation, high unemployment, Islamic restrictions and censorship, import impediments, Western embargo on export and import to Iran, and a lowering of gross domestic product. Many people simply could not afford to go to the movies, and many did not want to attend them because of the uninviting movie house conditions and movies. Many others found it necessary to hold more than one job to make ends meet, which cut down on their leisure time. In the meantime, other media whose uses were more favorable began competing with moviegoing. Television watching increased, as VVIR multiplied its channels to five, diversified its programming to reach women and youth, and increased its broadcast volume from 6,153 hours in 1976 to 30,000 hours in 2000. Video, satellite television, and the Internet also burgeoned as media for a population whose literacy rapidly increased to 80 percent. These electronic media transferred the favorite site of movie-watching from public to private sphere. This shift lowered the public patronage of movie houses, which went into decline, and many closed their doors (some thirty cinemas closed down in Tehran in the 2000s) or split into dingy multiplexes to appeal to different tastes. However, government impediments in importing foreign movies reduced the fare available to these movie houses and, more important, removed an essential source for improving the domestic movies—foreign competition. Without such competition and faced with increased censorship, domestic productions declined in quantity and quality. High-school and college students, whose populations grew rapidly in the 1990s and 2000s, were not only literate but also media literate. Disappointed with the film industry and its products, they not only turned away from commercial movie houses and domestic movies and flocked to the newer electronic media, but also became readers of a surging publishing industry, which produced nine times more books than during the Pahlavi era and six times more periodicals in Tehran alone. In the meantime, this media and media use shift brought on yet another fundamental shift: the youth changed from being passive consumers of big media and culture, such as movies and television, into being producers and users of smaller, interactive media and culture, such as videos, videogames, Internet sites, blogs, and social networks, with vast potential for effecting social change and achieving their democratic and emancipatory aspirations. With the turn toward electronic media censorship also shifted, from prior censorship of films to cyberspace surveillance and control of activists and their products.

To bring into the movie houses the youths (under twenty-five years of age), who were more educated, media savvy, and cinephilic than other social strata and who comprised some 60 percent of the population, moviemakers began making in the last years of the twentieth century and in the early years of the twenty-first century movies whose stories centered on young people's issues, producing films that critiqued restrictive social norms and a coterie of rising young stars. It was hoped that the changed stories—many involving love and cross-gender relationships, shunned in the previous years—and the presence of heartthrob stars—an emerging phenomenon—would bring in disaffected youths.

Mullah Vision: Television as an Instrument
of Public Education and Interpellation

Both the Pahlavi and Islamic states considered the broadcast media to be a vital force in shaping public opinion and forming national identity. Both took direct control of these media. In the heyday of the uprising, the revolutionary leader Ayatollah Khomeini and Sadegh Ghotbzadeh, the first director of VVIR (a.k.a. IRIB), each called the broadcast media a "public university."[62] Since Khomeini's opinions set policy in all institutions, it is helpful to deal with those concerning media.

Soon after the formation of the Islamic Republic, in a meeting with broadcast executives, Khomeini offered a comprehensive analysis of the role of media during the Shah's time and issued orders that molded the broadcast media henceforward. According to his protégé Ebrahim Yazdi, Khomeini had seldom watched television during the Shah's time, and he did not have a television set in his home (he did own a radio). It was only when in exile in France that Khomeini "learned the practical political value of the mass media" (quoted in Ghods 2002:30). He appeared frequently on television and in radio broadcasts, distributed audiocassettes, and issued telephonic pronouncements against the Pahlavi regime. Now in power at home, he accused the previous regime of having employed television, radio, theater, cinema, and the press to entertain the populace, to corrupt their morals, and to divert their attention from the country's problems. He saved his most virulent comments for music, calling it "treasonous" and a betrayer of the country's youths, and suggesting that there was "no difference between opium and music." Sounding like Shaikh Fazlollah Nuri almost a century earlier, Khomeini claimed that music attracted young people but also stupefied them, so that like addicts they could no longer concentrate on real social issues. His solution for ensuring the country's political independence from both East and West was to convert the broadcast media into an educational force and to remove music from them altogether. Several months later, apparently dissatisfied with the pace of change at VVIR, the ayatollah expressed the importance of the broadcast media in building an Islamic nation by reiterating his injection theory: "If this organization works well, our country will become well, and if it is corrupted, it might create a tremendous amount of corruption."[63] Ghotbzadeh had dismissed many NIRT staff members, but this was deemed to be insufficient (Jafari Lahijani 2008:vol. 1:94–95). He urged the new VVIR chief, Parviz Taqi Farrahi, who replaced Ghotbzadeh, to make the broadcast media "one hundred percent Islamic" by summarily removing all "deviant groups" and individuals tainted by their collaboration with the Shah's regime.

The purification of the broadcasting media was under way. The politically correct and blood relatives of the clerics were appointed to high positions within the vast broadcasting organization, to the point of turning its management at the highest level into a "family business" (Sreberny-Mohammadi and Mohammadi 1991:41).[64] Khomeini praised progressive domestic movies such as Mehrjui's *The Cow*, which he had viewed; however, he asked that television networks stop screening foreign movies, which he called "colonialist." He advocated talk shows, even those involving communists, because someone else could always counter their opinions, "right there and then." He asked that broadcast media remain independent from "interference from anyone" while urging on them increased Islamicization.[65] All the "non-Islamic" programs were removed from radio and television, and music, once taken off the air for Ramadan in 1980, was kept off thereafter. Religious and discussion programs flourished, and at first there was a great deal of tolerance for opposition viewpoints. However, by mid-1979, the PFOI was already charging VVIR with tampering with and censoring their representative's views.[66]

Khomeini initially had in mind a progressive function for broadcasting, as he reiterated in several meetings the idea that broadcasting must remain "independent," "neutral," and "completely impartial" (Khomeini 1981a:293). Whether he changed his mind, or by "neutral" he meant "Islamic," or whether exigencies moved him in the opposite direction, the fact remains that these noble ideas did not take root and the views of those opposing the Islamic Republic were soon excised from VVIR, turning the broadcast media into powerful instruments of public interpellation. The clerics' full-bearded faces so dominated the media, particularly the electronic screen, that people began to derisively call the television networks "glass wool," "woolly glass," or "mullah vision," and called the radio networks the "minaret" or "pulpit" of the regime (Hankey 1982; Saedi 1984a:17; Sreberny-Mohammadi and Mohammadi 1991). The noted writer Reza Baraheni in a scathing attack on the VVIR chief Ghotbzadeh charged that he engaged in censorship because he did not fully grasp the spirit of tolerance in Islam and did not trust that Islam could withstand discussion of rival ideologies in the broadcast media. He boldly predicted that if censorship were reinstituted, it would be followed by accusations, terror, imprisonment, secret trials, torture, and executions, and that "from among the ruins of the revolution will arise another Napoleon, Reza Khan, or mad Mohammad Reza Shah" (Baraheni 1981:187–94).

Television Confessions, Recantations, and Show Trials

As though on cue, soon, a string of television recantations and confessions by the regime's opponents began appearing, among them such notable clerical, secular, and leftist personalities as Ayatollah Kazem Shariatmadari, Foreign Minister Sadegh Ghotbzadeh, the Tudeh Party leader Nureddin Kianuri, the Tudeh writer Mahmud Etemadzadeh (a.k.a. M. A. Behazin), the Peykar leader Hosain Ruhani, and other key members of Mojahedin, Marxist, communist, and leftist organizations, all of whom were probably tortured and coerced into their self-incrimination and recantations. Some of them were executed anyway, while others were imprisoned or were confined to house arrest for years. Those who survived the ordeal of torture, confession, and repudiation of life-long beliefs suffered from various psychic and physical ailments, including anxiety, anomie, shame, and guilt.[67] M. A. Behazin, a well-known writer and translator and a member of the Tudeh Party's Central Committee, relates his forced television confession.

> The script that the young interrogator wanted to implement in my case was like a set of instructions. Prominent Central Committee members had been forced into performing such a scripted show before mine. Each had come before television stating the same content, even though in different words, that treason, espionage, and corruption was endemic to the party, expressing regret and sorrow for their actions, and in the end offering a fatherly advice to the young generation to learn and avoid deceitful traps. . . . At any rate, after painful internal hesitations and objections, I did appear before the television camera because I feared that if I did not, I might die in prison and my life be judged with the wrong yardstick. I did not, and do not, fear what others will think about this. But I cannot deny that avoiding further torture, and giving the injured soles of my feet a brief respite from lashing, was not a motivation, too. Fortitude and endurance are not infinite. . . . As for the charge of espionage for the Soviet Union, under the intolerable pressure that they exerted on my body and soul I told the lie they so insisted on my telling [that I was a spy], so that they would leave me be.
>
> When with my eyes blindfolded I was descending the stairs from the third floor, where this shameful televisual interrogation took place, I turned to the interrogator guiding me by the arm and said: "You must be satisfied like a butcher who has taken a fattened animal to the slaughterhouse and is now returning with its carcass." He pretended

not to understand me. I repeated it, but we both remained silent. Well, the ordeal was over, but there was no glory in it for any one. (Behazin 1991:26–32)

Such confessions, broadcast both nationally and inside prison, had profound effects on their intended populations. Houshang Asadi, an intellectual Tudeh member (and later, editor of *Gozaresh-e Film* magazine), who was tortured to falsely confess to spying for both the Soviet Union and Savak, painted a dramatic picture of the disempowering effect of hearing the Tudeh leaders' forced confessions on broadcast media while he was in the political block of a prison.

I fill up my jug as usual and am on my way back to my cell when I hear the voice of the main leaders being broadcast over the loudspeakers, announcing the Party's dissolution. I stop automatically. My knees are shaking and suddenly I collapse. I manage to get back on my feet, and drag myself to my cell. The Party leader's [sic] confessions are being broadcast and a deathly silence fills the block. When the loudspeaker is turned off, there is absolute silence for a few minutes and then someone, somewhere, starts crying and suddenly, the whole block is shaking with the sounds of weeping. The prisoners are crying in their cells. They are crying in corridors. There is no other sound, apart from the sound of weeping. I lean against the wall of my cell and my whole body is shaking. Someone is shouting: "Look what we wanted to achieve, and look what has happened. . . ." Again, a wave of crying starts and slowly dies down to intermittent sobs. I feel as if the ground underneath my feet has been pulled away and I am going down. My heart is empty and I have nothing to rely on. Everything has gone to the wind. . . . On that spring night of 1983, my world collapsed inside me. Not long before, I had pretended to repent my beliefs under horrific torture and now those beliefs had turned to ashes. When the lights were turned off, the sound of the last cries was still audible. I felt absolutely defenseless. For the first time in my life, I felt the need to pray. (Asadi 2010:217–18)

While the Mojahedin (PMOI) made anti-Islamic Republic videos and television in Iraq via its *Vision of Resistance* (*Sima-ye Moqavemat*) and in the United States and Europe via its *Vision of Freedom* (*Sima-ye Azadi*) television programs, on which victims exposed and denounced the government's torture practices, the Islamic Republic's television put on its own recantation shows of PMOI members and their families. In one such program, Masud Rajavi's sister and brother-in-law "confessed" to, and "repented," their sins on television, and his seventy-six-year-old mother pleaded with him to return from his foreign exile to "kiss the Imam's feet" (Abrahamian 1989:257).

More televisual self-incriminating confessions and recantation of opposition and reformists, which the critics called "show trials," ensued in later years, particularly after the massive protest against the disputed reelection of President Ahmadinejad in June 2009 (discussed in volume 4).

Although the Islamic Republic's constitution outlaws the use of torture to obtain confession, torture and coercions of various kinds were routinely applied to break down the intellectuals and opponents psychologically and to disgrace them publicly. There was no real right to remain silent and no law against self-incrimination. As a result, opponents had the choice of resisting self-incrimination, in the process giving their lives by torture or execution, which would immortalize them as indestructible and mythologized martyrs. Or they could earn the right to live—however ignominiously, as weaklings— but at the expense of confessing to crimes they may not have committed and rejecting sometimes their entire intellectual lives and accomplishments. However, as the dissident exile poet Majid Naficy rightly pointed out, "Both of these . . . are victims of the regime that holds little value for human rights but in two different ways. . . . I admire the first group and I sympathize with the second and oppose the policy of rejecting and isolating them" (2008).

Movies on Television

The purification of television went beyond executing the high-ranking NIRT officials Jafarian and Nikkhah, dismissing "deviant" personnel, exposing oppositional thinkers, and the other measures discussed above. It extended to purifying the broadcast schedule. In the early days, the television networks were turned into display windows for three types of programming: revolutionary news from inside Iran, war movies, and nature programs—the latter two mostly imported from the West. The war movies included the acclaimed British series on the Second World War, *World at War* (1973), and Peter Davis's hard-hitting Vietnam War documentary, *Hearts and Minds* (1974), which was critical of the U.S. administration's conduct of that war. Nature programming included the American series *Survival* and Frédéric Rossif's *Wildlife Opera* series (*Opera Sauvage*, 1975), which covered wildlife and human life in several countries, including Iran, with beautiful slow-motion photography. The networks also dipped into their archives of classic foreign movies. Masud Kimiai states in Robert Safarian and Ahmad Mir Ehsan's film about him,

Double Six (Joft Shish, 2007), that during his eight months as head of VVIR he screened all of John Ford's films that were in the network's archive.

Soon, other foreign feature movies began to appear on VVIR, but they were cut to reflect Islamicate values. As in the Pahlavi era, the television networks had their own censorship apparatus, separate from that at MCIG. American movies were shunned, and, after the "neither East nor West" policy was instituted, Soviet movies came to the same fate. In 1982 the government purchased fifty feature movies and thirty-nine short films from Cuba and India to air on VVIR networks.[68] In releasing the statistics on its activities for 1983, VVIR announced that its film acquisition council had approved purchasing 663 foreign movies and had rejected 349 films and television programs for that year, a better ratio of accepted-to-rejected than in the motion picture field. In 1983, the network aired a total of 2,270 hours of programs, of which 1,382 hours comprised domestic productions and 194.5 hours comprised foreign films. Subsequently, the acquisition department imported, with help from the Farabi Cinema Foundation, 397 documentaries, 20 documentary series, 70 children programs, 13 serials, and 49 feature movies. To illustrate the ratio of domestic productions to imports, the figures for the Second Network, which is a highbrow cultural network, are cited. Most of the domestic programming consisted of talk shows and religious lectures.[69]

Women's hijab in foreign feature movies posed a problem for television as well, necessitating purification similar to that instituted for theatrical movies. Hashemi Rafsanjani, speaker of the Majles, wrote in his published diary, that on 4 May 1984, he told his brother, Mohammad, who headed VVIR, "It is advisable to prevent the screening of foreign movies showing unveiled women in a repulsive manner, even though such images are not forbidden by Islam *(haram)*" (Hashemi Rafsanjani 2008:88). Within six days, the board of governors of VVIR had decided to reduce the volume of foreign movies aired and to stop screening movies that contained "repulsively unveiled women." More important, to offset this reduction the board decided to boost the domestic production of movies (ibid.:94). The reorientation of program sources, from foreign dominance to domestic dominance, continued over the years, and it can be summarized as follows: if the ratio of foreign imports to domestic productions broadcast by NIRT was three-to-one in 1976, that ratio was reversed by 1994 such that 85 percent of all television programs were produced domestically (Malek and Mohsenian Rad 1994:84).

Another reorientation was taking place at the level of the audiences, whose media menus showed a preference for television over the other media, particularly with regard to news. In 1974, 21 percent of the respondents in an audience survey said they used television as a "source of news"; this figure grew threefold by 1995, reaching 70 percent; and it rose even higher by 2003, peaking at 83 percent (Naini, Dehqan, and Moayedfar 2006:2). In addition, the use of all media increased in direct relationship to level of education, so that 61 percent of those with high-school diplomas watched television, compared with 66 percent of those with college degrees. Likewise, the figures for radio use went from 50 to 67 percent and for filmgoing from 6 percent to 18 percent according to level of education (ibid.:6).

VVIR aired on a weekly basis top-rated domestic art-house features and documentaries produced before the revolution, among them Mehrjui's *The Cow* (*Gav*, 1959), Shirdel's *The Night It Rained* (*Unshab keh Barun Umad*, 1963), Naderi's *Harmonica* (*Saz-e Dahani*, 1973), Shahid Saless's *A Simple Event* (*Yek Etefaq-e Sadeh*, 1973), Farmanara's *Prince Ehtejab* (*Shazdeh Ehtejab*, 1974), Baizai's *The Crow* (*Kalagh*, 1977), and Kiarostami's *Report* (*Gozaresh*, 1978). These films were safe to broadcast in the new Islamic atmosphere, as most could be said to either confirm Islamicate values or to offer criticism of life under the Pahlavi regime. The networks also showed many newsreel and compilation documentaries on the revolution and the war with Iraq.

VVIR grouped its cultural research and production efforts into several production units, each focusing on particular aspects of Iranian life. Units such as Research on Iran, Culture and People, Theater, Islamic Center for Amateur Filmmaking, House of Film Culture, and Animation Group were all involved in making films. There was also a unit charged with making films on the war with Iraq. Like its predecessor NIRT, VVIR supported the development of the film industry as a by-product of having to feed the voracious appetites of its expanding networks and to disseminate Islamicate culture through made-for-television films. Like NIRT with its Telfilm, VVIR created a film production company, Sima Film, to finance and produce features, some by auteur cineastes. The individual networks also produced or funded films of such filmmakers. For example, VVIR's First Channel produced Amir Naderi's *First Search* (*Jostoju 1*, 1982), Bahram Baizai's *Death of Yazdegerd* (*Marg-e Yazdegerd*, 1982), Reza Mirlohi's *Ghosts* (*Ashbah*, 1982), and Ali Hatami's *Haji Washington* (*Haji Vashangton*, 1982). The channel also produced Abolfazl Jalili's war movies *Milad* (*Milad*, 1984) and *Spring* (*Bahar*, 1985), as well as his powerful *Scabies* (*Gal*, 1988), which documented with formal rigor the panoptic structures of a reformatory for young boys, and by extension the panoptic structure operating in the society at large, which was conveniently relocated to Pahlavi times (fig. 37).

The final reorientation in the field of television had to do with the explosive

37 Poster for Abolfazl Jalili's *Scabies*,
a production of the First Channel of
the Voice and Vision of the Islamic
Republic. Collection of the author.

growth of the number of vvir channels available to Iranians. By 2010, the number of state-operated television channels for domestic and international audiences had reached fifteen, eight aimed at domestic and the rest at international audiences, including Iranians in diaspora. Most of these channels not only aired films they acquired from other producers, but also produced their own fiction movies, short films, animated and cartoon films, and documentary films. Dozens of foreign satellite television channels and Iranian exile satellite channels augmented the menu of movies available to domestic audiences, becoming part of the "cultural invasion" and public diplomacy soft war between Iran and the West.

Controlling Film Imports

After some deliberation, the government took control of all film imports. Farabi Cinema Foundation was given a monopoly over importation of films for cinemas based on their ideological suitability.[70] Table 5 shows the volume of imported movies in 1983–84 and their countries of origin.

Clearly, despite the "neither East nor West" policy, the Soviet Union dominated the imports; however, American and European movies increased their percentage. That the anti-Western rhetoric did not eliminate American im-

TABLE 5 Imported theatrical movies receiving
exhibition permits (1983–84)

Country of Origin	Year	
	1983	1984
U.S.S.R.	28	29
Italy	16	20
United States	12	24
United Kingdom	9	15
France	6	5
Yugoslavia	6	1
Poland	5	2
Japan	4	5
North Korea	2	2
Algeria	2	0
Hungary	2	1
People's Republic of China	1	9
Australia	1	2
Bulgaria	1	0
Czechoslovakia	1	2
East Germany	0	6
West Germany	0	4
Mexico	0	2
Spain	0	4
Hong Kong	0	1
Libya	0	1
Greece	0	1
Armenia	0	1
Lebanon	0	1
Total	96	131

Source: Ministry of Culture and Islamic Guidance 1985,
Appendix 5.

ports demonstrates the divisions over Islamicate values within the republic,
as well as the pragmatism of policymakers, film importers, and spectators.
Officials permitted a film regardless of its origin as long as it could be made
to fit Islamicate values. *Star Wars*, *Close Encounters of the Third Kind*, *Ten Com-
mandments*, and *A Bridge Too Far* screened in 1983; *War Hunt*, *Law and Disor-
der*, *Black Sunday*, and *The Chase* screened in 1984. Previously banned genres,
such as Westerns, were allowed, but they were manipulated during dubbing
and editing to give them an anti-American edge. Henry Hathaway's *Nevada*

Smith (1966) was so radically altered that a new "Iranian Western" resulted. In a more drastic instance, two movies with the same key actors were reportedly cut and assembled into a single new movie thanks to heavy editing and appropriate dubbing.[71]

Many Soviet movies underwent similar transformations, changing their communist features into neutral, Islamic, or Iranian ones. The remaking of a Soviet movie called *The Story of Siavash* (*Dastan-e Siavash*) offers a remarkable example of the audacity of such cultural realignments. According to the dubbing director Mahmud Qanbari, who was the Iranian "director" of the revised Soviet movie, the original had distorted the story of the famous Iranian warriors, as told by Ferdowsi in his epic *Shahnameh*. So, he set to "re-make it like the *Shahnameh*": the film was cut from eighteen reels (three hours) to something manageable. The character of the archetypal hero Rostam, who was shown to be "scrawny and frail," was bolstered by replacing his accompanying soundtrack with rhythmic battle music borrowed from Kimiai's toughguy movie, *Dash Akol*. Scenes involving Rudabeh and other women in various stages of undress were rephotographed by turning them into a series of freeze-frames that were lap-dissolved, one into another. Qanbari added to the film a voice-over of lines from the *Shahnameh*. The film's ending—Siavash committing suicide—was changed. Qanbari thought that this and more of the films he doctored were an improvement over the originals.[72]

While in the 1980s and the 1990s foreign movies were screened in commercial cinemas, these films were few and far between due to import bans of various sorts. Hollywood, the most powerful cinema in the world, traditionally regarded as a threat to national cinemas, was essentially banned. This was beneficial to the domestic cinema insofar as it removed a lethal competitor. Without such import bans, Iranian cinema would probably not have achieved the quality and quantity of productions it had reached by the end of the century, even though competition could have energized more innovation. Indeed, having been institutionalized, industrialized, and streamlined, Iranian cinema may now benefit from foreign competition.

Streamlining Domestic Productions out of the Transition Period

Until mid-1989, all film ideas were subject to the four-phase production review process at MCIG, during which they underwent many changes before their release.[73] The quality of the films was dismal. That only 25 percent of 202 screenplays reviewed in the early 1980s were approved testifies to the effectiveness of this review process and to the low quality of the movies. Even many movies that had received a production permit failed to receive an exhibition permit once they were made (Omid 1987:696–713). It was not the Supervisory Council of MCIG alone that gave a vote of no confidence to domestic screenplays and films. The authoritative film journal *Mahnameh-ye Sinemai-ye Film*'s 1985 ratings corroborated MCIG's dismal evaluation. Of 115 features it reviewed, it rated 35 as trite, 57 as bad, 22 as mediocre, 1 as good, and none as excellent.[74]

The major complaints against the Islamicate cinema's early films involved not only their low quality but also their ideological earnestness and moralistic somberness. Perhaps for a nation barraged by external wars and propaganda and gripped by internal violence and xenophobic hysteria, this was to be expected. However, even the speaker of the Majles, Ali Akbar Hashemi Rafsanjani, who would soon become president, acknowledged the necessity of lighter treatments: "It is true that a film must have a message, but this does not mean that we must deny its entertaining aspects. Society needs entertainment; lack of joy reduces one's effectiveness and involvement."[75] That a leading political and religious figure would have to authorize joy and entertainment points to the way the nation was gripped by grim violence and a culture of death.

Filmmakers, too, were critical and demanded reforms, and the government introduced new regulations that encouraged higher-quality productions. In the first six months of 1984, the municipal tax for domestic films was reduced from 20 percent to 5 percent, and it increased from 20 percent to 25 percent for imports. Ticket prices were increased by 25 percent. The Farabi Cinema Foundation was exempted from paying customs duties for its imports. And changes in the composition of the "screen committee," responsible for assigning films to theaters, allowed representatives of producers and exhibitors to partake in the proceedings.[76]

In April 1989, the government loosened its grip and began allowing previously censored films to be screened.[77] Barely a month later, for the first time in cinema history—during both Pahlavi and Islamic Republic periods—the requirement for screenplay approval was removed. Two chief reasons for this liberalization policy stood out. One was the confidence authorities felt that Islamicate values were sufficiently inculcated. The other was that a more self-assured and enlightened government wished to open cultural discourse and reduce criticism of its ironclad control, thereby boosting morale and film quality. It was hoped that this would liberate cinema, deflate the black market in screenplays, and diversify film topics.[78] While this seemed like an enlightened policy—and in many ways it was—it had a nefarious side effect, for it transferred, in a panoptic fashion, an external source of censorship, the government, to an internal source, the filmmakers themselves. Since film producers and directors could not afford to risk their investments by shooting films that would not get an exhibition permit, they tended to mind the Islamicate values and engage in self-censorship. Later, film policy underwent still further adjustments aimed at encouraging higher quality movies: A-list directors no longer had to submit their films for review, and their movies were assigned to "distinguished" movie houses.

To generate funds for the health, social security, and workers' compensation of entertainers and filmmakers, the Majles passed a resolution late in 1985 imposing a 2 percent tax on all box office receipts.[79] To bolster domestic cinema, the 1987 national budget included long-term bank loans for film production.[80] In June 1988, MCIG enabled highly rated producers to exhibit their films in high-class theaters for higher revenues. These producers were also granted television advertising, which became a bone of contention between MCIG and VVIR.[81] In May 1989, MCIG announced further measures: allocation of foreign exchange funds for importing chronically scarce technical equipment and supplies; availability of interest-free credits and long-term loans; sponsorship of domestic films in international film festivals; and, finally, the inauguration of a social-security system for film workers.[82]

Political consolidation, diversity of production centers, centralization of imports, passage of regulations governing production and exhibition, establishment of civil society and professional institutions of cinema, creation of movie and movie house rating systems, and enhanced coordination and cohesiveness within the industry all brought cinema into line both with Islamicate values and with industrialization, resulting in films of better quality and more quantity. The latter is reflected in table 6, which, containing thirty years of IRI film output, shows an initial dip and fluctuation, followed by a sustained pattern of an increasing number of productions coinciding with the aforementioned reforms, which brought the industry output to near the mid-1970s average.

With output hovering between sixty and seventy features annually in the last decade, Iran became one of the world's more prolific movie producers, pointing to the continued industrialization of the film industry. According to Ataollah Mohajerani, minister of Culture and Islamic Guidance, in 1998 Iranian cinema ranked tenth in the world in its annual output of feature movies, surpassing Germany, Brazil, South Korea, Canada, and Australia, and far exceeding the traditionally high-volume Middle Eastern film producers Egypt and Turkey.[83] Beyond features, MCIG's statistics show that between 1988 and

TABLE 6 Feature movies produced in the Islamic
Republic (1979–2009)

Production Year (Gregorian/Iranian)	Films Released
1979/1358	5
1980/1359	26
1981/1360	19
1982/1361	14
1983/1362	35
1984/1363	41
1985/1364	36
1986/1365	47
1987/1366	48
1988/1367	42
1989/1368	50
1990/1369	41
1991/1370	54
1992/1371	66
1993/1372	50
1994/1373	61
1995/1374	62
1996/1375	51
1997/1376	52
1998/1377	46
1999/1378	47
2000/1379	49
2001/1380	58
2002/1381	61
2003/1382	61
2004/1383	60
2005/1384	70
2006/1385	68
2007/1386	68
2008/1387	60
2009/1388	58
Total	1507

Source: Ladan Taheri of the Iranian National Film
Archive kindly prepared the table for this publication.
The data for films made between 1978 and 1994 are
based on Abbas Baharlu's filmography (2004); thereafter, it is based on Baharlu's new filmography (forthcoming). I thank both Taheri and Baharlu for their
valuable assistance.

1997 an average of between 23 and 31 shorts and documentaries were produced annually, a figure that spiked to 200 in 1998 (Ministry of Culture and
Islamic Guidance 2000:19). Very likely these MCIG figures do not include the
shorts, documentaries, and animated films made by the CIDCYA, VVIR, IATC,
IYPCS, DEFC, and other governmental and nongovernmental institutions. If
these are considered, the total industry output is much higher.

Taxonomy of Film Types

Iranian movies screened abroad in the 1990s and 2000s gave a false impression of homogeneity. However, postrevolutionary cinema is heterogeneous
and has evolved over the years to produce several types. Critics claimed it was
created by a "ruthlessly united" ideological apparatus controlled by the state;
however, this cinema grew out of considerable ideological work and negotiations. It is neither a militantly political "Islamist" cinema, nor an "Islamic"
cinema upholding the ruling religious ideology, nor a homogeneous art-house
cinema. Nevertheless, Islamist politics and Islamicate values as well as resistance to them are inscribed in the movies in various degrees and forms, leading to diverse film types. I identify and briefly discuss ten types here. Such
variety and diversity are emblematic of growing industrialization and modernity, which also demand quality and quantity.

The first to emerge was what I call the "official Islamist cinema," which
explicitly supported the government's ideology. This cinema consists of some
doctrinal features, including early Mohsen Makhmalbaf movies such as *Nasuh's Repentance* (*Towbeh-ye Nasuh*, 1983), but, more important, documentaries
and features about the revolution and war with Iraq. The second type, "popular Islamicate cinema," like the Pahlavi commercial cinema, is a commercially produced fiction cinema affirming Islamicate cultural values less mani-
festly than official cinema, but embedding them in plot, theme, character, and
mise-en-scène. "Art-house cinema," on the other hand, like the Pahlavi period's new-wave cinema, engages with dominant values and tends to critique,
implicitly and explicitly, social conditions and ruling Islamicate values; this
is recognized abroad as Iranian "national cinema." A much smaller "experimental cinema" also emerged, hovering on the margins. The revolution and
long war with Iraq propelled a new "documentary cinema" that was at first
concerned with these large issues but which later moved into more personal,
more intimate, and eventually more sociopolitical explorations. If documentaries about the revolution and the war were often supportive of the state, the

personal and social documentaries were critical and muckracking and left no stone unturned. Since the 1980s, following the massive exodus of Iranians to foreign countries, a sixth cinema, an Iranian "accented cinema," which is diverse in forms and contents and prolific in output, has emerged abroad. Gradually but forcefully there has also emerged a "women's cinema" inside Iran, produced primarily by women directors. What turns these nonhomogeneous films into a category is not only their directors' gender but also their women-centered worldviews, stories, and casts. A post–Cold War world and the new hot global War on Terror in the Middle East has primed the emergence of an "extraterritorial cinema," consisting of films Iranian residents made in other countries, and of an "ethnic cinema," comprising films Iranians made inside the country dealing with ethnic and ethnoreligious minorities. Finally, globalization, digitization, and the Internet have encouraged an entirely new type of cinema, "Internet cinema," whose films are often nonfictional, unedited, and made by anonymous, nonprofessional community journalists and filmmakers, and they are uploaded to the Internet social-networking sites or video-sharing sites.

The popular and art-house cinemas evolved almost simultaneously, as official cinema waned.[84] Art-house cinema provoked struggle because its filmmakers—at least in the decade after the revolution—were, like their new-wave predecessors, dependent on state financing even while trying to remain independent, even critical, of their chief sponsor. Few art films were made, comprising perhaps 10 to 15 percent of the national output; but in quality, prestige, and revenues, the art-house film is the most significant film type. With the exception of official and popular cinemas, all the other cinemas belong not only to their own category, but also to art-house cinema.[85]

By restricting imports, the government enabled the domestic film industry's growth. Because the industry was initially so weak, protectionism was necessary. Domestic films' captive audience gradually learned to like the films that were made for it, and in turn influenced filmmakers. The more than doubling of the population that has taken place since the revolution has extended the industry's audience, as has the increasing involvement of the private sector in filmmaking. Foreign films found their way in through pirated videos and illegal satellite television channels.

Heterogeneity extended to other realms of the industry. While Tehran remained the center for all things cinematic—production, distribution, publicity, advertising, exhibition, exporting, importing, archiving, publishing, and reviewing—film production increased in the provinces. These were mostly shorts and documentaries, but fiction features elbowed in occasionally. As early as 1983, features were being made in Ilam, Isfahan, Mashhad, and Nahavand. Film festivals moved to provincial centers: the Vahdat Film Festival to Tabriz and the Children's Film Festival in Isfahan. Provincial magazines weighed in with reviews and film criticism; particularly strong was *Zendehrud*, in Isfahan, which issued articles and special issues on cinema.[86] In another feat of decentralization, for the first time, the premiere exhibition of a first-run movie occurred in provincial capitals, rather than in Tehran.[87]

Linguistic diversity also increased, as feature movies were regularly dubbed into the local languages and dialects of ethnoreligious minorities, particularly Turkish and Kurdish. Hasan Mohammadzadeh made *Hesar* (1983), about the village named in the title, during the war with Iraq. It was made for the Foundation of Dispossessed branch in Urumiyeh, and it was dubbed into Turkish. *Trap (Dam*, 1983) was also dubbed into Kurdish. Both *Hesar* and *Trap* were screened in the Vahdat Film Festival.[88] However, increasingly features were not just dubbed, but also filmed in various regions of the country and in various Iranian languages and dialects, or they were filmed in foreign languages outside Iran, requiring subtitling. Powerful elements of multiculturalism and multilingualism crept into cinema, elements that had always been part of society but had been suppressed by Iranian modern nationalism, driven by a state-imposed homogeneous identity as a monolingual national identity. Baizai's *Bashu, the Little Stranger*, filmed inside Iran but almost entirely in Gilaki, with some Arabic and Persian dialogue, was a pioneer in this exploration of Iranian multilingualism and national diversity. Many of the extraterritorial and ethnic movies were also multilingual.

At the same time, in a post–Cold War globalized world and in a society whose leaders, particularly Ayatollah Khomeini, advocated "exporting" the Islamic Revolution elsewhere, these multilingual films provided both a counterdiscourse against official ideology by emphasizing the multiplicity of Persian and Iranian cultures predating and exceeding Islam, and a reminder of the earlier Persian empire, which contained those cultures. Finally, all these multiplicities and heterogeneities were part of what I have called the emerging multiplexity in cinema worldwide (2009).

Genres and Themes of Domestic Features

The nature of the times resulted in the emergence of certain film genres, in the context of the film types described. Early on action, adventure, war, comedy, and family melodrama genres dominated. The themes they embodied

TABLE 7 Themes of feature movies (1987)

Themes	No. of Films
Amnesia as a result of shock	5
Psychological disorders	9
Emigration or escape from the country	11
Problems and disputes within families	14
War as a principal and ancillary theme	12
Wealth does not bring happiness (Islamicate values)	20
Exposing the Pahlavi regime	11
Exposing antigovernment "grouplets" (*goruhakha*)	4

Source: Purmohammad 1987.

indicate social tensions, the way Islamicate values were playing out on the screen to create an overall Islamicate cinema, and the continual struggle with modernity. Masud Purmohammad's study of movie screenplays turned up some of these themes (table 7).

While this study focused on 1987 movies, its findings can be generalized to at least the entire first decade of the Islamic Republic, during which revolution and war with Iraq were paramount. The themes of shock and psychological disorders, split families, and war were explored particularly in family melodramas and war movies.[89] Given the long wake of the revolution, it was understandable for Islamicate cinema to dwell on the moral corruption, economic dependence, subservience to the West, and political suppression of the Pahlavi regime. The large number of films in this category (eleven), seven years after the fall of the Shah, points to the theme's continuing resonance. The prioritizing of spirituality over material rewards in Islamicate values figures large in table 7, with twenty movies. In fact, postrevolutionary cinema as a whole may be characterized as moralist, imbued with a generalized sense of ethics, pitting a moral-centric, religious world against a corrupting modern secular world. Like Pahlavi-period commercial movies, postrevolution popular movies favored traditional values of rural folks over the consumerist ideology of urban residents. But this moralist popular cinema, instead of concentrating on deeper Iranian and Islamic mystic values, catered chiefly to superficial morality, characterized by "easy hopes, cheap emotions, and inexpensive good deeds" (Karimi 1988). At the same time, the quality films of the ethical, humanist art cinema put postrevolutionary film on the map with its modernist concern for the individual.

Mehdi Sabbaghzadeh's *The Senator* (*Senator*, 1984), about graft and her-

38 Poster for Masud Kimiai's masculinist movie, *Razor and Silk*, combining war and international drug smuggling. Collection of the author.

oin smuggling, embodies the theme of corruption. It topped the box office of 1984 with sales of nearly $1 million. As drug smuggling and addiction loomed larger, Masud Kimiai explored them, with his characteristic masculinist style, in such movies as *Snake's Fang* and *Razor and Silk* (*Tigh va Abrisham*, 1987) (fig. 38).

Not surprisingly, spying and torture by Savak as well as armed struggle against the Shah were early favorite themes, leading to a genre of quickie political movies. Mehdi Ma'danian's *The Cry of a Mojahed* (*Faryad-e Mojahed*, 1979), perhaps the first postrevolution fiction feature movie, is about a young teacher who is politicized by anti-Shah clerical actions that caused the attack against the Faiziyeh Seminary in Qom in the early 1960s and the exile of the Ayatollah Khomeini. The teacher forms an urban guerrilla opposition group, which succeeds in the "revolutionary execution" of a torturer and a chief of police. Apparently vvir officials, including Director General Ghotbzadeh, campaigned against the "superficialities" of the film, causing it to be banned permanently. The film's producer and the producers' association claim that the ban was caused by the competition between vvir and mcig over the control of cinema in the country (Jafari Lahijani 2008:vol. 2:773). Such internecine rivalries, part of the consolidation process, continued for some time after the revolution. Aman Manteqi's *The Soldier of Islam* (*Sarbaz-e Eslam*, 1980) cen-

39 Poster for Aman Manteqi's *The Soldier of
Islam*, an example of "Savak films" turning into
an Islamic film. Collection of the author.

40 Poster for Habib Kavosh's "Savak film,"
Season of Blood. Collection of the author.

ters on an Islamist fighter whose sister falls in love with the son of a Savak
operative, who eventually joins the anti-Shah revolution (fig. 39). Mansur Tehrani's *From Shout to Assassination* (*Az Faryad ta Teror*, 1980) deals with three
men, former schoolmates, who collaborate in armed struggle against Savak
agents. Habib Kavosh's *Season of Blood* (*Fasl-e Khun*, 1981) is about fisher-
men's struggles in the port of Anzali against government fishery officers and
Savak agents who sow seeds of distrust among seamen (fig. 40). Copying
thrillers, these movies made the "revolutionaries" act like gangsters. Allamehzadeh rightly characterizes them as "religious filmfarsi" (1991:78). Others called them "Savak movies" or "guerrilla movies" and roundly condemned
them as phony and exploitive. One critic warned their producers, "If you are
not truthful, the audience will edit you out into the dust bin of history." He
called on the filmmakers to abandon commercialism and pick up the "pen of
the camera" to create accurate reports of life under the Pahlavis (Ebrahimian
1979).

An exception was Khosrow Sinai's first feature movie, *Long Live!* (*Zendeh Bad!*, 1980), depicting the way in which a professional, upscale engineer inadvertently becomes involved with anti-Shah forces when a demonstrator takes refuge in his house. The engineer's involvement ends in his death at the hands of police. This film was born from the events of the year preceding the revolution, and as Sinai relates, it was a home movie: 80 percent of it was filmed inside his own home; his children acted in it and his wife, Gizzela Varga, a painter, created the sets and costumes. Although at first MCIG praised the film—rating it "excellent," exhibiting it in commercial cinemas, and entering it into the Karlovy Vary Film Festival, where it received a top prize from an antifascist group—it canceled the film's exhibition permit after four days and seemingly for good (Baqerzadeh 1987:343–44). The permanent ban is partially due to women and actresses not wearing proper hijab in the film. Sinai thinks it is also due to his political impartiality, signified by the film's title, which does not specify the subject to which it refers, and by the exclamation mark that it carries (Jafari Lahijani 2008:vol. 2:756).

In the 1980s, several movies worked on "exposing" the activities of various antigovernment groups, particularly those of PMOI, which had become the most lethal threat against the regime, necessitating the mobilization of all media to blunt its impact. One was Said Hajmiri's movie *Suspicion* (*Tavvahom*, 1985), made for Channel Two Television, about two members of PMOI, which the Islamic Republic routinely labeled with the disdaining monikers of "hypocrites" or "grouplets" (Hajmiri was also co-producer and screenplay writer). The film is about two PMOI sympathizers living clandestinely in a "safe house" as they await instructions for their next operation. One of them is steadfast in his resolve to work with PMOI, while the other is wavering. At one point, they are led to believe that the security police have surrounded them: they burn their documents and prepare for a gun battle. The wavering guerrilla, meanwhile, makes up his mind to abandon PMOI and escapes the house, but in the course of various adventures, in a case of mistaken identity, he ends up murdering his friend. Because PMOI declared an armed guerrilla war against the Islamic Republic in 1981 and began to assassinate scores of high-ranking officials and clerics in spectacular terrorist acts, it was natural that a film made by the state-controlled television network would not be complementary to PMOI. In fact, it represents them as heartless criminals. PMOI's partisan exile publications countered by reporting a decidedly negative reaction to the film inside the country.

According to one of these publications, the movie was screened in Shahr-e Qashang (Beautiful City) Cinema in Tehran. In one scene, as soon as an image of PMOI's leader Masud Rajavi came on the screen, a spectator shouted, "Praise to Rajavi," whereupon the shouts of "Praise to Rajavi" ("dorud bar Rajavi") resounded in the cinema "like a bomb" among the spectators, who also rhythmically stamped their feet. At another point, when a picture of the "martyred" PMOI founder Mohammad Hanifnezhad was displayed, the crowd began shouting in unison, "Hanif's blood is boiling, Rajavi's anger is roiling ("Khun-e Hanif mijushad, Rajavi mikhorushad"). This caused the projectionist to stop the screening and the police to pour into the theater to calm the melee. But the paper reported, "One could observe in the faces and the eyes of the spectators the smiles of happiness and the sparkles of triumph over the abject enemy."[90] In another incident, in Ahvaz, during the screening of *Suspicion*, when a PMOI anthem and the audio logo of the Radio Mojahed were heard ("This is the voice of People's Mojahedin of Iran"), the entire audience rose to their feet and burst into clapping, singing, and displays of intense joy.

Shahriar Bohrani's anti-Mojahedin movie *Flag-Holder* (*Parchamdar*, 1984), made for the Shahed Cinema Group, also caused similar spectatorial demonstrations of antigovernment and pro-Mojahedin sentiments in the cities of Saqqez and Tabriz. These sentiments were apparently so strong and sustained that after two days of screening, the security agencies banned the movie. Some spectators read the movie against the grain, such as a supporter of the Mojahedin who claimed that he and his sister were so impressed by the PMOI members in this anti-Mojahedin movie that they had both joined the organization as full-fledged members.[91] Yet another film with an anti-Mojahedin and anti-Kurdish storyline was Ahmad Hasanimoqaddam's *The Epic of the Shiler Valley* (*Hamaseh-ye Shiler*, 1986), which dealt with the story of a revolutionary guardsman who defects to antigovernment forces and is sent on a mission to obtain weapons from Iraq. The revolutionary guards, who are onto the plot, however, attack and decimate the antigovernment group and rescue the repentant guardsman. The film was screened in Bahman Cinema in the Kurdish-dominated city of Sanandaj, where as the government's own "confidential" sources reported, "approximately 80 percent of the gathered audience favored" the murder of revolutionary guardsmen by the member of Democratic Party of Kurdistan.[92]

The former Ayat Film member and former MCIG official Mohammad Ali Najafi directed an anti–Tudeh Party movie, *Report of a Murder* (*Gozaresh-e Yek Qatl*, 1986), about the head of the Tudeh Party's military wing during the Pahlavi period who is released in Isfahan after twenty years of imprisonment. Bitter about his betrayal, he hunts for the stool pigeon who informed on him, finds him heading the official Resurgence Party branch within the giant steel mill, and murders him. A young leftist lawyer is appointed to the case and by befriending the Tudeh member's wife and daughter tracks him down during the revolutionary upsurge. The Tudeh Party had participated in both the revolution and the installation of the Islamic Republic regime, thus earning the anger both of the hard left, which felt betrayed by it, and of the Islamist right, which felt manipulated by it. The film was narratively and visually weak, partly because of its inability to portray the Pahlavi-era society in which professional women worked alongside men without wearing the hijab.

Another common movie theme was population displacement and migration (see table 7). The upheavals of the revolution, the Islamic Republic's reign of terror, and the violence of the protracted war with Iraq caused a massive displacement internally and also to foreign lands. Perhaps up to three million Iranians were driven to, or chose, external exile. As I have shown elsewhere (Naficy 1993), in its first decade the Islamic Republic took a highly antagonistic stance against this population of exiles, often characterizing them as anti-government, treasonous escapees and comfort-loving, pleasure-seeking, un-Islamic loafers and thieves. No wonder that several movies were made with these themes; however, interestingly, the films were less belligerent than the government rhetoric. After all, they depended on attracting spectators, many of whom had family members among the escapees, refugees, and exiles. Jamshid Haidari's *Escape* (*Farar*, 1984) deals with two families in Tehran's South End, the fate of whose sons represents the two antagonistic poles after the revolution. One family's son, Javad, chooses honorably to go to war, where he is martyred, while the other family's son, Ali, dishonors it by escaping to West Germany. Ashamed by his son's action, Ali's father joins the fighting front. After exilic difficulties, Ali gradually comes to his senses and returns to Iran, where he searches for his father, finds him injured on the war front, replaces him, and sends him back home happy. The veteran director Bahram Raipur's *Visa* (*Viza*, 1987) is about a physician who plans to emigrate to the United States. He first sends his family to Istanbul to obtain American visas, while he remains behind to sort out his affairs before joining them. Instead, he becomes aware of personal family problems (addiction, old age) and is then sent to the front as a physician, where through an encounter with a Basij Militia Force, he becomes aware of the problems within the nation. Realizing that his services are needed at home, he changes his mind and sends for his family (fig. 41).

With the continuation of repression and problems at home, the pace and scale of emigration increased, turning Iran into a major source of émigrés while providing a rich vein of topics for domestic filmmakers. On the other

41 Poster for Bahram Raipur's *Visa*, a film that mixes immigration and war themes. Collection of the author.

hand, many of the émigrés turned to filmmaking abroad, forming an active and growing accented cinema.[93] Likewise, the revolution and the war with Iraq, along with their sociopolitical aftermaths, continued to capture the imaginations of filmmakers and spectators, resulting in a wealth of documentaries and war-related movies.[94] With time other genres, themes, and types of movie emerged, two of the most vibrant of these being women's films and art-house films.[95] Finally, growing social discontent at home and globalization, digitization, and technological convergence created a perfect storm for the emergence of a new inchoate Internet cinema.[96]

Post-Khomeini, Postwar, Post–Khatami Era Cinema

Ayatollah Khomeini signaled his reluctance to agree to United Nations Resolution 598, which declared a cease-fire in the war with Saddam Hussein, by analogizing it to drinking a "chalice of poison." But this was a cruel war that lasted eight long years, during which both countries lost massive numbers of their youths and suffered colossal economic damage and social disruption without any apparent gain (the borders remained unchanged, both regimes remained in place, and no peace treaty was signed). As though the cease-fire, reached in 1988, had indeed been a slow poison, the ayatollah died within a year. Soon, the ideology of exporting the Islamic revolution, which Khomeini had advocated, was abandoned and was replaced with what might be called "Islamic nationalism." In the official discourse, Islamic community (*ummat-e eslami*) changed to Islamic nation (*mellat-e eslami*) and was further modified to accommodate ethnoreligious and nationalist diversity.

In the wake of these two important endings—of the war and of Khomeini's reign—and subsequent developments, Iranian politics, economy, and culture underwent significant transformations, which affected the film industry and cinema, ushering in the culturally more liberal if contentious reform period, which resulted in the restoration and strengthening of a professional hybrid production mode capable of producing and sustaining several new types of cinemas, which received wide national and international recognition.

Rebuilding and Privatizing the Film Industry

President Khatami took a more public role in cultural negotiations over cinema than had his predecessors, personally defending quality films and openness. For example, Davud Mirbaqeri's *The Snowman* (*Adam Barfi*, 1994), banned for several years, was released only after Khatami's election to presidency and Mohajerani's appointment to head MCIG. The film immediately became controversial and subject to attacks by Islamist toughs, causing Khatami and other reformists to come to its rescue.[97] The spectators, too, endorsed it, by flocking to the movie houses. During the reconstruction era, President Hashemi Rafsanjani had begun to privatize major industries, including cinema, leading to the reevaluation and partial removal of government subsidies to the film industry. Dire predictions of the industry's collapse failed to materialize. In fact, in the long run, privatization probably helped.[98] Khatami intensified Rafsanjani's privatization of the country's shattered economy and heightened relations of exchange with other national economies. In 1999, he offered a five-year plan to turn over the communications, post, railway, and tobacco industries to the private sector in a "total restructuring of the Islamic Republic's economy."[99] Privatization meant the reduction of government involvement in film financing, production, and exhibition. However, the exhibitors had complained for years about the high cost of running their movie houses, whose financial returns were not sufficient for continued operation, let alone expansion or improvement. They claimed that it was financially more rewarding to convert their cinemas into arcades, storage facilities, apartment complexes, or to just let them run down. They cleverly mobilized the argument of the conservative faction against themselves by stating that if the government wanted to successfully counter the cultural assault on Iran by Western culture industries, it must support cinema owners and exhibitors through low-interest loans, land grants, import credits for equipment and facilities, and permission to create commercial businesses within the movie houses, such as bookstores, video stores, and cafés, in order to attract both spectators and investors. They argued that increasing the ticket prices alone would not offset the losses. The shortage of cinemas was glaring in the light of the rapid rise in the country's population, the film industry's increased output, and statistics that showed one movie house per 220,000 persons. The general director of Farabi Cinema Foundation, Mohammad Hasan Pezeshg, concurred with the dire need for new cinemas, calculating that if every Iranian were to go the movies once every fifteen days, a minimum of 1,200 *new* cinemas were needed.[100]

Ironically, however, the inadequacy of the cinemas, their aging projection and sound systems, decrepit facilities, general grime, and rising ticket prices turned spectators away. The popularity of video, satellite television, and the Internet was also a factor, as were the low quality of most commercial movies and the esoteric attributes of most art-house films. As in the Pahlavi era, the spectators were bifurcated between popular movies, which attracted the majority, and art cinema movies, which smaller cosmopolitan audiences favored. A new factor was the large population of youth under thirty, the "youth bulge," for whom the film industry needed to make movies. The challenge, however, was that these films had to compete with satellite television, home video, video games, and the Internet, which offered this demographic potent entertainment, enlightenment, and worldliness. The end result was that moviegoing actually declined precipitously and alarmingly, to the point that attendance for Iranian movies in 1998 was half that of 1988 (Ministry of Culture and Islamic Guidance 2000:20).[101] The final irony is that the only domestic industry that in the 1990s had brought worldwide renown and respect to Iran, countering the negative global public diplomacy and mediawork about it, was unable to find enthusiastic general audiences inside its home country.

To open up the bottleneck that the shortage of movie houses had formed for the industry, MCIG placed movie house construction among its "top priorities" and promised in 1999 to build a hundred new movie houses within the year (Ministry of Culture and Islamic Guidance 2000:7). This was a shot in the arm but clearly inadequate, as it would bring the number of cinemas nationwide only to around 415, still less than what it had been over two decades earlier. Government assistance to cinema owners to convert their establishments into multiplexes was a positive new strategy, as was its interest-free loan to convert their sound systems to Dolby and to improve their exteriors.

To deal with unauthorized video and satellite television the government planned to relinquish its monopoly on video distribution by licensing local film producers and video distributors to import foreign movies on video. Up to this point, it had protected the domestic film industry from competition by essentially banning foreign imports. Under the new plan, domestic film producers could import four foreign movies for every feature they produced in Iran.[102] This was designed to raise the number and the quality of available films in order to bring in spectators. The long-term effects of privatization would probably be damaging, but fortuitously a new factor favoring domestic productions emerged. The foreign film market for Iranian films made possible a partially "independent cinema" with both national and transnational audiences and investors. If managed properly, the income from this market might be sufficient both to offset government pullback and to protect art cinema films against low domestic public taste and commercialization. Directors such as Abbas Kiarostami, Bahman Ghobadi, Majid Majidi, Jafar Panahi, Mohsen Makhmalbaf, Rakhshan Banietemad, and Samira Makhmalbaf were able to operate in the realm of independent cinema, self-financing and co-producing their own films with international funding.

Ideological Repositioning of Cinema

The major shifts in official and popular attitudes toward cinema were as significant as the aforementioned moves to rationalize and modernize the industry. Rejected as part of the corrupting Pahlavi *superstructure*, cinema was immediately adopted as part of the edifying Islamic Republic's *infrastructure*. Ayatollah Khomeini initiated this shift in the first speech he gave on his return from exile, in which he declared that he was not against cinema per se, but against its "misuse." Later, Fakhreddin Anvar, deputy minister of MCIG in charge of the Cinematic Affairs Department, explained how this was to be achieved: "Believing culture to be the structure undergirding all aspects of running a society . . . the department has directed all its efforts toward ensuring that cinematic activities and filmmaking are included in all legislation, laws, systems, and regulations."[103] Thus, the Islamic Republic began to "internalize" cinema by absorbing it into its interstices.

Moviegoing and working in film, once despised, became respectable. Hojjatoleslam Ali Akbar Hashemi Rafsanjani, then powerful speaker of the Majles, publicly put his stamp on this shift when he declared, in March 1987, "Our entertainers, male or female, did not enjoy the same esteem that they enjoy today from the lay and religious people. . . . This is a real revolution."[104] Reza Kianian, a popular postrevolution movie star, relates an anecdote about this changed public perception. He was invited to attend and to speak to audiences on several important religious events. On the occasion of the sacred Night of Power (a.k.a. the Night of Resurrection by the Shiites), the Ministry of Culture and Islamic Guidance organized a major celebratory event, for which a huge crowd gathered, so many in fact that, as the Persian saying goes, if you dropped a needle, it would not hit the ground.[105] On the stage, Kianian told the gathered crowd how appropriate the celebration was, for that night of religious resurrection was also a night marking the resurrection of actors, who some seventy years earlier had been called *motreb*, whose dictionary meaning is "dancer" or "entertainer," but whose popular interpretations were derogatory and disrespectful, suggesting someone who was cheap, lightweight, and tawdry. "That's how your ancestors regarded my ancestors." He then pointedly explained the changed public regard for actors and entertainers after the revolution.

> I don't know how they would feel if they knew that today their offspring not only invite the offspring of *motrebs*, but also invite them to climb the dais [*menbar*]. . . . Before, your predecessors would invite my predecessors to happy events, such as circumcision and wedding ceremonies, to entertain them, after which they would pretend not to know us. . . . Entertainers were part of what was forbidden. They were religiously forbidden. . . . Your ancestors did not allow my ancestors to be buried in the Muslims' cemetery. . . . I am surprised that on this night, which is worth a thousand other nights, you have invited a *motreb* to speak to the faithful. (Kianian 2008:65–66)

That this resurrection, or rehabilitation, of the entertainers was taking place on a night of religious significance made it highly symbolic.

Another indication of the changed public perception and general reorientation of cinema is that for the first time clerics were not only attending movie houses, but also acting in the movies. A midlevel cleric, Hojjatoleslam Rastegari, who appeared in Akbar Sadeqi's *Under Siege* (*Dar Mohasereh*, 1981), was probably the first to act in a fiction movie. (The film told the story of the son of an officer in the Shah's army who rises against both his family father and the nation's "crowned father," as the Shah used to be called.) Rastegari played the role because he believed in the pedagogical power of cin-ema, which he thought was untapped by the Islamist forces, but he was still unsure enough to consult with Ayatollah Ali Khamenei and with his prayer beads (estekhareh) before daring to participate.[106] Clerics also directed cine-matic and cultural institutions: Mohammad Ali Zam, head of the Islamic Propaganda Organization, produced many movies, and Mohammad Kha-tami, minister of Culture and Islamic Guidance, for a decade supervised all cultural, artistic, and cinematic spheres of the country. Significantly, how-ever, with few exceptions—among them, Seyyed Reza Mir-Karimi's *Under the Moonlight* (*Zir-e Nur-e Mah*, 2002) and Kamal Tabrizi's *Lizard* (*Marmulak*, 2004)—clerics were glaringly absent from fiction movies, particularly art cin-ema films. And these exceptions were highly critical of the clerics. This was not an accidental absence, but a structured absence, which could be attributed both to the filmmakers' resistance to clerics and their values and to a strategy of avoiding controversy and censorship, which filmic treatment of the clerics, like that of women, would have invited. Foreign visitors whose image of the country is based solely on Iranian movies screened abroad would surely be very surprised on arriving in the country and noting the dominance of the clerics in society, politics, and official media. On the other hand, the clerics and other religious figures colonized the screens of government television networks, not only in newscasts but also in documentaries, particularly bio-graphical documentaries, inspiring the comic moniker "glass wool."

Immediately after the revolution, films were judged solely on political pu-rity and instructional values; gradually they began to be assessed for their ability to entertain and enlighten. Again, it was Hashemi Rafsanjani who ac-knowledged the necessity of a lighter treatment of themes in cinema, in 1985, authorizing joy and entertainment as important to a productive life. The MCIG minister Khatami, too, declared this shift in perception and repositioning of cinema in no uncertain terms: "I believe that cinema is not the mosque. . . . If we remove cinema from its natural place, we will no longer have cinema. . . . If we transform cinema to such an extent that when one enters a movie house one feels imposed upon or senses that leisure time has changed to become homework time, then we have deformed society."[107]

The same tripartite policy of support, supervision, and guidance that gov-erned the reemergence of cinema was applied by MCIG to help reinvigorate the music industry (Youssefzadeh 2001:253). The Islamicate morality codes, which had become a straitjacket for cinema, limiting the portrayal of women and men and the use of music, were eased considerably after December 1987, when Ayatollah Khomeini issued an edict relaxing their application.[108] Music returned to public spaces, but with some restrictions and institutional specialization. While MCIG seemed to support mostly Persian classical music, VVIR tended to support the reemergence of a new Islamicate pop music. The television networks broadcast both art music and pop music as long as the musicians were not shown playing the instruments, and they aired women's singing voices as long as they were not shown singing. These limitations were to expand and contract over the years, depending on politics and personalities in charge of culture industry institutions. Comedy entered the quality cinema as well. The immense popularity and revenues that Mehrjui's social satire *The Tenants* (*Ejareh Neshinha*, 1986) generated (highest in the history of Iranian cinema up to that date) were testimony that the public, too, wanted movies to be well made, entertaining, and enlightening. In fact, as Mohammad Beheshti, director of Farabi Cinema Foundation, observed in an interview with me, "A new and unprecedented situation has developed in postrevolutionary Iran, whereby the best quality films are also the most popular films" (Naficy 1991b). While this was not true of the official movies, it was true of an increasing number of art cinema and populist films. An example of the latter was *Bride* (*Arus*, 1991), made by the Islamist filmmaker—later to become a reformist member of parliament—Behrouz Afkhami (d. 2010). About the courtship of a young, attractive couple (played by Niki Karimi and Abolfazl Pourarab), the film emphasized love, celebratory sentiments, and the beauty of Karimi, who became one of the postrevolutionary cinema's first new female movie stars. That the film became the top box office draw, surpassing Mehrjui's *The Tenants*, sent an unmistakable message. Imitations followed quickly: in the Fajr International Film Festival of 1994, some thirty movies contained a scene with a bride in a wedding gown (Tahaminejad 2001:89).

In its first year under the Islamic Republic, cinema was regarded as an agent of corruption and draconian purification policies were applied to it. As a result of these measures, certain immoral and corrupting practices and people were removed from the screen and from the industry. That real change, in addition to changed perceptions, opened the film industry to new audiences and fresh talent. If religious people did not attend the cinemas during the Pahlavi period, they did now. If parents did not allow their children, particularly daughters, to work in the film industry as a career, they were now willing to consider that option. The family mode of production, which developed after the revolution and by which members of a nuclear family participated in filmmaking—exemplified by Mohsen Makhmalbaf's and Rakhshan Banietemad's families—is emblematic of this ideological shift about cinema. Filmmakers dealt with this shift in their movies, as well. Mohsen Makhmalbaf, for example, in his *Salaam Cinema* (1995) played with this changed perception. He placed a casting-call ad, and five thousand young people swarmed the audition. The entire film is about the director (played by Makhmalbaf himself) interviewing and auditioning various eager would-be actors—male and female—for undefined parts. The applicants give all sorts of reasons, concoct all types of tales, and endure all kinds of hypothetical situations, indignities, abuses, and tests at the hand of the self-important, autocratic director in order to get his cherished nod to act in the movie. If nothing else, the film demonstrates at once the humor and resourcefulness of the applicants as well as the love of cinema among young people in a country that began the revolution by burning down movie houses. Ironically, and unexpectedly, the biggest beneficiaries of such general repositioning were women, who became an indispensable part of the new Iranian cinema, both behind and before the cameras. Likewise, Abbas Kiarostami's *Close-Up* (1989) offers an intriguing portrait of one ordinary person's love and respect not only for auteur cinema, but also for the auteur, particularly for Mohsen Makhmalbaf, a love that caused the person to pass himself off as Makhmalbaf, a fraudulent impersonation for which he was tried in court and in the film.

Such ideological repositioning of cinema was commensurate with other ideological and sociopolitical reorientations and transformations that favored values of liberal democracy, secular modernity, and individualism. This in turn resulted in another social bifurcation, which expressed itself in dividing the filmmakers into insiders (*khodi, mahram*) and outsiders (*gharibeh, namahram*), with the former, who made pro-regime films, worthy of support, and the latter deserving of scorn.

Under the premiership of Mir Hosain Musavi, the cabinet in its session on 3 July 1982 (12 Tir 1361) approved the following regulations governing the exhibition of movies, videos, and slides, which the MCIG had proposed (proposal no. 2422, dated 30 October 1982/8 Aban 1361). These regulations contain seventeen articles, some of which originally had notes attached, which I have turned into endnotes for clarity (Ministry of Culture and Islamic Guidance 1985:appendix 1:40–44). These regulations apply to producers who submit movies for license.

1. What is meant by film and video in these regulations is any type of film, video, or slide in various gauges and lengths, whether educational, documentary, or fictional.

2. All movies and videos shown publicly must bear an exhibition permit from MCIG; otherwise, MCIG or its representatives in the provinces will call upon the police to stop unauthorized screenings.

3. Sale and public screenings of all movies containing the following provisions are forbidden nationwide.

— If they deny or weaken the principle of monotheism and other sacred Islamic principles, or if they insult them in any manner.

— If they deny, manipulate, or damage other fundamentals [*Foru-e din*] of the sacred religion of Islam.[1]

— If they insult directly or indirectly the heavenly prophets, the innocent imams, supreme jurisprudent [*velyat faqih*], the ruling council, or the jurisprudents [*mojtaheds*].

— If they blaspheme the values and personalities held sacred by Islam and other religions recognized in the constitution.

— If they negate the equality of all people regardless of color, race, language, ethnicity, and belief, or if they incite racial and ethnic differences or make fun of them.

- If they negate or violate the high value of humans.[2]
- If they encourage wickedness, corruption, and prostitution.
- If they encourage or teach dangerous addictions and earning a living from unsavory means such as smuggling.
- If they facilitate foreign cultural, economic, and political influence contrary to government's "neither West nor East" policy.[3]
- If they express or disclose anything that is against the interests and policies of the country, which might be exploited by foreigners.
- If they show details of scenes of murder, violent crimes, and torture in such a way as to disturb or mislead viewers.[4]
- If they misrepresent historical and geographical facts.
- If they present rough and abnormal images and sounds, be they caused by technical or other problems, in such a way that endangers the health and security of spectators.
- If they lower the taste of spectators through low production and artistic values.

4. Exporting Iranian movies for sale, rent, or entry into festivals requires a separate license.

5. To review the films for the purpose of issuing exhibition licenses based on the provisions of these regulations, the deputy minister of Islamic Guidance must form the Supervisory Council [Haiat-e nezarat], approved by the minister of Islamic Guidance, consisting of the following persons who hold the necessary expertise in film and cinema. One cleric familiar with artistic issues; three people with political, sociological, and Islamic insight and familiar with cinematic and filmic issues; and one expert in domestic and foreign cinematic matters.[5]

6. The Supervisory Council will draw up its own internal procedures for its operation and upon approval of the minister of Islamic Guidance will implement them.

7. When necessary, the Supervisory Council may invite content experts from various fields to attend its sessions.

8. The parts of the films that do not conform to these regulations must be altered or cut. Films may be granted exhibition license if such alterations do not harm their contents and forms.

9. If the council rejects a film and the applicant disagrees, he can request another review by the High Council of Supervision [Showra-ye ali-ye nezarat]. Films may be brought to the high council whose rejection by the supervisory council was not unanimous.[6]

10. The minister of Islamic Guidance appoints the members of High Council of Supervision from among the following persons: One deputy minister from MCIG or his authorized representative; one representative from the Ministry of the Interior, upon approval of MCIG minister; one representative from the High Council of Propaganda, upon approval of MCIG minister; chair of the review coun-

cil will participate in the High Council of Supervision's meetings to answer questions, without the right to vote.[7]

11. The exhibition licenses are valid for two years. To renew licenses, proper application must be made as specified in these regulations.

12. The exhibition license is valid for the entire country unless otherwise noted.

13. The applicant for an exhibition license must fill in all the relevant information about the film in appropriate forms provided by the General Department of Supervision and Exhibition and turn over these along with a complete print of the film (either dubbed into Persian or with its original soundtrack) to the General Department of Supervision and Exhibition.

14. The number and date of exhibition licenses for Iranian or foreign movies must legibly and audibly appear in the films along with their titles.

15. Movie trailers must have exhibition licenses from the General Department of Supervision and Exhibition.

16. Any person who exhibits movies, videos, and slides without a permit from the General Department of Supervision; or any person who engages in fraud and deception and provides fraudulent or wrong documents and information at the time of application for exhibition license; or any person who during the screening of a movie cuts scenes or adds the scenes that the authorities had previously removed from the film; or any person who at the time of his application removes certain scenes and having received exhibition permit restores those scenes; and in general all persons who violate any of these regulations will be prosecuted according to the laws of the country. In the first instance, they will lose their exhibition license. If the violation is repeated, in addition to legal prosecution, the business license of the applicant and of the exhibitor will be revoked.

17. All exhibition licenses for films, videos, and slides, which have been issued up to the date of these regulations are valid for their duration.

Regulations Governing Exhibition of Movies, Videos, and Slides

Some of the articles in these regulations are similar to those governing issuing of exhibition licenses to producers. However, these apply to film exhibitors and most are different, interjecting in fascinating and more forceful ways the Islamicate values, derived from the new constitution, giving the postrevolutionary cinema its Islamicate cast. To preserve the historical integrity of these regulations, they are presented here fully, despite some repetition. These regulations contain nine articles, with their notes transferred to the endnotes for clarity (Ministry of Culture and Islamic Guidance 1985:appendix 1:45–49).

1. Since unlike reading books and periodicals, during film watching there is not sufficient time for precise and complete thinking, the film's attitude is trans-

ferred to the spectators. As a result, not only the technical clarity of sounds and images but also the general impact of the movies on the revolutionary society's culture must be considered.[8]

2. The exhibition of any segment of a film or the entire film that denies, manipulates, or damages the following points is forbidden in the entire country.

— Monotheism and submission to God and to his authority and laws.
— Role of divine revelation and its fundamental function in expressing laws.
— Resurrection and its role in the evolution of humans toward God.
— Justness of God in creation and in law.
— The importance of Imamate [religious leadership by the imams] and its fundamental function in maintaining the Islamic revolution.
— The role of Islamic Republic of Iran under the leadership of Ayatollah Khomeini in ridding the Muslims and the downtrodden of the clutches of world imperialism.[9]
— The lofty dignity and merit of human beings along with their freedom and responsibility before God, which come to fruition and are revealed in the following manner.
  — Continuous *ejtehad* (independent judgment) of qualified religious scientists based on Islam's sacred book and tradition.
  — Utilization of the advanced human sciences and technologies and effort to advance them further.
  — Obtaining justice and political, economic, social, and cultural independence.
— The constitution of the Islamic Republic, or sections thereof, and the fruits of the Islamic revolution.
— The sanctity of the family as the fundamental unit of Muslim society and the firmness of family relations based on the rights and ethics of Islam.
— The constructive and effective function of Muslim women in social affairs and in training committed, saved, and responsible children.
— The equality of all humans regardless of color, race, language, and ethnicity before God almighty.
— The Islamic dimensions of the Iranian revolution and the rights of all social strata that were involved in the revolution.
— The right of self-determination of all nations and people, which belongs to them.
— Involvement of the Muslims in political, cultural, social, economical, and military affairs in the Iranian Muslim society under the authority of the constitution, which is the duty of each Muslim.
— Struggle against racism and oppression by superpowers and world imperialism at any place and any time, according to Islamic regulations and criteria.
— Constant effort and struggle for the purpose of achieving a world society that is entirely ruled by Islam.

3. The exhibition of a segment or all of a film that contains one of the following is forbidden in the entire country.

— Any movie that attempts to directly or indirectly exert cultural, political, and ethnic influence of foreigners in the Islamic Republic of Iran.[10]
— Any movie that makes fun of the languages or dialects of various ethnicities and official minorities.
— Movies made by government-authorized parties and groups which are not congruent with the laws governing political parties and groups.[11]
— Any movie that creates false sensation and has no redeeming social and cultural value.
— Any movie that propagates *taquti* [idolater, decadent] values and the corrupt ideals of imperialists.
— Movies that appear to be religious but deceive viewers out of opportunism, or movies that due to their strict Islamism damage and lower the lofty intellectual and spiritual status of Muslims.
— Movies that deny the role of women in constructing a progressive and divine society and use them as commodities or means to satisfy sexual desires.[12]
— Movies that use music for prurient, pleasurable, and debauched purposes [*lahv va la'ab va ghena*] that go beyond plots and narratives and whose sole purposes are to emotionally attract spectators and propagate such music in society.
— Movies that show details of murder.
— Movies that show the murder, torture, or general cruelty to animals in such a way as to disgust viewers.[13]
— Movies that manipulate historical and geographical facts in such a way as to lead the spectators astray.
— Presenting images and sounds that damage, or have an abnormal effect on, the vision or hearing of viewers.
— Movies that deny the productivity, self-sufficiency, and economic independence of society.
— Prints of damaged movies whose projection would inconvenience the spectators.
— Old film prints on nitrate stock, the slightest negligence in the handling of which can cause fire, explosion, and suffocation.

4. To evaluate the appropriateness of the movies for children and young adults, a committee must be formed consisting of representatives of the Ministry of Education, administrators of school districts, Islamic Society of Teachers, Islamic Parents and Teachers Association, and Islamic Society of Home and School. The Supervisory Council may take into consideration their opinions in its evaluations.

5. Religious minorities and people from various regions of the country are permitted to produce and exhibit movies in their own languages and dialects, provided they follow all the legal procedures.

6. The export of Iranian movies for sale, rent, or nonprofit participation in film festivals requires an additional review and a separate license.

7. The Supervisory Council should divide the movies into six categories: Distinguished, Excellent, Good, Mediocre, Bad, Very bad.[14]

8. If excision of a segment, or segments, of a movie contrary to these regulations does not damage the content or form of the movie, then that movie may be exhibited after the designated segment or segments are removed.

9. If these regulations are violated, the violators will be punished according to the regulations for the issuance of exhibition permits.

Chapter 1: Transition to "Islamicate Cinema"

1 The Rex Cinema fire was naturally a hot topic in the press, where the tragedy and trials of Takabalizadeh and the other accused arsonists were extensively reported. While multiple versions of the incident emerged, varying the number and names of the apparent and real culprits, the number of dead victims, and the details of the event, Mostafa Abkashak's narrative seems to be more authoritative. Abkashak, a leftist worker in Abadan, was condemned to three years' imprisonment during the Shah's period for antigovernment activities. He participated in the revolution and subsequently joined the underground opposition to the Islamic Republic. According to his obituary in the Los Angeles periodical *Rayegan* (16 June 1989, n.p.), he had intimate knowledge of the circumstances surrounding the Rex Cinema fire, the personalities involved, and the ensuing trial. He wrote his account in 1984, after he had escaped Iran and settled in Los Angeles, where he died in an automobile accident, in 1989.

In addition, Ali Sajjadi, of Radio Farda, an American government–funded radio based in Prague, Czech Republic, produced a comprehensive thirteen-part series about this fire and its aftermath. Called *Conflagration of Rex Cinema* (*Atashsuzi-ye Sinema Rex*), the series, each of whose episodes lasted from eight to ten minutes, was first aired near the twenty-seventh anniversary of the fire, 10 August 2005. Radio Farda's website, http://www.radiofarda.com, has links to these episodes. Finally, Hosain Boroujerdi's tome of a confession about his revolutionary terrorism in the run-up to the revolution and in supplying the fuel to Takabalizadeh and cohort proved useful (2002).

Unless otherwise noted, my narrative of the fire and its aftermath is based primarily on these three sources, although I also used numerous newspaper clippings from *Kayhan*; unfortunately, many of these are without dates and page numbers. These clippings can be found at the Alefbe in Exile website, http://www.alefbe.com. See also "Mohakemeh-ye Atashsuzi-ye Sinema Rex-e Abadan," *Kayhan Havai*, 3 September 1980/12 Shahrivar 1359.

2 "Theater in Iran Drawn into Area's Vortex of Terror," *Variety*, 23 August 1978, 1, 85.

3 Khomeini's message can be found on the Markaz-e Asnad-e Enqelab-e Eslami website under the title "Faje'eh-ye Atashsuzi-ye Sinema Rex-e Abadan Tavasot-e Ommal-e Rezhim-e Pahlavi," http://www.irdc.ir.

4 See, for example, *Asnad va Tasaviri az Mobarezat-e Khalq-e Mosalman-e Iran* vol. 1, part 3 (Tehran: Abuzar, 1357/1978).

5 Also see "Iran's Film Biz Nipped in the Bud by Islamic Belief," *Variety*, 5 September 1979, 1.

6 In the early days of the revolution, Hosain Boroujerdi had been involved in compiling a list of assassination targets from among prominent Shah supporters and the upper classes, tracking and photographing these targets, violently eliminating them, setting fire to Baccarat Cabaret and Atlantic Cinema in Tehran, and supplying Takabalizadeh and cohorts with their fuel.

7 There was talk under the Islamic Republic of constructing across the street from the half-ruined site of Rex Cinema a memorial both to the victims of the tragedy and to the "popular struggle" against the monarchy, but this did not materialize. The site itself remained as a memorial of ruin for over twenty years, until April 2004, when the cinema was completely burned down in another fire, which had started in an adjacent building. See "Baqaya-ye Sinema Rex-e Abadan dar Atash Sukht," *Iran Times*, 23 April 2004/4 Ordibehesht 1983.

8 The original slogans are "Qatel-e azizan-e ma e'dam bayad gardad," "Na zellat, na khari, azadi, azadi," and "Tup, tofang, mosalsal digar asar nadarad."

9 Samaneh Qadar Khan's short film *The Lalehzar that Was* (*Lalehzari Keh Bud*, 2008) deals with the disappearance after the revolution of movie houses lining this famous avenue. See the film at Jadid Online, http://www.jadidonline.com.

10 In *Velayat-e Faqih*, Khomeini hammers on the theme of cinema and entertainment as the direct cause of prostitution, corruption, and political dependence.

11 The term *taqut* (idol, sorcerer, oppressor) became popular immediately after the revolution and referred to the Shah himself, his cult of personality, his entire establishment, and the culture he propagated; it was also used as an adjective, to describe anybody who made a name under his regime.

12 The original phrase is *mellat-e hamisheh bar sahneh*, which means "the nation that is always on the stage."

13 Interestingly, Ali Khamenei, who replaced Khomeini after the latter's death, in 1989, carried only one of the three titles bestowed on his predecessor: the leader.

14 One such primer issued during the war with Iraq, *Learning the Alphabets with Painting* (*Alefba ra ba Naqqashi Baiyamuzim*) (Entesharat-e Sepideh, 1984),

drawn by a person with only one name, Samadian (no place of publication), provides an example. It is a large-format book, each page containing one large letter of the alphabet and a large picture of the word that begins with that letter. The opposite page mirrors the first page in outline form, ready for the pupils to color them in. The prevalence of technological and war-related images and words is astonishing. Clearly this is to prepare children for martyrdom in war. Some of them also refer to the Islamicate values. Here are the Persian alphabets, followed by Persian words that begin with each letter of the alphabet, followed by the English translations of the words in parentheses (which are pictured in the book): Alef, *otomobil* (automobile); B-e, *bazuka* (bazooka); P-e, *padegan* (garrison); T-e, *tank* (tank); S-e, *sana* (eulogy, prayer); Jim, *jebheh* (war front); Ch-e, *chatrbaz* (parachutist); H-e, *hamleh* (attack); Kh-e, *khalaban* (pilot); Dal, *daryanavard* (sailor); Zal, *zowb* (to melt, incinerate); R-e, *radar* (radar); Z-e, *Zerehpush* (armored tank); Zh-e, *zh-e 3* (G3 rifle); Sin, *sarbarz* (soldier); Shin, *shamshir* (sword); Sad, *sayyad* (hunter); Zad, *zedd-e havai* (anti-aircraft gun); Ta, *tabl* (drum); Za, *zarf* (soldier's cooking pot); Ain, *edalat* (justice); Ghain, *ghavvas* (diver); F-e, *fantom* (phantom jet); Qaf, *qayeqran* (boatman); Kaf, *komando* (commando); Gaf, *goluleh* (bullet); Lam, *Laleh* (tulip, symbol of martyrdom); Mim, *min* (explosive mine); Nun, *neizeh* (spear); Vav, *veda'* (farewell on the front); H-e, *haft tir* (pistol); Y-e, *uzi* (Uzi machine gun).

15 For example, Sreberny-Mohammadi and Mohammadi note that the "true Islam" and "neither East nor West" concepts became the "criteria for televisual content and the weapon of the emergent state" (1994:170–71).

16 For an assessment of the new vocabulary that Khatami interjected into Iranian politics and public sphere, and a critical evaluation of its promise and failures, see Boroumand and Boroumand 2000.

17 Hosseini is now a commentator on the U.S. government–funded anti-Islamic Republic Radio Free Europe/Radio Liberty's Persian Service, Radio Farda. To see the clip of his 11 February 1979 announcement and his commentary about it, see the Iranian.com website, http://www.iranian.com.

18 The Tabriz events followed large demonstrations in Qom to protest the publication of a Savak-planted article in *Ettela'at* newspaper (7 January 1978), which cast aspersions on Ayatollah Khomeini's true nationality (he was born in India), close ties to the British, and writing of Sufi poetry. Many credited the publication of this article as the spark that ignited the revolution. Dariush Homayoun, then minister of information, later claimed that the article was printed at the personal order of the Shah (Sreberny-Mohammadi and Mohammadi 1994:139).

19 See Radio Farda's series *Conflagration of Rex Cinema*, available at http://www.radiofarda.com.

20 "Zad O' Khord-e Movafeqan va Mokhalefan-e Tahasson-e Vabastegan-e Shohada-ye Sinema Rex," *Iranshahr* 2, no. 20 (8 August 1980/17 Mordad 1359), 10. Also see "Mosahebehi ba Khanevadeh-e Qorbanian-e Faje'eh-ye Sinema Rex-e Abadan," *Mojahed*, no. 93 (21 June 1980/31 Khordad 1359), 7.

21 Parviz Sayyad wrote and directed a play about this trial, *Trial of Cinema Rex* (*Mohakemeh-ye Sinema Rex*), widely performed in the 1980s in Europe and the United States, in which, among other criticism of the conduct of the trial, he accused the film director Masud Kimiai, who after the revolution briefly served as general manager of a national television network, of suppressing the truth of the trial.

22 See the Radio Farda website, http://www.radiofarda.com.

23 "6 Amelan-e Faje'eh-ye Sinema Rex Tirbaran Shodand," *Kayhan Havai*, 10 September 1980/19 Shahrivar 1359. Also see "6 Tan az Amelin-e Asli-ye Atashsuzi-ye Sinema Rex Tirbaran Shodand," *Jomhuri-ye Eslami*, 15 Shahrivar 1359.

24 The burning and destruction of cinemas and other establishments were figured in the postrevolution art and literature. Hushang Golshiri's short story "Fathnameh-ye Moghan," for example, dealt graphically and powerfully with the destruction of cinemas and taverns as revolutionary tactics, a destructiveness that soon befell its perpetrators and squelched their revolutionary aspirations for freedom. See "Fathnameh-ye Moghan," *Kargah-e Qesseh*, no. 1 (n.d.), 1–6. For its English translation, see Golshiri 2005.

25 "Theater in Iran Drawn into Area's Vortex of Terror," *Variety*, 23 August 1978, 85.

26 I have compiled these figures from the following sources: "Iran's Film Biz Nipped in the Bud by Islamic Belief," *Variety*, 9 May 1979, 91; "Sadha Sinema dar Barabar-e Atash Bidefa'and," *Kayhan*, 6 September 1978/15 Shahrivar 1357; "Iran Theaters to Ban Sex on Their Own," *Variety*, 23 May 1979, 7; "300 Sinema-ye Keshvar Fa'aliat-e Khod ra az Sar Gereftand," *Kayhan*, 14 July 1979/23 Tir 1358; Hazel Guild, "Lots of Mullah in Iran's Show Biz," *Variety*, 13 June 1979, 1 (Guild estimates that 40 percent of cinemas burned down). The figures quoted in *Kayhan* are official figures issued by the Society of Theater Owners. Abbas Malek and Mehdi Mohsenian Rad report the destruction of 120 theaters, or 26 percent of all movie houses (1994:87).

27 "Tabdil-e Sinema beh Kahdani," *Iran Times*, 26 April 1985/6 Ordibehesht 1984; *Mojahed*, no. 3 (3 January 1985/13 Day 1363).

28 I discuss this in more detail in *A Social History of Iranian Cinema, Volume 4*.

29 "Moscow Gets Tehran's Oscar," *Iran Times*, 2 April 1982/13 Farvardin 1361. Although table 1 has a different set of figures, it shows a rise in 1981 in Eastern-bloc imports.

30 "Salshomar-e Sinema-ye Pas az Enqelab-2," *MSF*, no. 6 (October 1983/Mehr 1362), 43.

31 "Sokhani Kutah dar Bareh-ye Namayesh-e Filmha-ye Khareji," *Enqelab-e Eslami*, 3 June 1980/13 Khordad 1359.

32 "Yaddashthai bar Mas'aleh-ye Sinemaha-ye Darbasteh dar Iran," *Enqelab-e Eslami*, 2 July 1980/10 Tir 1359.

33 "Sinema-ye Enqelab, Dafahsh-e Basij va Rowshangarist," *Nameh-ye Mardom*, 10 May 1980/20 Ordibehesht 1359.

34 See "Az Vorud va Kharid-e Filmha-ye Khareji Jelowgiri Mishavad," *Ayande-gan*, 8 July 1979/17 Tir 1358; "Vorud va Kharid-e Filmha-ye Khareji Mamnu' Shod," *Kayhan*, 9 July 1979/18 Tir 1958.

35 "Iran's Islamic Regime Kicks Out Bruce Lee and 'Imperialist' Films," *Variety*, 18 July 1979, 2. Also see "Sinema-ye Iran dar Rah-e Tazeh," *Ettela'at*, 18 March 1980/28 Esfand 1350; "Dowlat Varedat-e Filmha-ye Khareji ra beh Ohdeh Mi-girad," *Ettela'at*, 9 April 1981/20 Farvardin 1360.

36 "Salshomar-e Sinema-ye Pas az Enqelab-2," *MSF*, no. 6 (October 1983/Mehr 1362), 42.

37 "Iran Theaters to Ban Sex on their Own," *Variety*, 23 May 1979, 7.

38 "Magic Marker Cinema Censor," *Iran Times*, 29 June 1979/8 Tir 1358, 16.

39 "Yek Ebtekar Bara-ye Sabt Dar Jarideh-ye Tarikh-e Sinema," *MSF*, no. 40 (July 1986/Mordad 1365), 4.

40 "Sinema dar Nimeh-ye 63," *MSF*, no. 18 (November 1984/Aban 1363), 19.

41 "Nemayesh-e Film-e Bedun-e Parvaneh dar Sinemaha Mamnu' Shod," *Ettela'at*, 28 February 1980/9 Esfand 1358.

42 "Filmhai keh Rang-e Pardeh ra Nadidehand!," *MSF*, no. 37 (May 1986/Khor-dad 1965), 14. Also see Sadr 2003:254; "Salshomar-e Sinema-ye Pas az En-qelab-2," *MSF*, no. 6 (October 1983/Mehr 1362), 42; "Salshomar-e Sinema-ye Pas az Enqelab-5, 1359," *MSF*, no. 17 (October 1984/Mehr 1363), 28. For films banned in 1979, see Mehrabi 1978:184.

43 Almost a decade later, in 1989, Mehrjui's *Hayat-e Poshti-ye Madreseh-ye Adl-e Afaq* was retitled *Madreseh-i keh Miraftim* (*The School We Went To*) and released.

44 For more on Kimiai's postrevolution movies, see Qukasian 1999b.

45 "Aineh-i keh Tab'id ra Tasvir Mikonad," *Kayhan* (London), 5 July 1984/14 Tir 1363.

46 "Zavabet-e Modavan-e Namayesh-e Film Bezudy Bara-ye Tasvib Taslim-e Majles Mishavad," *Kayhan*, 10 May 1980/20 Ordibehesht 1360.

47 "Namayesh-e Filmha-ye Hendi va Torki Mamnu' Shod," *Ettela'at*, 17 March 1980/27 Esfand 1358.

48 "Sinema-ye Iran dar Rah-e Tazeh," *Ettela'at*, 18 March 1980/28 Esfand 1358.

49 "Barzakhiha: Dahankaji Vaqihaneh be Khun-e Shahidan," *Javanan-e Emruz*, 17 Khordad 1361.

50 "Owj-e Ebtezal Beravayat-e Tasvir," *Javanan-e Emruz*, 17 Khordad 1361.

51 "Tarafdari-ye Vazir-e Ershad-e Eslami az Film-e 'Barzakhiha,'" *Iran Times*, 9 July 1982/18 Tir 1361.

52 "Ekhtelaf-e Nazar Bar Sar-e Film-e Sinemai-ye 'Barzakhiha,'" *Iran Times*, 2 July 1982/11 Tir 1361.

53 In Mehrdad Shabikhan's documentary *Black Green White* (*Siah Sabz Se-fid*, 2004), Karimi says that he was imprisoned four times for the film *Go-Between*. While in prison, he organized a film class for thieves, generals, and murderers, attendance numbering some sixty inmates.

54 "Iran's Film Biz Nipped in the Bud by Islamic Belief," *Variety*, 9 May 1979, 91.

55 Misaqiyeh was by some accounts a third- or even a fourth-generation convert from Judaism to Baha'ism. According to Mehrdad Amanat, who wrote a dissertation on Jewish conversions to Baha'ism in Iran (Amanat 2005), Misaqiyeh's great-grandfather was the influential Hakim Harun, who was associated with the Babi/Baha'is. His grandmother and father were known Baha'is, and rather prominent ones, even though Misaqiyeh himself did not associate with the Baha'i community much (Naficy 2006c).

56 "Yek Modir-e Sinema Beh Etteham-e Dayer Kardan-e Eshratkadeh Bazdasht Shod," *Kayhan*, 31 May 1979/10 Khordad 1358.

57 What happened to Saedi in his Parisian exile was equally harrowing psychologically, and will be addressed in the last chapter of *A Social History of Iranian Cinema, Volume 4.*

58 The prominent Jewish businessman Habib Elqanian was arrested as an "industrial feudalist" by the Shah's regime in its waning days (Abrahamian 1982:497) and was executed by a revolutionary court, on 9 May 1979, for "contact with Israel and Zionism" (Fischer 1980:228).

59 "Enhedam-e Bozorgtarin Shabakeh-ye Fesad va Ertesha,'" *Zan-e Ruz*, 14 December 1991/23 Azar 1370.

60 "Iran Executes Six Men on Brothel Charges," *Los Angeles Times*, 14 July 1979. The use of the term *pornography* for movies in Iran, particularly by Muslim traditionalists, is highly exaggerated. It does not mean that they were actually "porno" films, showing actors engaged in sexual acts or even in kissing and necking. Films showing sexual acts or deep kissing were always illegal in Iran. As a result, a "porno" film in general discourse means only that it contained female nudity, sexualized situations and teasing, and scopophilic gazing and filming.

61 The other woman had killed her husband and had had an affair with a younger man. See "Iran: Information on Women, Religious Freedom, and Ethnic Minorities," *Refworld*, http://www.unhcr.org/refworld.

62 See "Murderer, Adulteress Wife Stoned in Evin Prison," 21 July 2001, http://www.netnative.com.

63 I discuss Parviz Nikkhah's recantations in *A Social History of Iranian Cinema, Volume 2.*

64 The Boroumand Foundation's database of human-rights violations in Iran lists the charges against both Jafarian and Nikkhah to have been "association with the Shah's idolatrous regime" and "corruption on earth," noting that they were both executed by firing squad in Tehran's Qasr Prison on the same day. See "One Person's Story: Mr. Mahmud Ja'farian," at the Human Rights and Democracy for Iran website, http://www.iranrights.org.

65 Both Zabihi and Ruhani were apparently assassinated by Payam-e Mostazaf, one of many shadowy revolutionary terrorist groups known as Towhidi groups (Boroujerdi 2002:118). For more on Zabihi's trial and assassination, see Jafari Lahijani 2008:vol. 1:669–70. Zabihi was arrested by IRGC, condemned to five years' prison, and later pardoned by Ayatollah Khomeini, whereupon he was

assassinated. Parviz Nabavi made a film about him, called *Trial of Seyyed Javad Zabihi* (1978–79).

66 "Karkonan-e Savaki-ye Radio va Televizion ra Mo'arefi Konid," *Kayhan*, 6 May 1979/16 Ordibehesht 1358.

67 There were other accounts of why Ghotbzadeh was executed, none more strange that the one involving a film, whose existence, if it were true, would be worth a movie thriller of its own. Jafar Shafi'zadeh, Ayatollah Khomeini's chief bodyguard in Neauphle-le-Château, France, claimed in his memoirs that Ghotbzadeh had engineered a film of the alleged debauchery of Seyyed Ahmad Khomeini (Ayatollah Khomeini's son) and Mohammad Montazeri (son of Ayatollah Hosain Ali Montazeri, Khomeini's heir apparent) in Paris before Khomeini's triumphant return to Iran from exile. According to his unverified account, the film showed these two rising religious figures and sons of prominent leaders of the revolution changing their clerical attire for Western cloths, smoking opium in Ghotbzadeh's Paris office along with his lover, Beatrice, then going to a nightspot, near the Champs-Elysées, called Rasputin Club, where they became wildly drunk on alcohol and cavorted with topless women—activities strictly forbidden by Islam. After leaving the club, they went to a "plush building" where the two religious figures took the women to bed. Shafi'zadeh relates that in the meantime, in the living room, Ghotbzadeh showed him the video footage that his photographer had filmed of the clerics' nighttime escapades. He claims that the shots were framed so that neither the bodyguard nor Ghotbzadeh nor his girlfriend was shown, effacing them entirely from the scenes of debauchery. Shafi'zadeh claims that Ghotbzadeh used this clandestine film to ensure his survival and rise to power in Iran by blackmailing both Ahmad Khomeini and his father, an action for which he lost his life (Shafi'zadeh 2000:91–96). According to Shafi'zadeh, Ghotbzadeh engineered the making of other incriminating films to discredit other leaders and opponents of Khomeini, such as, allegedly, Seyyed Jalal Tehrani, the head of the Regency Council, which the Shah had set up in his last months in power. The film supposedly forced Tehrani to resign from the post (ibid.:113–15). Cosroe Chaqueri, a university professor and scholar in Paris, who was an opposition student leader in France at the time and who Shafi'zadeh mentions in his memoir, stated in an e-mail to me, "I have read almost everything that has come out on the revolution and have had special graduate seminars on it for several years. I really do not believe in the accuracy of this kind of cheap rumours. . . . I tend to think that Shafi'zadeh, if he really exists, has concocted the whole thing to make money and 'earn' fame" (Naficy 2006b).

Many criticized Ghotbzadeh's reign at the helm of vvir, but the journalist Carole Jerome, who covered Iran-related news for European, Canadian, and American newspapers and television networks while maintaining a passionate love affair with Ghotbzadeh, reported a different version. According to her, soon after the success of the revolution, Ghotbzadeh became disappointed and distressed at the ascendance of the Islamists and fundamentalists both at vvir and in the rest of the government. From his office on the thirteenth floor of the vvir Tower, high atop a hill in North Tehran, "Sadegh could see the city fanning out below, and from here he considered his dilemma. A nightmare he was not in control of was closing around him" (Jerome 1987:116). In her memoir about him, she does not mention either Ghotbzadeh's involvement in making incriminating films or his use of such films to blackmail officials as the cause of his execution; rather, she correctly ascribes his demise to the fact that he had led an effort to launch a coup against the Islamic government.

68 *Mojahed*, no. 266 (8 November 1985/17 Aban 1364), 4–6. Also see *Shohada-ye Javdan-e Azadi, Parchamdaran-e Enqelab-e Novin-e Khalq-e Qahreman-e Iran*, published as a supplement to *Mojahed*, no. 261 (12 September 1986/21 Shahrivar 1365), 159.

69 The preceding quotations are from the transcripts of the Trades Union Congress, which I obtained through correspondence with tuc's International Department, dated 3 October 1985.

70 I discuss tough-guy movies in more detail in chapter 5 in *A Social History of Iranian Cinema, Volume 2*.

71 "Fardin, Honarpisheh-ye Sinema va Golpaygani, Khanandeh-ye Mar'ruf Dastgir Shodand," *Iran Times*, 1 April 1985/14 Dey 1363; "Nematollah Aghasi Khanandeh-ye Ma'ruf 50 Zarbeh-ye Shallaq Khord va Tab'id Shod," *Iran Times*, 13 September 1985/22 Shahrivar 1364.

72 See the film at Jadid Online, http://www.jadidonline.com.

73 "Gozareshi az Dayereh-ye Monkarat," *Kayhan Havai*, 3 December 1980/12 Azar 1359.

74 "Iraj Qaderi Ejazeh-ye Kargardani Gereft," *Kayhan Havai*, 27 October 1993/5 Aban 1372.

75 See her interview with Behnud Mokri of Voice of America Persian service television, Seda-ye Emrika, on YouTube, http://www.youtube.com/watch?v=PrJdbxSY9Dw&feature=player_embedded#.

76 Enayat Fani, "Susan Taslimi: Deltang-e Tamashachi-ye Irani Hastam," bbc *Persian*, 23 August 2010, http://www.bbc.co.uk/persian.

77 "Sinemagaran-e Motoahed va Mobarez-e Iran," *Mojahed*, 8 Mordad 1361/30 July 1982, 31.

78 These are discussed in the chapters that follow in this volume, as well as throughout *A Social History of Iranian Cinema, Volume 4*.

Chapter 2: Documenting the Uprising

1 This narrative is primarily based on a one-hour audiotape that Moshiri sent me (Naficy 2005d); all quotations in this section are from this tape, unless otherwise noted.

2 Parviz Nabavi filmed many other events of the revolution, among them, *Prime Minister Hoveyda's Trial, Trial of Nikkhah and Jafrian, Trial of Seyyed Javad*

Zabihi, Demonstration of Unveiled Women, and *Prisons*, all circa 1978–79. For description of these television news films, see Jafari Lahijani 2008:vol. I:411–14.

3 This, the Shah's last speech on television, is viewable at "Shah's Last Speech (uncensored)," opus125arts channel, YouTube, posted 25 October 2009, http://www.youtube.com.

4 See "Mohammad Reza Ghotbi's Handwriting," available at the Persian Photo Fotopages website, 11 February 2004, http://persian.fotopages.com.

5 Moini escaped Iran and joined the POMI's Camp Ashraf, in Iraq, where, ironically, he reportedly became a jailhouse interrogator for the organization (Jafari Lahijani 2008:vol. I:411).

6 An important documentary cameraman, who filmed both the emerging revolution and the war with Iraq, Bahadori died from a heart attack in 2002 (Dey 1381). Shahdust emigrated to Sweden in 1984, where he worked in the field of medical photography.

7 Hamid Jafari made *The Footage that Disappeared* (*Namahai keh Napadid Shodand*, 2010), a documentary in which he scours the various television archives for the forty hours of rushes of *The Pulse of History*, to no avail.

8 The latter are discussed in chapter 5 in *A Social History of Iranian Cinema, Volume 4*.

9 The other cinematographers in addition to Najafi himself were Fakherddin Anvar, Mohammad Reza Alipayam, Hojatollah Saifi, and Mohammad Aladpush.

10 The French filmmakers' guild, ANAC, also sent a telegram to the Iranian ambassador in Rome, protesting Kimiavi's arrest ("International Sound Track," *Variety*, 29 November 1978, 36).

11 Haritash died soon after the revolution.

12 This case study is based on a published interview, which Mahvash Kianersi conducted with Shirdel (2005) and on my own correspondence with Shirdel (Naficy 2005b, 2005c).

13 Shirdel's three Pahlavi-era banned documentaries, later dubbed "The Captivity Trilogy," were *Fortress: The Red Light District, Women's Prison*, and *Tehran, Iran's Capital*. They were finally screened publicly at the first Milad Film Festival, soon after the revolution. Subsequently, they found their way into international film festivals.

14 See also Sattareh Farman Farmaian's account of the Qaleh fire, when she was director of Iran Social Service Organization (Farman Farmaian and Munker 1992:301–2).

15 Nejatollahi was later hailed as a revolutionary martyr, and Villa Street, a key Tehran thoroughfare along which many foreign airlines offices are located, was renamed Ostad Nejatollahi Street in his honor.

16 "Shadi-ye Yek Filmsaz," *Ayandegan*, 22 April 1979/2 Ordibehesht 1358.

17 The American networks paid for these hostage films. The NBC news special

The Hostages at Easter, aired on 8 April 1980, stated that the network had paid Iranians $12,000 for the film.

18 Mary's real name is Masumeh (Nilufar) Ebtekar, who after the hostage taking attended Beheshti University, where she received a doctorate in immunology. In 1990, she became the first woman appointed as deputy president of the Islamic Republic for environmental protection (Dezham 2005:45–46).

19 Shirdel's *The Genaveh Project*, on the construction of underwater oil pipelines from Genaveh to Khark Island, stood out because of the footage of laborers working under bombardment from Iraqi forces and furious oil fires. Like the Golestan and Pendry classic *Wave, Coral, Rock*, Shirdel's is a process film, showing the details of the operations involved, accompanied by a verbose voice-over narration. Unlike its predecessor, however, the film showed the world of war beyond the inexorable pipeline process, and it contains sharply observed snippets of native life around it.

20 Among important filmmakers who made documentaries on commission for the Mobarekeh Steel Company, in addition to Shirdel, were Khosrow Sinai, Farshad Fadaian, Pirooz Kalantari, and Mohammad Reza Moqaddasian.

21 In the late 1970s, after his film *The Night It Rained* received the Grand Prix in the Third Tehran International Film Festival, after more than six years of being banned, Shirdel was commissioned by Mehrdad Pahlbod, minister of Culture and Art, to make a series of documentaries on the Persian Gulf Emirates and Sheikhdoms. "That was considered to be the first attempt for an Iranian team to make films abroad and to see the world through an Iranian eye," wrote Shirdel to me in an e-mail (26 October 2009). He completed only two forty-minute films on 35mm stock, on Kuwait and Dubai, as the overwhelming summer heat and other factors prevented further filming. *Dubai: Pearl of the Persian Gulf* (*Dubai, Morvarid-e Khalij,* 1975) was thought lost for over thirty years, until, thanks to Shirdel's sleuthing, it was discovered in the mid-2000s in the Ministry of Culture and Islamic Guidance's vaults. In 2007 Shirdel was invited to show the film in Dubai, in the presence of over three hundred people and dignitaries, including Sheikh Mohammad, the ruler, and the royal family. "It was a great success and became an icon for the government of Dubai," stated Shirdel. This film—containing a narration (written by the poet Ismail Nuriala) that waxes alternately lyrical and informational—is of particular historical interest. Elegantly filmed and edited with verve, the film contains much footage both of the city life before its rapid development and modernization and of the former rulers, including the late Sheikh Rashed, the main architect of today's Dubai; Sheikh Maktoum, his crown prince; and Sheikh Mohammad, then defense minister, who piloted the helicopter carrying the film crew over the city of Dubai and landed among his tribespeople. More than thirty years later, the film's prediction of a vast leap forward for Dubai seems prescient. The version I have seen has an English voice-over narration by an anonymous announcer; the Persian version is read by the famed radio personality Asadollah Payman.

22 For example, Shirdel made two versions of *Gas, Fire, Wind*, in which he both documented and critiqued the wastage of valuable gases produced during oil extraction. One contained interviews with experts and was fifty-seven minutes long; the other contained no interviews and was forty-five minutes. The released version was even shorter, at thirty-eight minutes (Mehrabi 1996:324). The long version, which I have seen, offers its critique via man-on-street interviews with area natives, particularly one with an old man who is eloquent about how the country's resources, such as the gases produced during oil extraction, are being wasted, instead of harnessed. The film shows this process at various sites, including at Paris, Khuzestan. Unlike in Shirdel's other films, the voice-over narration is political, strident, and clichéd, referring, for example, to the extraction of oil from Iran by Western oil concerns as "pillaging" the land of its "black gold" and "sucking the blood" of the country—phrases that were de rigueur under the Islamic Republic.

23 Shirdel was featured prominently in 2003 in the Cinéma du Réel festival in Paris, and the International Festival of Film Societies held a retrospective of his documentaries in Reggio Calabria, Italy, in June 2002. He is a consultant and jury member of the latter festival. For a recent article on his works as a "subversive" filmmaker, see Hachard-Sébire and Orléan 2004. For a biographical article calling him "lion-hearted" (which is a translation of his last name), see Tahaminejad 2003.

24 "Towzih-e Radio Televizion dar Bareh-ye Sansur-e Yek Film," *Kayhan*, 5 May 1979/15 Ordibehesht 1358; see also "Dar Payan-e Hafteh," *Ayandegan*, 2 August 1979/11 Mordad 1358.

25 The cinematographers of *For Freedom* were Feraidun Raypur, Karim Davami, Ali Sadeqi, Hosain Kamalinafar, Farajollah Zohurian, Manuchehr Haqqaniparast, Ebrahim Qazizadeh, Hosain Rafii, and Haidarqoli Khodabandehlu.

26 Torabi claims that an Austrian filmmaker offered to purchase his footage of the tearful Shah at the Mehrabad airport for up to $100,000, but "we did not sell it" (quoted in Tahaminejad 2000:157).

27 The Persian language original is "Ey Shah-e Kha'en avareh gardi/ mam-e vatan ra viraneh kardi."

28 It did not help that Taheri was associated with the political left and was from a Baha'i family. Before his escape, he had officially separated from his wife, with whom he had two children, so as not to "taint" them (Sullivan 2001:211). Several years later, they rejoined in Los Angeles, where Taheri worked as a cameraman and a filmmaker.

29 According to the film historian Mohammad Tahaminejad, over fifty hours of 16mm and 8mm film is stored in the VVIR archive alone (2000:125).

30 Tehrani's historical documentary *Till Revolution (Ta Azadi*, 1980), made in exile, is discussed in chapter 5 in *A Social History of Iranian Cinema, Volume 4*.

31 "Beh Donbal-e Sarab, Ali Abbasi," *MSF* (21 Shahrivar 1379), 103.

32 "Posht-e Pardeh-ye Sinemaha-ye Iran Cheh Migozarad?," *Ettela'at*, 6 July 1980/ 15 Tir 1359.

33 "Yadnameh-ye Fadai-ye Shahid Said Soltanpur, Setarh-ye Sorkh-e Adabiat-e Enqelabi-ye Iran," *Jahan* 3, no. 21 (July 1984/Tir 1363), 26–27, 12.

34 "Akhbar-e Jonbesh-e Daneshjui," *Jahan* 3, no. 21 (July 1984/Tir 1363), 22–23.

35 Some of these titles are my translations from the Persian titles printed in the organization's flyers and thus may not be the actual film titles.

36 For an illustrated article detailing pmoi radio's new antenna and programming, see "Vizhehnameh-ye Sevvomin Salgard-e Eftetah-e 'Seda-ye Mojahed,'" *Mojahed*, no. 214 (July 1984/Mordad 1363), 9–13, 37–40. See also "This Is the Voice of Mojahed . . . ," *NLA Quarterly* (autumn 1988), 98–103.

37 "Nehzatha-ye Borun Marzi," *Iran Times*, 15 March 1991. The figure of 120,000 "members and sympathizers" murdered appeared in full-page ad pmoi placed in the *New York Times* on 23 June 2006, in which it argued that the "terrorist" label should no longer be applied to its organization.

38 This discourse on the tortured body was dialogic, for the Islamic government also contributed to it. For example, in 1984 and 1986 the Tehran prosecutor general published a two-volume book reproducing in compulsive detail the capture and torture to death of three high-ranking Pasdaran (Revolutionary Guards) by the Mojahedin in Iran. The books contain handwritten confessions of pmoi torturers who were captured. They also bear gruesome photos of the tortured and mutilated bodies of victims (Dadsetani-ye Enqelab-e Eslami-ye Tehran 1984–86).

39 These were New York City (Columbia University), Chicago (Northwestern University), Washington, D.C. (American University), San Jose (First Presbyterian Church), Los Angeles (University of Southern California), Dallas (Ramada Inn), and Houston (University of Houston).

40 "Smuggled Film of Iran Hanging Shocks Western Viewers," *Iran Focus*, 31 May 2005, http://www.iranfocus.com.

41 See "Stoning to Death in Iran: A Crime against Humanity Carried Out by the Mullahs' Regime," available at the Iran-e Azad website, http://www.iran-e-azad.org.

42 See Iran National tv, http://www.iranntv.com.

43 See http://besoyepirozi.com; and see Mojahedin pmoi's Channel on YouTube, http://www.youtube.com.

44 These films included the following titles and the locations in which they were exhibited. Documentaries: Dorudian's *Blood Will Triumph Over the Sword*, at usc; *The Crusade in the War Front* (*Jahad dar Jebheh*, 1980), at ucla; and an untitled Palestinian film, at ucla. Fiction movies: Mehrjui's *The Cow*, at usc; Pontecorvo's *The Battle of Algiers*, at ucla; *Ten Days that Shook the World*, at ucla; *Viva Zapata*, at ucla; and Costa Gavras's *State of Siege*, at ucla.

45 The films they screened in the 1980s included the following titles, all screened at ucla: Reconstruction Crusade's documentaries *Confessions of Treasonous Leaders of the Tudeh Party*, *Al-Fajr Military Operations* (*Amaliat-e Val-Fajr*), *Bloody Victory* (*Fath-e Khunin*), *Bloody Urban Front* (*Jebheh-ye Khunin-e Shahr*),

The People's War (Jang-e Mardomi), Triumph of Blood (Fath-e Khun) What Hap-pened to Palestine (Bar Felestin Cheh Gozasht), and Alireza Davudnezhad's *Pahlavi's Justice.*

46 See the "'Terrorist' Lists" at http://www.statewatch.org/terrorlists/terrorlists
.html.

47 The Kurds also produced slide-tapes such as *Crimes of Khomeini Regime in Kurdistan (Jenayat-e Rezhim-e Khomeini dar Kordestan)*, which contrasted posi-tively life in Kurdish-held areas with that elsewhere in Iran. This slide-tape was shown at UCLA in July 1981 (Naficy 1984b:79).

48 For the Kurdish Film Festival in London, see the festival's website, http://www.kurdishfilmfestival.com. For the Douarnez Film Festival, which an-nually features sections on linguistic and ethnic minorities cinema, see the Kerys.com website, http://www.kerys.com.

49 See *A Social History of Iranian Cinema, Volume 2.*

50 I thank Amir Hassanpour for putting at my disposal a list of Tayfur Patai's films, which Patai had prepared (Naficy 2005a).

51 See "Part 1/4 Human Rights in Iran and the Plight of the Bahais," Ensan Doost channel, Vimeo, 29 April 2010, http://vimeo.com.

52 Mona was apparently the last, and the youngest, of ten Baha'i women executed that day. For the *Mona with the Children* video, see the YouTube video, http://www.youtube.com/watch?v=kQ-UxEbuPag. For the video's lyrics, which are by Doug Cameron, see the Seals and Crofts website, http://www.sealsandcrofts
.com.

53 See "Damning Report on an Ignored Issue: Discrimination against Ethnic and Religious Minorities in Iran," 21 October 2010, 26, available in PDF form on the International Federation for Human Rights website, FIDH, http://www
.fidh.org.

54 The film is posted as "March 8, 1979, International Women's Day in Tehran," 7 February 2007, on the Iranian.com website, http://www.iranian.com.

Chapter 3: Consolidating "Islamicate" Cinema

1 I noted this in *A Social History of Iranian Cinema, Volume 1.*

2 "Degarguni dar Zamineh-ye Sinema, ba 'Dizolv' Ettefaq Mioftad nah ba 'Kat,'" *MSF*, no. 46 (February 1987/Bahman 1365), 4.

3 "300 Sinema-ye Keshvar Fa'aliat-e Khod ra az Sar Gereftand," *Kayhan*, 8 Feb-ruary 1982/23 Tir 1358.

4 "Dah Sinema-ye Tehran Ta'til Shod," *Etella'at*, 20 February 1980/29 Bahman 1358.

5 *Iranshahr*, 20 June 1980/30 Khordard 1359; *Iranshahr*, 4 July 1980/13 Tir 1359; and "Sinemaha-ye Sarasar-e Keshvar Ta'til Shod," *Kayhan Havai*, 2 July 1980/11 Tir 1359.

6 "Chera ba Mostazafan Chenin Mikonand?," *Ayandegan*, 7 August 1979/16 Mor-dad 1358.

7 "Karnameh-ye Dowlat-e Jomhuri-ye Eslami dar Zamineh-e Siasatha-ye Kolli-ye Keshvar va Arzeshha-ye Hakem bar an," *Soroush*, no. 252 (3 Shahrivar 1365/1984), 22.

8 "Degarguni dar Zamineh-ye Sinema, ba 'Dizolv' Ettefaq Mioftad nah ba 'Kat,'" *MSF*, no. 46 (February 1987/Bahman 1365), 9.

9 "Ja-ye Sinema dar 'Barnameh-ye Panj Sal-e Avval' Kojast?," *MSF*, no. 6 (October 1983/Mehr 1362), 4–5.

10 *Ettela'at*, 30 January 1980/10 Bahman 1358; emphasis added.

11 "Nameh-ye Sargoshadeh-ye Sinemagaran-e Iran beh Mellat va Dowlat," included as a flier inside *Daftarha-ye Sinema*, no. 4 (March 1981/Ordibehesht 1360).

12 The key role of kinship in perpetuating the economic and political life of the Islamic Republic is apparently a highly controversial subject, whose academic study was "strictly forbidden." As an anonymous Iranian professor told *Prospect* magazine, "They don't want us to know about these ties because this is where the real power lies. It is within these family-linked networks that the real decisions are taken—often at funerals, weddings and other private functions" (quoted in Porteous 2006).

13 As a college student, Shariati loved to go to the movies with his friends in Mashhad, particularly to see Ken Maynard's cowboy movies. Shariati was so enamored of this actor, who packed two pairs of revolvers and also physically resembled him, that his friends called Shariati "Ken with two Mausers" (*Ken-e do mowzeri*), referring to the Mauser, a German gun well known among Iranians. In 1971, at the University of Mashhad, Shariati was involved with a group of secular students that created a highly successful political play, *Once Again Abuzar*, based on a revolutionary Muslim historical figure (Rahnema 2000:75, 186–89).

14 See Rahnema 2000:319; also "Biographi-e Vaziran-e Kabineh-ye Rejai," *Kayhan Havai*, 10 September 1980/19 Shahrivar 1359.

15 "Iranian Film Biz Revisited: Lotsa U.S. Cassettes, Picture Backlog," *Variety*, 6 June 1984, 2.

16 "Sinema-ye Iran Nimeh Melli Mishavad," *Kayhan*, 6 May 1979/16 Ordibehesht 1358.

17 "Namayesh-e Filmha-ye Karatehi Mamnu' shod," *Kayhan*, 3 July 1979/12 Tir 1358.

18 "The Most Persistent Cultural Director in Iran Was Dismissed," *Film International*, no. 35 (summer 2002), 9.

19 Political connections and cronyism may have played a part in Khatami's longevity, as they did in the longevity of heads of MCA and NIRT during the Shah's time. In his youth, Khatami had been a student and disciple of Khomeini in Qom, and a close friend of his son, Ahmad. Khatami's brother, Mohammad Reza, later married one of Khomeini's granddaughters, while Khatami himself married the cousin of Ahmad's wife, and Khatami's own sister, Maryam,

married an influential cleric and an aide to Khomeini in exile in Paris (Scio-lino 2000:80).

20 For more on organizations devoted to amateur and short films, see Safarian 2004a.

21 The government may have also attempted to guide and supervise film pro-ductions in indirect and clandestine ways, such as by secretly funding certain filmmakers and their films. There were rumors in 1999 that a high-ranking member of the Ministry of Information and Security, Said Emami, who would later die mysteriously in a prison bathhouse, had attempted to threaten and cajole auteur filmmakers Baizai and Kimiai into some sort of collaboration, and may have even invested in five films of the art cinema directors. See the separate thirty-six-page supplement to *Gozaresh-e Film*, no. 141 (5 January 2000/15 Dey 1378), titled "Bazjui-ye Said Emami az Kimiai va Baizai."

22 "Moruri bar Vizhegiha-ye Moshtarak-e Filmah-ye Irani-ye Emsal," MSF, no. 68 (July 1989/Mordad 1368), 12–13.

23 These figures are based on the list of companies and labs in *Taqvim-e Sinemai-ye 1378*, published by MSF.

24 According to the *Washington Post*, the New York branch of the FOD, which re-possessed the Pahlavi Foundation's thirty-six-story building on Manhattan's Fifth Avenue, changed its name from the Mostazafan Foundation to the Alavi Foundation in 1992. The paper reported that this foundation was acting as a "front organization for the Iranian regime that is engaged in covert intel-ligence activity" (Mintz 2003). The Islamic Revolutionary Guard Corps runs the FOD in Iran. According to the *New York Times*, the Alavi Foundation prede-cessor, the Pahlavi Foundation of New York, a "shadowy" and "murky" orga-nization, was set up by the Shah as a tax-exempt "charitable" entity in 1973 in a "tale of international intrigue," involving "influence peddling, greed, brib-ery attempts, and duplicity" (Crittenden 1976). The original Pahlavi Founda-tion was established in Iran in 1957, which allegedly held between 10 and 90 percent of the Shah's assets and owned "merchant ships, hotels, a toll bridge, banks, factories, and even orphanages, which provided the excuses for all the rest." The foundation paid huge sums to U.S. politicians, diplomats, and me-dia organizations in the 1960s to facilitate securing American loans for Iran, including $500,000 to Henry R. Luce, president of Time Life Incorporated, which published *Time, Life*, and *Fortune* magazines, to muffle criticism of the Shah's regime (Richards 1975:14–15). Apropos this history of cinema, the foundation also paid $1 million to William Warne, director of the Point Four program in Iran, which ran the country's documentary film production and training programs in the early 1950s. In 2009, the U.S. government seized the Alavi Foundation's properties in the country and charged it with spending "millions of dollars to obtain and develop the properties, in violation of federal laws that ban trade with Iran." The foundation promised to fight the action (Weiser 2009).

25 "Boniad-e Mostazafan Miliardha Dolar beh Bankha Bedehkar Ast," *Iran Times*, 9 December 1983/18 Azar 1362, "Boniad-e Mostazafan 45 Miliard Rial Bedehi Darad," *Iran Times*, 24 February 1984/5 Esfand 1362.

26 "Az Ravayat va Qesas-e Quran Film-e Sinemai Sakhteh Mishavad," *Iran Times*, 29 July 1983/7 Mordad 1362.

27 Also see chapter 4 in *A Social History of Iranian Cinema, Volume 4*.

28 "Zarar-e Mostazafan az Kar-e Sinemaha," *Iran Times*, 18 May 1984/28 Ordibehesht 1363; "Videotapes of Iranian Films for Export," MSF, no. 49 (April 1987/ Ordibehesht 1366), 1 English section.

29 *"Khunbaresh*, Filmi dar Hiteh-ye Zhornalism-e Tasviri," *Ettela'at*, 14 August 1979/23 Mordad 1358.

30 From a leaflet titled "Reconstruction Crusade-1," put out in early 1980s by the Muslim Students' Association of the United States.

31 "Fa'aliatha-ye Nuzdah Mahheh-ye Jahad-e Sazandegi dar Majles E'lam Shod," *Kayhan Havai*, 4 March 1981/13 Esfand 1359.

32 *Ettela'at*, 7 May 1981/7 Farvardin 1360.

33 "Kholaseh-i az Eqdamat-e Jahad-e Sazandegi-ye Shahr-e Rey," *Jomhuri-ye Islami*, 15 April 1981/26 Farvardin 1360.

34 "Dar Keshtzar-e 'Jahad' Khushehha-ye 'Sazandegi' Miruyad," *Jahad Sazandegi*, 17 August 1980/26 Mordad 1359.

35 "Jahad-e Sazandegi," *Ettela'at-e Haftegi*, January 1981/Bahman 1359.

36 The film was screened at USC in 1980.

37 The British Council and the USIA film programs are extensively treated in *A Social History of Iranian Cinema, Volume 2*, chapters 1 and 2.

38 For a history of CIDCYA in its early years, see Ebrahim Forouzesh's film, *Gozaresh: Kanun-e Parvaresh-e Fekri-ye Kudakan va nojavanan* (1973), 30 min., see "1973 Kanoon Film 1/3," "1973 Kanoon Film 2/3," and "1973 Kanoon Film 1/3," kuroshv channel, YouTube, 4 May 2010, http://www.youtube.com.

39 "Karnameh-ye Dowlat-e Jomhuri-ye Eslami dar Zamineh-ye Parvaresh-e Fekri-ye Kudakan va Nojavanan," *Soroush*, no. 252 (3 Shahrivar 1363/1984), 18–21.

40 See the Iranian Youth Cinema Society website, http://www.iycs.ir.

41 See the Documentary and Experimental Film Center website, http://defc.ir.

42 See the bibliographies of the various volumes of *A Social History of Iranian Cinema* for references to Abbas Baharlu/Gholam Haidari's extensive publications.

43 For more on the history, evolution, regulations, and statistics of the national archive, see Muzeh-ye Sinema-ye Iran 2004a.

44 "Sinema-ye Iran: Eqbal-e Ziad, Arzeh-ye Kam," *Hamshahri*, 18 February 1998/ 29 Bahman 1376.

45 See the Iranian Alliance of Motion Picture Guilds, http://www.khanehcinema .ir/fa/Indexfa.aspx.

46 "Gozaresh-e Jashvareh-ye Jahani-ye Film-e Fajr," *Film* (March 1984/Esfand 1362), 73.

47 "Gozaresh-e Jashnvareh-ye Film-e Vahdat," MSF, no. 9 (January 1984/Dey

1362), 22–23. Also see "Moruri bar Nokhostin Jashnvareh-ye Film-e Vahdat," *Kayhan*, 31 December 1983/10 Dey 1362.

48 "Gozaresh-e Jashnvareh-ye Film-e Tolu,'" MSF, no. 13 (May 1984/Khordad 1363), 52–53.

49 I discuss the Festival of the Imposed War Films in *A Social History of Iranian Cinema, Volume 4*, chapter 1.

50 For critical reviews of festivals, see Lashgaripur 2002, chaps. 1 and 7.

51 For a full list and bibliographic information about these film publications, see Mahmoudi 2004b.

52 *Gozaresh-e Film*, no. 1 (April 1990/Ordibehesht 1369), 2–4.

53 For more on film periodicals in 1980s, see Naficy 1992.

54 For the web addresses of Iranian domestic and exile media, including periodicals, radios, and televisions, see the WebGuide available at http://www .iranian.com.

55 For censorship of theatrical plays by MCIG, see Mahmood Karimi-Hakkak 2003, which describes the MCIG's various censorship phases and details the tale of censoring his production of Shakespeare's *A Midsummer Night's Dream* in 1991. For comparison with earlier censorship, see Gholamhosain Saedi's play *Othello in Wonderland* (*Otello dar Sarzamin-e Ajayeb*), which dramatizes the censorship of Shakespeare's *Othello* at the beginning of Islamic Republic (Saedi 1996). This version contains a critical essay by Kaveh Safa.

56 In 1999, Tehran had 18 commercial movie houses rated distinguished, 28 rated first class, 17 rated second class, and 9 rated third class, totaling 72 movie houses. The movie house rating in provinces was as follows: 19 distinguished, 77 first class, 88 second class, 39 third class, making a total of 223 movie houses (Ministry of Culture and Islamic Guidance 1999:25–26).

57 "Azmun va Khata, Pas az Bist Sal," MSF 16, no. 226 (October 1998/Aban 1377), 28–30.

58 I discuss the Pahlavi censorship codes in chapter 3 in *A Social History of Iranian Cinema, Volume 2*.

59 I deal with these issues extensively in chapter 2 in *A Social History of Iranian Cinema, Volume 4*.

60 A popular form of political activism and creativity was the chanting of rhythmic slogans, manufactured in the ideological factories of the revolution and shouted during anti-Shah demonstrations. Such slogans were bandied about in the cinemas as well, both during and after the revolution.

61 This population statistics is from Population Reference Bureau's website, http://www.prb.org, under "Data by Geography>Iran>Summary: Demographic Highlights."

62 "Man Qatiyat Daram, Diktator Nistam," *Kayhan*, 6 August 1979/15 Mordad 1358.

63 "Esharat-e Ayatollah Khomeini dar Bareh-ye Barnamehha-ye Musiqi-ye Radio-Televizion," *Iran Times*, 3 August 1979/11 Mordad 1358. Also see *Los Angeles Times*, 24 July 1979.

64 This "family business" ethos would later find expression in what I have identified as the "family mode of production" in cinema. See *A Social History of
Iranian Cinema, Volume 4*, chapter 2.

65 "Emam: Radio va Televizion Bayad ba Esteqlalash Mahfuz Bashad," *Enqelab-e
Eslami*, 17 May 1980/27 Ordibehesht 1359.

66 "Barnamehha-ye Ghair-e Eslami az Radio Televizion Hazf Mishevand," *Kayhan*, 4 September 1979/13 Shahrivar 1358, "Pasokh-e Ravabet-e Omumi-
ye Seda va Sima-ye Jomhuri-ye Eslami," *Etella'at*, 6 August 1979/15 Mordad 1359; "Sazman-e Radio Televizion E'teraz-e Cherikha-ye Fadai-ye Khalq
ra Rad Kard," *Ayandegan*, 6 August 1979/15 Mordad 1258; and "Radio Televizion E'terazat-e Cherikha-ye Fadai-ye Khalq ra Rad Kard," *Kayhan*, 6 August
1979/15 Mordad 1358.

67 In June 1983, a group calling itself the American Friends of Revolutionary
Iran organized a news conference in Chicago, at which physicians and other
experts analyzed videotapes of television confessions by Tudeh Party Central
Committee members, including those of Kianuri and Etemadzadeh. Based
on their medical knowledge, these experts concluded that both individuals
had probably been tortured and drugged to confess to treasonous acts and to
repudiate both the party they had built over the years and their "deeply held
convictions," causing their bodily immobility, slurred speech, and breathing
difficulties before the cameras (from the eighteen-page booklet *Text of the
Press Conference Called by American Friends of Revolutionary Iran*, 6 June 1983,
Chicago).

68 "Televizion-e Jomhuri-ye Eslami Filmha-ye Kubai va Hendi Namayesh Mide-
had," *Iran Times*, 6 February 1982/7 Esfand 1360.

69 "Gozaresh-e Amalkard-e Televizion dar Sale-e 62," *MSF*, no. 17 (September
1984/Mehr 1363), 15.

70 "Iranian Film Biz Revisited: Lotsa U.S. Cassettes, Picture Backlog," *Variety*, 6
June 1984, 2.

71 "Yek Ebtekar Bara-ye Sabt Dar Jarideh-ye Tarikh-e Sinema," *MSF*, no. 40 (July
1986/Mordad 1365), 4.

72 "Kargardan-e Penhan-e Filmha-ye Irani va Khareji," *MSF*, no. 25 (May 1985/
Khordad 1364), 10–11.

73 "Doshvariha-ye Filmsazi dar Sali keh Gozasht," *MSF*, no. 23 (March 1985/Far-
vardin 1364), 5–7.

74 "Movafaqiyatha-ye Eqtesadi va Natayej-e Kaifi," *MSF*, no. 32 (December 1985/
Azar 1364), 9.

75 "Khamenei ba Sinema Mokhalef ast va Rafsanjani ba an Movafeq," *Kayhan*
(London), 30 May 1985/9 Khordad 1364.

76 "Sinema-ye Iran-1358–1363," *MSF*, no. 18 (November 1984/Aban 1363), 293–94.

77 "Sansur az Do Negah," *MSF*, no. 76 (April 1989/Ordibehesht 1368), 10–11.

78 "Green Light to Screenwriters," *MSF*, no. 66 (August 1988/Mordad 1367), 1
English section.

79 "Poshtvaneh-ye Ta'min-e Ejtemai va Herfehi-ye Dast Andarkaran-e Sinema," *MSF*, no. 35 (March 1986/Farvardin 1345), 6–8.

80 "Vam-e Banki Bara-ye Filmsazan," *MSF*, no. 52 (August 1987/Mordad 1366), 18. Also see "Rahi Besu-ye Esteqlal-e Eqtesadi-ye Filmsazan," *MSF*, no. 60 (January 1988/Bahman 1366), 5–8.

81 "Goruhbandi-ye Filmha-ye Irani va Sinemaha dar Sal-e Jari," *MSF*, no. 63 (April 1988/Ordibehesht 1367), 12–13. Also see "Iranian Films Rated According to Merit," *MSF*, no. 49 (April 1987/Ordibehesht 1366), 1 English section.

82 "New Policies for a Year of Challenge," *MSF*, no. 77 (May 1989/Khordad 1368), 1 English section.

83 "Iran Dahomin Keshvar-e Donia," *MSF*, no. 239 (August 1999/Shahrivar 1378), 38.

84 On the popular films' discursive formation, see Seyyed Majid Hosseini's doctoral dissertation (2009).

85 I discuss these film types in *A Social History of Iranian Cinema, Volume 4.*

86 See, for example, *Zendehrud*, nos. 6–7 (spring 1994/1373), a special issue devoted to cinema.

87 "Baray-e Avvalin bar dar Shahrestanha," *MSF*, no. 10 (February 1984/Bahman 1362), 10.

88 "Filmsazi-ye Herfehi dar Shahrestanha," *MSF*, no. 10 (February 1984/Bahman 1362), 12.

89 Family melodramas and war movies are discussed in *A Social History of Iranian Cinema, Volume 4*, in the two chapters that cover women's cinema and war movies.

90 "Gozareshi az Aksolamal-e Tamashachian Nesbat beh yek Film-e Zedd-e Mojahedi Benam-e 'Tavvahom,'" *Nashrieh Ettehadi-yeh Anjomanha-ye Daneshjuian-e Mosalman-e Kharej az Keshvar* no. 84 (27 February 1987/18 Esfand 1365), 28.

91 Ibid.

92 "Bahr-e Bardari-ye Zed-e Enqelab az Film-e Sinemai," *Khabarnameh-ye Farhangi-Ejtemai*, [zamimehye Andisheh va Paykar no. 2] (April 1989/Farvardin 1368), 52.

93 See chapter 5 in *A Social History of Iranian Cinema, Volume 4.*

94 See chapter 1 in *A Social History of Iranian Cinema, Volume 4.*

95 On women's films, see chapter 2 in *A Social History of Iranian Cinema, Volume 4*. On art-house films, see chapter 3 in *A Social History of Iranian Cinema, Volume 4.*

96 See chapter 4 in *A Social History of Iranian Cinema, Volume 4.*

97 I discuss this in more detail in chapter 5 in *A Social History of Iranian Cinema, Volume 2.*

98 Factors that threatened the film industry during Rafsanjani's term were high inflation (30–50 percent) and unemployment (12–20 percent), low investment in non-oil industries, and slow rationalization of foreign exchange policies (three different rates competed with each other) (Wright 1993).

99 "Iran's President Would Privatize Big Industries," *New York Times*, 16 September 1999.

100 "Bara-ye har 220 Hezar Nafar Yek Sinema Darim!," *Hamshahri*, 8 June 1997/18 Khordad 1376; "Haif Ast keh Roshd-e Sinema-ye Ma Motovaqef Shavad," *Hamshahri*, 17 January 1998/17 Dey 1376.

101 "Chera Mardom Sinema Nemiravand?," *Hamshahri*, 13 September 2001/22 Shahrivar 1388.

102 "Sakht-e Sad Sinema ta Payan-e Emsal," *MSF*, no. 239 (August 1999/Shahrivar 1378), 27.

103 "Sinema-ye Pas az Enqelab, dar Aghaz-e Dahe-ye Dovvom," *MSF*, no. 75 (March 1989/Noruz 1368), 73.

104 "Sinema Jozv-e Zendegi-ye Mardom Shodeh ast," *MSF*, no. 48 (March 1987/Noruz 1366), 73.

105 Night of Power (Lailatul Qadr) is the night that the Quran was revealed to Prophet Mohammad; for Shiites this night is doubly sacred, as on this day Imam Ali, the first of the twelve Shiite imams, was fatally injured with a sword.

106 "Sinema Vasileh-ye Khubi Bara-ye Enteqal-e Afkar-e Eslami Ast," *Javanan-e Emruz*, no. 787 (15 March 1982/24 Esfand 1360), 12, 56.

107 "Ma Agar Sinema ra az Ja-ye Khodash Kharej Konim Digar Sinema Nakhahim Dasht," *Kayhan Havai*, 24 October 1984/2 Aban 1363.

108 "Nazar-e Emam Khomeini dar Bareh-ye Film-ha, Serial-ha, Ahang-ha, va Pakhsh-e Barnameh-ha-ye Varzeshi E'lam Shod," *Kayhan Havai*, 30 December 1987/9 Dey 1366, 3.

Appendix

1 Note: Judgment on articles 1 and 2 is with the clerical member of the review council.

2 Note: The review council is responsible for devising the criteria for the presence of women in the movies in such a way that matches religious criteria and does not lower their merit. This would be applied to all films, domestic or foreign. These criteria should be given to domestic filmmakers and foreign film importers.

3 Note: Films that are designed to familiarize viewers with the ethnic traditions and customs of various people, the literature, arts, and sciences of nations, the different natural, geographical, and human science environments, and the various filmmaking techniques, or films that are designed to improve the capacity for thinking and imagination for such purposes as education and entertainment can receive exhibition licenses provided they do not promote imperialist or colonialist aims.

4 Note: Educational, scientific, and research films may be shown to special audiences in specialized places.

5 Note: An employee of the General Department of Supervision and Exhibition of Ministry of Culture and Islamic Guidance will be appointed as secretary to the council.

6 Note 1: Owners of Iranian movies may request a review of their films by the council after they have corrected them. Note 2: If a film is rejected because of conditions and exigencies of the time, the council may review it again, upon owner's request, after the mitigating circumstances have been removed.

7 Note 1: The High Council of Supervision may revise any rulings of the Supervisory Council. Note 2: All of High Council of Supervision's rulings are final. Note 3: The High Council of Supervision may invite experts for consultations. Note 4: The General Director of the General Department of Supervision and Exhibition will be the secretary of the High Council of Supervision. Note 5: If there is a need for the presence of representatives of governmental agencies in the supervisory council's meetings, upon prior invitation of the minister of Islamic Guidance, the relevant agencies are duty-bound to appoint representatives.

8 Note 1: By general impact of foreign movies on the society's culture is meant the following:

— Familiarizing the Muslim and committed Iranian nation with foreign cultures in such a way that their movies' non-Islamic cultures are not imposed on spectators.
— Familiarizing the Muslim and committed Iranian nation with the modes of thinking in other societies apart from imperialist and colonialist aims.
— Familiarizing the Muslim and committed Iranian nation with the national customs, rituals, arts, and literatures of other countries in accordance with the audiovisual considerations in these regulations.
— Familiarizing the Muslim and committed Iranian nation with the prevalent film production techniques.
— Reinforcing the power of imagination in cases involving educational, ethical, and entertaining movies.

Note 2: All foreign movies exhibited in Iran must be controlled in terms of their annual numbers.

9 Note 1: All Muslims have the duty of exporting the Islamic revolution by means of exporting the culture of the Islamic revolution. Note 2: All committed Muslims have the duty to propagate and guide other Muslims and dispossessed people of the world provided they follow Islamic regulations.

10 Note: A committee consisting of representatives of the foreign affairs committee of the Majles, Ministry of Foreign Affairs, Ministry of Culture and Higher Education, and Ministry of Culture and Islamic Guidance will investigate the movies that in the opinion of the Review Council propagate imperialistic tendencies. The vote of this committee is binding.

11 Note: The name and identity of the producing groups must appear in the movies' titles and in their advertising posters and brochures.

12 Note: Regarding the limits of modesty, the Supervising Council is required to determine these limits in terms of make-up, clothing, and acting for close-up, medium-shot, and long-shot cinematography, and relay them to domestic producers and importers of foreign movies.

13 Note: The Supervisory Council may issue special licenses for the exhibition of documentary films about slaughterhouses, serum-producing labs and clinics, and hunting to cinemas for viewing by special audiences.

14 Note: These rankings must appear clearly, visually, and aurally in all the advertising for the movies, including on posters, brochures, newspaper and magazine ads, and in the movie trailers.

Abkashak, Mostafa. 1985. "Mossabebin-e Vaqeie'-ye Faje'eh-ye Howlnak-e Sinema Rex-e Abadan Cheh Kasani Hastand?" Privately published manuscript.

Abrahamian, Ervand. 1993. *Khomeinism: Essays on the Islamic Republic.* Berkeley: University of California Press.

———. 1989. *The Iranian Mojahedin.* New Haven, Conn.: Yale University Press.

———. 1982. *Iran between Two Revolutions.* Princeton: Princeton University Press.

Adams, William C., and Phillip Heyl. 1981. "From Cairo to Kabul with the Networks, 1972–1980." *Television Coverage of the Middle East,* ed. William Adams, 1–39. Norwood, N.J.: Ablex Publishing.

Alamdari, Kazem. 2005. "The Power Structure of the Islamic Republic of Iran: Transition from Populism to Clientelism and Militarization of the Government." *Third World Quarterly* 26, no. 8, 1285–301.

Allamehzadeh, Reza. 1991. *Sarab-e sinema-ye Eslami-ye Iran.* Utrecht, Holland: Nashr-e nawid / Take 7.

Althusser, Louis. 1971. "Ideology and Ideological State Apparatuses: Notes toward an Investigation." *"Lenin and Philosophy" and Other Essays,* 127–89. Trans. Ben Brewster. New York: Monthly Review Press.

Amanat, Mehrdad. 2005. "Negotiating Identities: Iranian Jews, Muslims and Baha'is in the Memoirs of Rayhan Rayhani (1859–1939)." PhD diss., University of California, Los Angeles.

Andersson, Matilda, Marie Gillespie, and Hugh Mackay. 2010. "Mapping Digital Diasporas @ BBC World Service: Users and Uses of the Persian and Arabic Websites." *Middle East Journal of Culture and Communication* 3, 256–78.

Appadurai, Arjun. 1996. *Modernity at Large: Cultural Dimensions of Globaliza-tion*. Minneapolis: University of Minnesota Press.

Ardekani, Ahmad Sadeqi. 1981/1360. "Barresi va Rahyabi-ye Moshgelat-e Film va Sinema." *Ettela'at*, 27 Farvardin, 10.

Arjomand, Said Amir. 1988. *The Turban for the Crown: The Islamic Revolution in Iran*. New York: Oxford University Press.

Asadi, Houshang. 2010. *Letters to My Torturer: Love, Revolution, and Imprison-ment in Iran*. Oxford: Oneworld.

Asgard, Ramin. 2009. "Excerpt from U.S.-Iran Cultural Diplomacy Report." America.gov, 16 July, http://www.america.gov.

Asgari, Mirza Aqa, ed. 2005. *Khoniagar-e Khun: Dar Shenakht va Bozorgdash-te Fereydoun Farrokhzad*. Bochum, Germany: Human.

Asgharzadeh, Alireza. 2007. *Iran and the Challenge of Diversity: Islamic Funda-mentalism, Aryanist Racism, and Democratic Struggles*. New York: Palgrave Macmillan.

Asnad va Tasaviri az Mobarezat-e Khalq-e Mosalman-e Iran. 1978/1357. Vol. 1, part 3. Tehran: Abuzar.

Avini, Seyyed Morteza. 1992/1371. "Chera Rowshanfekran Mowred-e Etteham Hastand?" *Sureh* 4, no. 4 (Tir), 4–9.

Azimi, Negar. 2007. "Hard Realities of Soft Power," *New York Times*, 24 June, 50–55.

Baharlu, Abbas (Gholam Haidari). Forthcoming. *Filmshenakht-e Iran: Filmshe-nasi-ye Sinema-ye Iran 1373–1388*. Tehran: Nashr-e Qatreh.

———. 2004/1383. *Filmshenakht-e Iran: Filmshenasi-ye Sinema-ye Iran 1358–1372*. Vol. 2. Tehran: Nashr-e Qatreh.

———. 2000/1379. "Kanunha-ye Film dar Iran." *Tarikh-e Tahlili-ye Sad Sal Sinema-ye Iran*, ed. Abbas Baharlu (Gholam Haidari), 177–200. Tehran: Daftar-e Pazhuheshha-ye Farhangi.

Ball, Warwick. 2011. *Towards One World: Ancient Persia and the West*. Northamp-ton, Mass.: Olive Branch.

Banisadr, Masoud. 2004. *Masoud: Memoirs of an Iranian Rebel*. London: Saqi.

Baqerzadeh, Mohsen, ed. 1987/1366. "Goftogu ba: Gizlla Varga Sinai, Naqqash; Khosrow Sinai, Filmsaz; Gholamhosain Nami, Naqqash va Ostad-e Honarha-ye Tajassomi." *Ketab-e Tus* (summer), 335–84.

Baraheni, Reza. 1981/1360. *Dar Enqelab-e Iran Cheh Shodeh Ast va Cheh Khahad Shod*. Tehran: Ketab-e Zaman.

Basmanji, Kaveh. 2005. *Tehran Blues: Youth Culture in Iran*. London: Saqi.

Batty, David. 2010. "Guardian Journalist Wins Award for Iranian Protest Cover-age," *Guardian*, 24 November.

Bauer, Janet L. 2000. "Desiring Place: Iranian 'Refugee' Women and Cultural Politics of Self and Community in the Diaspora." *Comparative Studies of South Asia, Africa and the Middle East* 20, no. 1, 180–99.

Beeman, William O. 2005. *The "Great Satan" vs. the "Mad Mullas": How the United States and Iran Demonize Each Other.* Westport, Conn.: Praeger.

Behazin, M. A. 1991/1370. *Bar-e Digar va In Bar. . . .* Tehran: n.p. Available as a PDF file at http://www.ketabfarsi.org.

Black, Ian. 2009. "Iran Should Face Smarter Sanctions, Says Mohsen Makhmalbaf." *Guardian*, 25 November.

Bordewich, F. 1980. "Fascism without Swastikas." *Harpers*, July, 65.

Boroujerdi, Hosain. 2002. "Posht-e Pardehha-ye Enqelab: E'terafat-e Hosain Boroujerdi." Interview conducted and edited by Bahram Chubineh. Unpublished manuscript.

Boroumand, Ladan, and Roya Boroumand. 2000. "Illusion and Reality of Civil Society in Iran: An Ideological Debate." *Social Research* 67, no. 2 (summer), 303–44.

Brown, P. H. 1980a. "Ayatollah as Comic Foil." *Los Angeles Times*, 20 January, 7.
———. 1980b. "'Take My Ayatollah, Please': Breaking the Gag Barrier." *Los Angeles Times Calendar*, 20 January, 1.

Brunette, Peter. 2010. "The Hunter—Film Review." *Hollywood Reporter*, 2 February.

Chelkowski, Peter J. 1987. "Stamps of Blood." *American Philatelist* 101, no. 6, 556–66.

Chelkowski, Peter J., and Hamid Dabashi. 1999. *Staging a Revolution: The Art of Persuasion in the Islamic Republic of Iran.* New York: New York University Press.

Crittenden, Ann. 1976. "The Shah in New York." *New York Times*, 26 September.

Dabashi, Hamid. 2007. "The '300' Stroke." *Al-Ahram Weekly*, 2–8 August.

Dadsetani-ye Enqelab-e Eslami-ye Tehran. 1984–86/1363–65. *Joz'iat-e Shekanje-ye Seh Pasdar-e Shahid-e Komiteh-ye Markazi-ye Enqelab-e Eslami Beh Dast-e Monafeqin.* 2 vols. Tehran.

Dargis, Manohla. 2010. "World Events Rumble at Cannes." *New York Times*, 20 May.

Devictor, Agnès. 2002. "Classic Tools, Original Goals: Cinema and Public Policy in the Islamic Republic of Iran (1979–1997)." *The New Iranian Cinema: Politics, Representation and Identity*, ed. Richard Tapper, 66–76. London: I. B. Tauris.

Dezham, Ozra. 2005/1384. *Avvalin Zanan.* Tehran: Nashr-e Elm.

Dizard, Wilson P. Jr. 2004. *Inventing Public Diplomacy: The Story of the U.S. Information Agency.* Boulder: Lynne Rienner.

Dobson, William J. 2010. "Needles in Haystack." *Newsweek*, 6 August.

Dorman, William A., and Mansour Farhang. 1987. *The U.S. Press and Iran: Foreign Policy and the Journalism of Deference.* Berkeley: University of California Press.

Dorman, William A., and Ehsan Omeed (Mansour Farhang). 1979. "Reporting Iran the Shah's Way." *Columbia Journalism Review* (January–February), 27–33.

Dundes, Alan. 1981. "Many Hands Make Light Work, or Caught in the Act of Screwing in Light Bulbs." *Western Folklore* 40, no. 3 (July), 261–66.

Ebrahimian, Mohammad. 1979/1358. "Aqayan! Motma'en Bashid Mardom Shoma ra Qaichi Mikonand!" *Ettela'at*, 2 April/2 Ordibehesht.

Ehteshami, Anoushiravan. 1995. *After Khomeini: The Iranian Second Republic*. London: Routledge.

El Gody, Ahmed. 2007. "New Media, New Audience, New Topics, and New Forms of Censorship in the Middle East." *New Media and the Middle East*, ed. Philip Seib, 213–34. New York: Palgrave.

Elling, Rasmus Christian. 2008. "State of Mind, State of Order: Reactions to Ethnic Unrest in the Islamic Republic of Iran." *Studies in Ethnicity and Nationalism* 8, no. 3, 481–501.

Esfandiari, Golnaz. 2010. "The Twitter Devolution." *Foreign Policy*, 7 June.

Esfandiari, Haleh. 2009. *My Prison, My Home: One Woman's Story of Captivity in Iran*. New York: HarperCollins.

Etemadi, Fariborz, Sanaz Haqqani, Nazanin Salamat, Farimah Sharifirad, Mehrzad Fotuhi, and Bita Qavidel, eds. 1999/1378. *Doktor Mohajerani: Az Ra'i-ye E'temad ta Estizah*. Tehran: Nashr-e Elm.

Fani, Enayat. 2010. "Susan Taslimi: Deltang-e Tamashachi-ye Irani Hastam." *BBC Persian*, 23 August .

Farabi Cinema Foundation. 1987. *A Selection of Iranian Films*. Tehran: Farabi Cinema Foundation.

Farhi, Farideh. 2003. "Improvising in Public: Transgressive Politics of the Reformist Press in Postrevolutionary Iran." *Intellectual Trends in Twentieth-Century Iran: A Critical Survey*, ed. Negin Nabavi, 147–79. Gainesville: University Press of Florida.

Farman Farmaian, Sattareh, and Dona Munker. 1992. *Daughter of Persia: A Woman's Journey from Her Father's Harem through the Islamic Revolution*. New York: Anchor Books.

Fassihi, Farnaz. 2009a. "Iranian Crackdown Goes Global." *Wall Street Journal*, 4 December.

——. 2009b. "Revolutionary Guards Extends Reach to Iran's Media." *Wall Street Journal*, 5 November.

Fathi, Nazila. 2005. "Unrest in Iran's Kurdish Region Has Left 17 Dead; Hundreds Have Been Wounded." *New York Times*, 14 August.

Fischer, Michael M. J. 1980. *Iran: From Religious Dispute to Revolution*. Cambridge: Harvard University Press.

Foster, Hal. 1985. *Recodings: Art, Spectacle, Cultural Politics*. Port Townsend, Wash.: Bay Press.

Freud, Sigmund. 1965. *The Interpretation of Dreams*. Trans. James Strachey. New York: Avon.

Fullerton, Jami A., and Alice G. Kendrick. 2006. *Advertising's War on Terror-*

ism: The Story of the U.S. State Department's Shared Values Initiative. Spokane: Marquette.

Ghods, Reza. 2002. "Conversation with a Revolutionary." *MESA Bulletin* 36, no. 1 (summer), 27–32.

Golestan, Shahrokh. 1995/1374. "Sinema-ye Iran Dar Goftogu-ye Bahram Baizai va Shahrokh Golestan." *Chesmandaz* (Paris), no. 15 (autumn), 43–56.

Golmakani, Houshang. 2002. "Iran: Stars within Reach." *Being and Becoming: The Cinemas of Asia,* ed. Aruna Vasudev, Latika Padgaonkar, and Rashmi Doraiswamy, 186–203. Delhi, India: Macmillan.

Golshiri, Hushang. 2005. "The Victory Chronicle of the Magi." *Strange Times, My Dear: The Pen Anthology of Contemporary Iranian Literature,* ed. Nahid Mozaffari and Ahmad Karimi Hakkak. New York: Arcade, 11–36.

Green, Jerrold D. 1982. *Revolution in Iran: The Politics of Countermobilization.* New York: Praeger.

Grieshaber, Kirsten. 2010. "AP Exclusive: Iranian Says He Was Kidnapped." Iranian.com, 10 June, http://www.iranian.com.

Grognou, Virginie. 2009. "Iranian Filmmaker Hits Out at Tehran Regime." Yahoo! News, 20 September, http://news.yahoo.com.

Gurney, David. 2011. "Infectious Culture: Virality, Comedy, and Transmediality in the Digital Age." PhD diss., Northwestern University.

Hachard-Sébire, Gabrielle, and Matthieu Orléan. 2004. "Splendeurs méconnues du cinéma iranien des années 1960, Autour de Kamran Shirdel." *Cinéma 07* (printemps), 73–82.

Haidari, Gholam (a.k.a. Abbas Baharlu). 1997/1376. *Khaterat va Khatarat-e Film-bardaran-e Sinema-ye Iran.* Tehran: Daftar-e Pazhuheshha-ye Farhangi.

———. 1986/1365. "Javanan va Sinema." *Mahnameh-ye Sinemai-ye Film,* no. 44 (Dey), 6–9.

Hakakian, Roya. 2005. "Religion and Choice," *Boston Globe,* 8 May.

Hakarimoran, Ken. 2005. "Aghdashloo quits '24.'" *Hollywood Reporter,* 1 April.

Hakimzadeh, Shirin. 2006. "Iran: A Vast Diaspora Abroad and Millions of Refugees at Home." Migration Information Source, September, http://www.migrationinformation.org.

Hankey, Charles J. 1982. "Life in Tehran Slows to Half-Step as Residents Cope with Shortages." *Los Angeles Times,* 11 December.

Hashemi Rafsanjani, Akbar. 2008/1387. *Omid va Delvapasi: Karnameh va Khaterat-e Sal-e 1364.* Edited by Sara Lahuti. Tehran: Daftar-e Nashr-e Mo'aser.

Hassanpour, Amir. 2003. "Diaspora, Homeland and Communication Technologies." *The Media in Diaspora,* ed. Karim H. Karim, 76–88. London: Routledge.

———. 1996. "The Creation of Kurdish Media Culture." *Kurdish Culture and Identity,* ed. Philip Kreyenbroek and Christine Allison, 48–84. London: Zed.

———. 1992. *Nationalism and Language in Kurdistan, 1918–1985.* San Francisco: Mellen Research University Press.

Higgins, Andrew, and Jay Solomon. 2006. "Strange Bedfellows: Iranian Imbroglio Gives New Boost to Odd Exile Group." *Wall Street Journal*, 29 November.

Hilburn, R. 1981. "Tie a Yellow Ribbon Round the Ole Oak Tree." *Los Angeles Times*, 29 January.

Hodgson, Marshall G. S. 1974. *The Venture of Islam: Conscience and History in a World Civilization*, vol. 1., *The Classical Age of Islam*. Chicago: University of Chicago Press.

Hosseini, Seyyed Majid. 2009. "Tahavvol-e Farhang-e Siasi dar Iran Pas az Enqelab bar Asas-e Tahlil-e Filmha-ye Sinemai-ye Pormokhatab." PhD diss., Tehran University.

Huntington, Samuel P. 1996. *The Clash of Civilizations and the Remaking of World Order*. New York: Simon and Schuster.

Jafari Lahijani, Majid. 2008/1387. *Honar dar Garmagarm-e Enqelab 1357–1359: Sinema va Televizion*. 2 vols. Tehran: Entesharat-e Pazhuheshgah-e Farhang va Ma'aref.

Jalaeipour, Hamidreza. 2003. "Religious Intellectuals and Political Action in the Reform Movement." *Intellectual Trends in Twentieth-Century Iran: A Critical Survey*, ed. Negin Nabavi, 136–46. Gainesville: University Press of Florida.

Jerome, Carole. 1987. *The Man in the Mirror*. Toronto: Key Porter.

Kalantari, Pirooz. 2004/1382. *25 Sal Sinema-ye Iran: Gozideh-ye Filmha-ye Mostanad*. Tehran: Muzeh-ye Sinema-ye Iran.

Kamalipour, Yahya R. 2010. *Media, Power, and Politics in the Digital Age: The 2009 Presidential Election Uprising in Iran*. New York: Rowman and Littlefield.

———. 1998. "Window of Opportunity: Images of Iranians in the U.S. Media." Iranian.com, 11 August, http://www.iranian.com.

Kamrava, Mehran. 2008. *Iran's Intellectual Revolution*. New York: Cambridge University Press.

Kar, Mehrangiz. 2001/1380. "Moruri bar Eslahat az Manzar-e Hoquqi." *Iran Nameh* 19, no. 4 (autumn), 453–78.

Karimi, Iraj. 1988/1367. "In Nakoja Abad Kojast?" *Mahnameh-ye Sinemai-ye Film*, no. 72 (December/Dey), 52–54.

Karimi-Hakkak, Ahmad. 1983. "Of Hail and Hounds: The Image of Iranian Revolution in Recent Persian Literature." *State, Culture and Society* 1, no. 3 (spring), 148–80.

Karimi-Hakkak, Mahmood. 2003. "Exiled to Freedom: A Memoir of Censorship in Iran." *Drama Review* 47, no. 4, 17–50.

Katouzian, Homa. 2009. *The Persians: Ancient, Medieval and Modern Iran*. New Haven: Yale University Press.

Kelley, Ron, and Jonathan Friedlander, eds. 1993. *Irangeles: Iranians in Los Angeles*. Berkeley: University of California Press.

Kellner, Douglas. 1979. "TV, Ideology, and Emancipatory Popular Culture." *Socialist Review*, no. 9 (May–June), 13–53.

Kelly, John, and Bruce Etling. 2008. "Mapping Iran's Online Public: Politics and

Culture in the Persian Blogosphere." Berkman Center for Internet and Society, 26 April, http://cyber.law.harvard.edu.

Kempster, Norman. 1987. "CIA Saw Rebel Group Winning in Iran." *Los Angeles Times*, 19 March.

Khalili, Nader. 1990. *Racing Alone: Fire and Earth and a Visionary Architect's Passionate Quest for the Ultimate House*. Los Angeles: Burning Gate.

Khalkhali, Sadeq. 2001/1380. *Khaterat-e Ayatollah Khalkhali, Avvalin Hakem-e Shar'-e Dadgahha-ye Enqelab*. 4th ed. Tehran: Nashr-e Sayeh.

Khamenei, Seyyed Ali. 1994/1373. *Farhang va Tahajom-e Farhangi*. Tehran: Sazman-e Farhangi-ye Enqelab-e Eslami.

Khameneipour, Fereydoun. 1997. "The Case of the National Film Archives of Iran." Unpublished manuscript. 1–12.

Khomeini, Ruhollah. 1984/1363. *Seda va Sima dar Kalam-e Emam Khomeini*. Tehran: Sorush.

———. 1981a. *Islam and Revolution: Writings and Declarations of Imam Khomeini*. Trans. Hamid Algar. Berkeley: Mizan Press.

———. 1981b/1360. *Velayat-e Faqih: Hokumat-e Eslami*. Tehran: Entesharat-e Amir Kabir.

———. n.d.a. *Kashfol Asrar*. No place of publication: no publisher.

———. n.d.b. *Towzi al-Masael (ba ezafat va masael-e jadid)*. No place of publication: no publisher.

Khonsari, Mehrdad. 2010. "Akharin Monaqeshat miyan-e BBC va Dolat-e Shahanshahi-ye Iran." BBC Persian, 24 December, http://www.bbc.co.uk.

Khorrami, Masud, ed. 1997/1376. *Hoviyat*. Tehran: Moasesseh-ye Farhangi-Entesharati-ye Hayyan.

Khoshnevis, Mohammad Hasan. 1989/1368. "Introduction," *Nameh-ye Filmkhaneh-ye Melli-ye Iran* 1, no. 1 (autumn), 6–7.

Khosravi, Shahram. 2003. *The Third Generation: The Islamic Order of Things and Cultural Defiance among the Young of Tehran*. Stockholm: Stockholm University.

Kianian, Reza. 2008/1387. *In Mardom-e Nazanin: Qessehha-ye Reza Kianian ba Mardom*. Tehran: Nashr-e Mishki.

Klady, Leonard. 1979. "Farmanara and Spectrafilm Part Ways: Exec's Return to Production, Preceded by Detention in Iran." *Variety*, 4 July, 36.

Kraidy, Marwan, and Joe F. Khalil. 2009. *Arab Television Industries*. London: Palgrave Macmillan.

Kurzman, Charles. 2009. "Reading Weber in Tehran." *Chronicle of Higher Education*, 1 November.

Lancaster, John. 1998. "Barbie, *Titanic* Show Good Side of 'Great Satan.'" *Washington Post Foreign Service*, 27 October.

Lashgaripur, Pezhman. 2002/1381. *Tathir-e Sinema*. Tehran: Moasesseh-ye Farhangi-ye Sana-e Del.

Leyda, Jay. 1964. *Films Beget Films: A Study of the Compilation Film*. New York: Hill and Wang.

Lewis, Michael. 2002. "The Satellite Subversives." *New York Times*, 24 February.

Limbert, Mandana. 2002. "Visions of Iran: Persian-Language Television in the United States." *Social Constructions of Nationalism in the Middle East*, ed. Fatma Müge Göçek, 251–71. New York: State University of New York Press.

MacAskill, Ewen, and Julian Borger. 2006. "Bush Plans Huge Propaganda Campaign in Iran." *Guardian*, 16 February.

Macedo, Diane. 2010. "Iranian Rockers Tear Down 'The Wall.'" Fox News, 11 August, http://www.foxnews.com.

MacFarquhar, Neil. 2010. "Far from Iran, a Struggle to Stay Involved." *New York Times*, 27 July.

Mackey, Robert. 2010a. "Beirut Festival Pulled Film to Spare Ahmadinejad's Feelings." *New York Times*, 14 October.

———. 2010b. "Iranian Filmmaker Speaks Out on Prisoners." *New York Times*, 9 March.

———. 2010c. "Iran Jails Leading Filmmaker for Six Years." *New York Times*, 20 December.

———. 2010d. "Long Jail Term for Iran's 'Blogfather.'" *New York Times*, 28 September.

Mahmoody, Betty. 1998. *Bedun-e Dokhtaram Hargez*. Trans. Mohammad Zarrinbal. Annotated by Minu Badii. Tehran: Nashr-e Atiyeh and Nashr-e Sales.

Mahmoody, Betty, and William Hoffer. 1987. *Not Without My Daughter*. New York: St. Martins.

Mahmoudi, Alireza. 2004a/1382. *25 Sal Sinema-ye Iran: Gozideh-ye Filmha-ye Kutah*. Tehran: Muzeh-ye Sinema-ye Iran.

———. 2004b/1382. *25 Sal Sinema-ye Iran: Nashriat va Ketabha-ye Sinemai*. Tehran: Muzeh-ye Sinema-ye Iran.

Mahtafar, Tara. 2009. "The Week in Green with Hamid Dabashi." PBS Tehran Bureau, 24 October, http://www.pbs.org.

Malek, Abbas, and Mehdi Mohsenian Rad. 1994. "Iran." *Mass Media in the Middle East: A Comprehensive handbook*, ed. Yahya R. Kamalipour and Hamid Mowlana, 74–95. Westport, Conn.: Greenwood Press.

Maltzahn, Nadia Von. 2009. "The Case of Iranian Cultural Diplomacy in Syria." *Middle East Journal of Culture and Communication* 2, 33–50.

Mann, R. 1979a. "Evans Takes a Rugged Turn." *Los Angeles Times*, 22 November.

———. 1979b. "The Shah's Story: Half a Truth." *Los Angeles Times*, 23 October.

Markaz-e Amar-e Iran. 2001/1380. *Salnameh-ye Amari-ye 1379*. Tehran: Sazman-e Modiriat va Barnamehrizi-ye Keshvar.

———. 1985a/1364. *Iran dar A'ineh-ye Amar*. Tehran: Markaz-e Amar-e Iran (Mordad/August).

———. 1985b/1364. *Salnameh-ye Amari-ye 1363*. Tehran: Vezarat-e Barnameh va Budjeh.

———. 1984/1363. *Salnameh-ye Amari-ye 1362*. Tehran: Vezarat-e Barnameh va Budjeh.

Matin-Asgari, Afshin. 2000. "Tehran Memoirs and Diaries: Winter 1979 and Summer 1997." *Comparative Studies of South Asia, Africa and the Middle East*, vol. 20, nos. 1 and 2, 171–79.

Mehrabi, Masud. 1996/1375. *Farhang-e Filmha-ye Mostanad-e Iran az Aghaz ta Sal-e 1375*. Tehran: Daftar-e Pazhuheshha-ye Farhangi.

———. 1978/1357. *Tarikh-e Sinema-ye Iran az Aghaz ta 1357*. Tehran: Mahnameh-ye Sinemai-ye Film.

Mehran, Golnar. 2007. "Iran: A Shi'ite Curriculum to Serve the Islamic State." *Teaching Islam: Textbooks and Religion in the Middle East*, ed. Eleanor Abdella Doumato and Gregory Starrett, 53–70. Boulder: Lynne Rienner.

Millet, Kate. 1982. *Going to Iran*. Photos by Sophie Keir. New York: Coward, McCann and Geoghegan.

Ministry of Culture and Islamic Guidance. 2000/1379. *Shakhesha-ye Farhangi: Vaz'iat-e Sinema dar Keshvar Tey Salha-ye 1367–1368*. Tehran: Daftar-e Tarh va Barnameh Nevisi.

———. 1999/1377. *Siasatha va Raveshha-ye Ejrai-ye Sinema-ye Jomhuri-ye Eslami-ye Iran*. Tehran: Moavenat-e Omur-e Sinemai va Sam'ibasari.

———. 1985/1364. In response to my requests, Hosain Tusi, director general of the Office of Research and Cinematic Affairs, Ministry of Culture and Islamic Guidance, sent me on 6 July 1985/15 Tir 1364, a letter (no. 63,1415), containing information as well as two appendixes: appendix 1 contained "Marahel-e Mokhtalef-e Nezarat bar Sakht va Namayesh-e Film," 34–49, an unpublished internal memo; appendix 5 contained statistics and lists of titles of foreign movies receiving exhibition permits in 1983–84.

———. 1984. *Sinema-ye Iran 1358–1363*. Tehran: Ministry of Culture and Islamic Guidance.

Mintz, John. 2003. "U.S. Keeps Close Ties on Muslim Cleric." *Washington Post*, 1 January.

Moaddel, Mansoor. 2009. "The Iranian Revolution and Its Nemesis: The Rise of Liberal Values among Iranians." *Comparative Studies of South Asia, Africa and the Middle East* 29, no. 1, 126–36.

Mobasher Mostafavi, Mohsen. 2006. "Cultural Trauma and Ethnic Identity Formation among Iranian Immigrants in the United States." *American Behavioral Scientist* 50, no. 1 (September), 100–177.

———. 1996. "Class, Ethnicity, Gender, and the Ethnic Economy: The Case of Iranian Immigrants in Dallas." PhD diss., Southern Methodist University.

Modaqeq, Hamidreza. 2007/1386. "Kurosh va Khayyam beh Sinema Miravand." *MSF*, no. 367 (Shahrivar), 8–16.

Mohammadi, Majid. 2010. "Nofuz-e M'muran-e Sepah va Etella'at dar Marakez-e Pazhuheshi-ye Iran." Radio Farda, 4 December 2010/13 Azar 1389, http://www.radiofarda.com.

Mohassesi, Mohammad Said. 2008/1387. "Panjah Sal Mostanadsazi-ye San'ati." *Peyk-e Mostanad*, http://www.peykemostanad.com.

Mojahedin-e Khalq-e Iran. 1985/1364. *Shohada-ye Javidan-e Azadi, Parchamda-ran-e Enqelab-e Nevin-e Khalq-e Qahreman-e Iran.* Supplement to *Mojahed*, no. 261.

Morgan, David. 2005. *The Sacred Gaze: Religious Visual Culture in Theory and Practice.* Berkeley: University of California Press.

Mostofi, Babak. 2010. "Sinema-ye dar Tab'id-e Iran." BBC Persian Service, 8 July, http://www.bbc.co.uk.

Muzeh-ye Sinema-ye Iran. 2004a/1382. *25 Sal Sinema-ye Iran: Filmkhaneh-ye Melli-ye Iran.* Tehran: Muzeh-ye Sinema-ye Iran.

———. 2004b/1382. *25 Sal Sinema-ye Iran: Video va Resanenha-ye Tasviri.* Tehran: Muzeh-ye Sinema-ye Iran.

Nabavi, Shayda. 1999/1378. "Abadan, 28 Mordad 1357, Sinema Rex." *Cheshman-daz*, no. 20 (spring).

Naficy, Hamid. 2011. "Interstitial Filmmaking and the Politics and Poetics of Risktaking." *Film and Risk*, ed. Mette Hjort. Wayne State University Press.

———. 2010. "Faster than a Speeding Bullet, More Powerful than a Locomotive: Mutual Instrumentalization of Culture, Cinema, and Media by Iran and the U.S." *Media, Power, and Politics in the Digital Age: The 2009 Presidential Election Uprising in Iran*, ed. Yahya R. Kamalipour, 205–20. New York: Rowman and Littlefield.

———. 2010. Roxana Saberi, reporter. Interview by author. Doha, Qatar, 21 September.

———. 2009. "From Accented Cinema to Multiplex Cinema." *Convergence Media History*, ed. Janet Staiger and Sabine Hake, 3–13. New York: Routledge.

———. 2008. Dariush Mehrjui, filmmaker. Interview by author. Chicago, 24 October.

———. 2006a. Badi'eh Misaqiyeh (Eshraghian), niece of film producer Mehdi Misaqiyeh. Interview by author. Los Angeles, California, 6, 12 January.

———. 2006b. Cosroe Chaqueri, scholar. Personal correspondence with author. Paris, France, 29–30 March.

———. 2006c. Mehrdad Amanat, scholar. Personal correspondence with author. Los Angeles, California, 1 January.

———. 2006d. Mehrnaz Saeed-Vafa, filmmaker and professor. Personal correspondence with author. Chicago, Illinois, 8 August.

———. 2005a. Amir Hassanpour, professor, Kurdish media scholar. Personal correspondence with author. University of Toronto, Canada, 18 August, 5–6 September.

———. 2005b. Kamran Shirdel, documentary filmmaker. Personal correspondence with author. Tehran, Iran, 16 August, 18 September.

———. 2005c. Kamran Shirdel, documentary filmmaker. Personal correspondence with author. Tehran, Iran, 17 August.

———. 2005d. Manuchehr Moshiri. Tape correspondence with author. Tehran, Iran, 2 November.

———. 2005e. Parviz Navi. Personal correspondence with author. Switzerland, 8 August.

———. 2005f. Poori Soltani, Senior Research Librarian, National Library of Iran. Personal correspondence with author. Tehran, Iran, 27 April.

———. 2003. "Narrowcasting and Diaspora: Middle Eastern Television in Los Angeles." *The Media of Diaspora*, ed. Karim H. Karim, 51–62. London: Routledge.

———. 2002a. "Identity Politics and Iranian Exile Music Videos." *Music, Popular Culture, Identities*, ed. Richard Young, 249–67. Amsterdam: Editions Rodopi.

———. 2002b. "Making Films with an Accent: Iranian Émigré Cinema." *Framework* 43, no. 2 (fall) 2002, 15–41.

———. 2002c. "Narrowcasting in Diaspora: Iranian Television in Los Angeles." *Planet TV: A Global Television Reader*, ed. Lisa Parks and Shanti Kumar, 376–401. New York: New York University Press.

———. 2001a. Alireza Shojanoori, former director of international relations, Farabi Cinema Foundation. Interview by author. London, U.K., 6 May.

———. 2001b. *An Accented Cinema: Exilic and Diasporic Filmmaking*. Princeton: Princeton University Press.

———. 2000. "Self-Othering: A Postcolonial Discourse on Cinematic First Contact." *The Pre-Occupation of Post-Colonial Studies*, ed. Fawzia Afzal-Khan and Kalpana Seshadri-Crooks, 292–310. Durham: Duke University Press.

———. 1998. Mohammad Hasan Khoshnevis, director of Iran's National Film Archive. Interview by author. Tehran, Iran, 1 August.

———. 1995. "Mediating the Other: American Pop Culture Representation of Postrevolutionary Iran." *U.S. Media and the Middle East: Image and Perception*, ed. Yahya R. Kamalipour, 73–90. Westport, Conn.: Greenwood.

———. 1993. *The Making of Exile Cultures: Iranian Television in Los Angeles*. Minneapolis: University of Minnesota Press.

———. 1992. "Cultural Dynamics of Iranian Post-Revolutionary Film Periodicals." *Iranian Studies* 25, nos. 3–4, 67–73.

———. 1991a. Houshang Golmakani, editor of *Mahnameh-ye Sinemai-ye Film*. Interview by author. Tehran, Iran, 11 September.

———. 1991b. Mohammad Beheshti, director of Farabi Cinema Foundation. Interview by author. Tehran, Iran, 21 August.

———. 1989. "Sabk-e Pishtaz-e Sinema-ye Kimiavi." *Simorgh* (Los Angeles) 1, no. 2 (March), 92–95.

———. 1988a. Barbod Taheri, filmmaker and cinematographer. Interview by author. Los Angeles, California, 10 February, 12 August.

———. 1988b. Mohammad Reza Allamehzadeh, filmmaker. Interview by author. Los Angeles, California, 7 October.

———. 1987. "The Development of an Islamic Cinema in Iran." *Third World Affairs 1987*, 447–63. London: Third World Affairs Foundation.

———. 1985a. Bahman Farmanara, film director. Telephone interview by author. Toronto, Canada, 10 July.

———. 1985b. Barbod Taheri, filmmaker. Interview by author. Los Angeles, California, 10 September.

———. 1984a. Ali Mortazavi, critic and editor of the film magazines *Setareh-ye Sinema* and *Film va Honar*. Interview by author. Los Angeles, California, 25 October.

———. 1984b. *Iran Media Index*. Westport, Conn.: Greenwood.

———. 1983. Mojahedin sympathizer, who requested anonymity because of possible political prosecution. Interview by author. Los Angeles, California, 28 August, 10 October, 15 October.

———. 1979a. Fuad Badie, head of Tehran's Badie Film Studio (later known as Iran Center for Film Industries). Interview by author. Los Angeles, California, 5 June, 23 July, 9 August.

———. 1979b. Hosain Rajaiyan, film director. Interview by author. Los Angeles, California, 23 June.

———. 1979c. "Iranian Feature Films: A Brief Critical History." *Quarterly Review of Film Studies* 4, 443–64.

———. 1979d. Khosrow Haritash, film director. Interview by author. Los Angeles, California, 10 October.

———. 1979e. Mohammad Tehrani, film director. Interview by author. Los Angeles, California, 8 December 8.

———. 1979f. Shahriar Farahvashi, filmmaker. Interview by author. Los Angeles, California, 12 March.

———. 1979g. Susumo Tokomo, soundman. Telephone interview by author. Los Angeles, California, 13 August.

———. 1978. Hosain Rajaiyan, film director. Interview by author. Los Angeles, California, 10 January.

Naficy, Majid. 2008/1387. "Behazin va Haqq-e Khamushi." 11 June/22 Khordad, http://www.iranian.com/main/2008-234.

Nafisi, Azar. 2003. *Reading Lolita in Tehran: A Memoir in Books*. New York: Random House.

Nafissi, Mohammad. 2007. "Before and Beyond the Clash of Civilization." *ISIM Review* 19 (September), 46–47.

Naini, Hushang, Alireza Dehqan, and Said Moayedfar. 2006. "Tahsilat, Resanehha va Aqahiha," Persian Edition, 12 pages, http://dcsfs.ut.ac.ir/gmj/3.asp.

Najmabadi, Afsaneh. 1987. "Depolitisation of a Rentier State: The Case of Pahlavi Iran." *The Rentier State*, ed. Hazem Beblawi and Giacomo Luciani, 211–27. New York: Croom Helm in association with Methuen.

Nateq, Homa. 1987/1366. "Yaran-e Mottahed dar Kudeta va Enqelab." *Zaman-e Now* (Paris), no. 8 (April/Ordibehesht).

National Movement of Iranian Resistance. 1983. *Iran: In Defense of Human Rights*. France: L'imprimerie ch. Corlet.

Navvab Safavi, Mojtaba. 1978/1357. *Jameheh va Hokumat-e Eslami*. Qom: Entesharat-e Hejrat.

Netherby, Jennifer. 2000. "Uncensored TV Channel Targeting Iranian Audience." *San Fernando Valley Business Journal*, 26 June, 10.

Nichols, Bill. 2001. *Introduction to Documentary*. Bloomington: Indiana University Press.

Nobari, Ali-Reza, ed. 1978. *Iran Erupts*. Stanford, Calif.: Iran-America Documentation Group.

Nye, Joseph. 2002. *The Paradox of American Power: Why the World's Only Superpower Can't Go It Alone*. Oxford: Oxford University Press.

Omid, Jamal. 1987/1366. *Farhang-e Sinemay-e Iran*, vol. 2, *Az 1351 ta 1366*. Tehran: Entesharat-e Negah.

Papan-Matin, Firoozeh. 2009. "The Case of Mohammad Khordadian, an Iranian Male Dancer." *Iranian Studies* 42, no. 1 (February), 127–38.

Plotskin, H. 1985. "Flashy. Gutsy. Unpredictable. Incisive. Appalling," *TV Guide*, 30 November, 16.

Porteous, Tom. 2006. "Reading Iran." *Prospect Magazine*, no. 118, 22 January.

Powers, Charles T. 1979. "News Film Leaving Iran Faces 'Review.'" *Los Angeles Times*, 16 March.

Powers, J. 1985. "Landis Grows Up (a Little)." *L.A. Weekly*, 29 March–4 April, 39.

Priest, Dana, and William M. Arkin. 2010. "Top Secret America: The Secrets Next Door." *Washington Post*, 21 July.

Purahmad, Kumars. 2001/1380. *Kudaki-ye Nimeh Tamam: Zendegi va Filmha*. Tehran: Nashr-e Elm.

Purmohammad, Masud. 1988. "Ebteda Sang-ha-ye Kuchak." *Mahnameh-ye Sinemai-ye Film*, no. 64 (June/ Khordad 1367), 4–8, 64.

Qasemfar, Mehrdad. 2010. "Akharin Pasokh-e Ghobadi: Aqa-ye Kiarostami, Masir-e Bahs ra Monharef Kardid!" Radio Farda, 4 December/11 Azar 1388, http://www.radiofarda.com.

Qasemlu, Abdolrahman. 1984/1362. *Gozaresh-e Komiteh-ye Markazi beh Kongereh-ye Seshom-e Hezb-e Demokrat-e Kordestan-e Iran* (January/Bahman). Democratic Party of Iranian Kurdistan. No place of publication.

Qukasian, Zaven. 1999/1378. *Majmue-ye Maqalat dar Naqd va Moarrefi-ye Asar-e Masud Kimiai: Az Khat-e Qermez ta Faryad*. Tehran: Nashr-e Didar.

Rahnema, Ali. 2000. *An Islamic Utopian: A Political Biography of Ali Shariati*. London: I. B. Tauris.

Richards, Helmut. 1975. "America's Shah Shahanshah's Iran." *Merip Reports*, no. 40 (September), 3–22, 24, 26.

Rohani, Talieh. 2009. "Nostalgia without Memory: Iranian-Americans, Cultural Programming, and Internet Television." Master's thesis, Massachusetts Institute of Technology.

Rosenberg, Howard L. 1980a. "Iran: The Ayatollah Television." *Los Angeles Times*, 23 January.

———. 1980b. "Unplugged in Iran: The Network Shuffle." *Los Angeles Times*, 14 January.

Rouhani, Farhang. 2004. "Multiple Sites of Fieldwork: A Personal Reflection." *Iranian Studies* 37, no. 4 (December), 685–93.

Rusta, Mahin, Mahnaz Matin, Sirus Javidi, and Naser Mohajer. 2008/1387. *Goriz-e Nagozir: Si Ravayat-e Goriz az Jomhuri-ye Eslami*. Vol. 1. Germany: Nashr-e Noqteh.

Saberi, Roxana. 2010. *Between Two Worlds: My Life and Captivity in Iran*. New York: HarperCollins.

Sabri-Laqai, Azarakhsh. 2002. "Chera Mardom Kantar beh Sinema Miravand?" *Sanat-e Sinema* (September/Mehr), 16–17.

Sadr, Hamid Reza. 2006. *Iranian Cinema: A Political History*. London: I. B. Tauris.

———. 2003/1381. *Dar Amadi bar Tarikh-e Sinema-ye Siasi-ye Iran (1280–1380)*. Tehran: Nashr-e Nay.

Saedi, Gholamhoseyn. 1996. *Othello in Wonderland and Mirror-Polishing Storytellers*. Edited by M. R. Ghanoonparvar. Translated by Michael Phillips. Critical essay by Kaveh Safa. New York: Bibliotheca Iranica.

———. 1986. "Sharh-e Ahval." *Alefba* (Paris) 7 (fall), 3–6.

———. 1984a. "Iran under the Party of God." *Index on Censorship* 3, no. 1 (February), 16–20.

———. 1984b/1363. "Namayesh dar Hokumat-e Namayeshi." *Alefba* (Paris), no. 5, new series (winter), 1–9.

———. 1982/1361. "Farhang Koshi va Farhang Zada'i dar Jomhuri-ye Eslami." *Alefba*, new ed. (winter), 7.

Saeidi, Ali A. 2004. "The Accountability of Para-Governmental Organizations (bonyads): The Case of Iranian Foundations." *Iranian Studies* 37, no. 3 (September), 479–98.

Safai, Reza. 2001/1380. *Man va Sinema*. Tehran: Gol-e Yakh.

Safarian, Robert. 2004a/1382. *25 Sal-e Sinema-ye Iran: Gozideh-ye Filmha-ye Kutah*. Tehran: Muzeh-ye Sinema-ye Iran.

———. 2004b/1382. *25 Sal-e Sinema-ye Iran: Khaneh-ye Sinema: Jame'eh-ye Asnaf-e Sinema-ye Iran*. Tehran: Muzeh-ye Sinema-ye Iran.

Said, Edward W. 1981. *Covering Islam: How the Media and the Experts Determine How We See the Rest of the World*. New York: Pantheon.

Salehi-Isfahani, Djavad, and Daniel Egel. 2007. *Youth Exclusion in Iran: The State Education, Employment and Family Formation*. Middle East Youth Initiative Working Papers no. 3 (September). Wolfensohn Center for Development, Dubai School of Government. Dubai, United Arab Emirates.

Saltzman, B. 1980. "Cagney, O'Brien to Meet Royalty." *Los Angeles Times*, 29 November.

Savage, Charlie. 2010. "U.S. Pushes to Ease Technical Obstacles to Wiretapping." *New York Times*, 18 October.

Schrag, P. 1980. "Politics." *Inquiry Magazine*, 7–21 January, 10.

Sciolino, Elaine. 2000. *Persian Mirror: The Elusive Face of Iran*. New York: Free Press.

Scott, Catherine. 2000. "Bound for Glory: The Hostage Crisis as Captivity Narrative in Iran." *International Studies Quarterly* 44, 177–88.

Semkus, Charles Ismail. 1979. *The Fall of Iran 1978–1979: An Historical Anthology*. New York: Copen Press.

Sepanloo, Mohammad Ali. 2002. *Sargozasht-e Kanun-e Nevisandehgan-e Iran*. Sweden: Nashr-e Baran.

Setoodeh, Ramin. 2003. "It's Prime Time for Persians." *U.S. News and World Report*, 15 September, 48.

Shafi'zadeh, Jafar. 2000/1379. *Dar Posht-e Pardehha-ye Enqelab: E'terafat-e Jafar Shafi'zadeh*. 2nd ed. Essen, Germany: Nima Verlag.

Shahab, Cameron J., and Reza Mousoli. 2010. "Cat and Mouse in Cyberspace: A Case Study of China vs. Iran." Iranian.com, 10 September, http://www.iranian.com.

Shales, T. 1985. "Networks Love TV Newsmagazines." *Los Angeles Times*, 31 May.

Shane, Scott. 2005. "A T-Shirt-and-Dagger Operation." *New York Times*, 13 November.

Shay, Anthony. 2000. "The 6/8 Beat Goes On." *Mass Mediations: New Approaches to Popular Culture in the Middle East and Beyond*, ed. Walter Armbrust, 68–87. Berkeley: University of California Press.

Siamand. 2010/1389. "Patak-e Narm-e Televizioni." Roozonline, 24 Khordad, http://www.roozonline.com.

Siavoshi, Sussan. 1997. "Cultural Policies and the Islamic Republic: Cinema and Book Publication." *International Journal of Middle East Studies* 29, no. 4, 509–30.

Simpson, Cam. 2006. "Airwave Blitz on Iran." *Chicago Tribune*, 31 May.

Simross, L. 1980. "Frustration Goes Public in a Climate of Crisis." *Los Angeles Times*, 23 January.

Slackman, Michael, and Nicholas Kulish. 2010. "Iran Continues Focus on Outside Provocateurs, Now Blaming Germany," *New York Times*, 27 January.

Soltanpur, Said. 1970/1349. *No'i az Honar, No'i az Andisheh*. Tehran: n.p.

Sontag, Susan. 1980. "Fascinating Fascism." *Under the Sign of Saturn: Essays*, 73–108. New York: Farrar, Strauss, and Giroux.

Spellman, Kathryn. 2004. *Religion and Nation: Iranian Local and Transnational Networks in Britain*. New York: Berghahn.

Sreberny, Annabelle. 2000. "Media and Diasporic Consciousness: An Exploration among Iranians in London. "*Ethnic Minorities and the Media: Changing Cultural Boundaries*, ed. Simon Cottle, 179–96. Buckingham: Open University Press.

Sreberny, Annabelle, and Gholam Khiabany. 2010. *Blogistan: The Internet and Politics in Iran.* London: I. B. Tauris.

Sreberny-Mohammadi, Annabelle, and Ali Mohammadi. 1994. *Small Media, Big Revolution: Communication, Culture, and the Iranian Revolution.* Minneapolis: University of Minnesota Press.

———. 1991. "Hegemony and Resistance: Media Politics in the Islamic Republic of Iran." *Quarterly Review of Film and Video* 12, no. 4, 33–59.

Stewart, G. 1979. "Songs Vent U.S. Frustration over Iran." *Los Angeles Times,* 20 December.

Sullivan, Zohreh, ed. 2001. *Exiled Memories: Stories of the Iranian Diaspora.* Philadelphia: Temple University Press.

Tahaminejad, Mohammad. 2003. "Kamran Shirdel, Coeur de lion." *Forum des images* (le programme du 10 septembre au 19 octobre), 36–43.

———. 2001/1380. *Sinema-ye Iran.* 2nd ed. Tehran: Daftar-e Pazhuheshha-ye Farhangi.

———. 2000/1381. *Sinema-ye Mostanad-e Iran: Arseh-ye Tafavotha.* Tehran: Soruch.

Tait, Robert. 2009a. "Iran Activist Sentenced to Death for Election Protests." *Guardian,* 8 October.

———. 2009b. "Iranian Police Arrest Pornographic Film Actors." *Guardian,* 4 March.

———. 2008. "Hollywood Film Accused of Insulting Iran." *Guardian,* 13 December.

———. 2006. "Iranian Actor in Sex Video Scandal Says Ex-Fiancé Faked Footage." *Guardian,* 22 November.

Talebinezhad, Ahmad. 1987. "Raval-e Kar dar Nahadha-ye Filmsazi-ye Iran." *Mahnameh-ye Sinemai-ye Film,* no. 53 (September 1987/Shahrivar 1366), 6–11.

Tammadon, Nima. 2010. "Pre-Islamic Past Pushes into Present." Iranian.com, 28 November, http://www.iranian.com.

Tehrani, Hamid. 2008. "Iran: A Long and Painful Story of Jailed Bloggers." Global Voices, 18 December, http://globalvoicesonline.org.

Theodoulou, Michael. 2008. "Iranian 'Blogfather' Hossein Derakhshan Is Arrested on Charge of Spying for Israel." *Sunday Times* (U.K.), 20 November.

Tiedeman, Anna. 2004. "U.S. Public Diplomacy in the Middle East: Lessons Learned from the Charlotte Beers Experience." usc Public Diplomacy News, 4 May, http://uscpublicdiplomacy.org.

Tofreh, Massoumeh, and Annabelle Sreberny. 2010. "The BBC Persian Service and the Islamic Revolution of 1979." *Middle East Journal of Culture and Communications,* no. 3, 216–41.

Torabi, Hosain. 2000/1379. "Shayad Ayandegan ra Beh Kar Ayad," *Mahnameh-ye Sinemai-ye Film* no. 258 (21 Shahrivar), 132–36.

Vahabzadeh, Peyman. 2010. *A Guerilla Odyssey: Modernization, Secularism, Democracy, and the Fadai Period of National Liberation in Iran, 1971–1979.* Syracuse, N.Y.: Syracuse University Press.

Vahdat, Farzin. 2002. *God and Juggernaut: Iran's Intellectual Encounter with Modernity*. Syracuse, N.Y.: Syracuse University Press.

Van Dyck, D. 1980. "Iranian in Iowa Feels Sting of Baker's Jab in TV Ad." *Los Angeles Times*, 18 February.

Veisi, Morad. 2010. "Sardaran-e Sepah-e Pasdaran dar Timha-ye Futbal-e Iran." Radio Farda, 9 September, http://www.radiofarda.com.

Wehrey, Frederic, et al. 2009. *The Rise of the Pasdaran: Assessing the Domestic Role of Iran's Islamic Revolutionary Guards Corps*. Santa Monica: Rand Corporation.

Weiser, Benjamin. 2009. "U.S. Moves to Seize Properties Tied to Iran," *New York Times*, 12 November.

Weisman, J. 1985. "Network News Today: Which Counts More—Journalism or Profit?" *TV Guide*, November 26, 8.

Werba, Hank. 1979. "Contrasting Views on Iranian Pic Biz." *Weekly Variety*, 30 May, 5, 30.

Wiedner, R. 1981. "Hostagemania." *Penthouse*, July, 75–79.

Wright, Robin. 1993. "Losing Faith." *Los Angeles Times Magazine*, 25 April.

Yong, William. 2010. "Iran's Divorce Rate Stirs Fears of Society in Crisis." *New York Times*, 6 December.

Yong, William, and Robert F. Worth. 2010. "Iran Expatriates Get Chilly Reception." *New York Times*, 7 August.

Young, William. 2010. "Iran Halts Production of 'Neda' Figures." *New York Times*, 9 June.

Youssefzadeh, Ameneh. 2001/1380. "Musiqi dar Iran-e Pas az Enqelab." *Iran Nameh* 19, no. 3 (summer), 247–62.

"Zad O' Khord-e Movafeqan va Mokhalefan-e Tahasson-e Vabastegan-e Shohada-ye Sinema Rex." 1980/1359. *Iranshahr* 2, no. 20 (8 August/17 Mordad).

Zakariai, Mohammad Ali. 2000/1379. *Konferans-e Berlin: Khedmat ya Khianat*. Tehran: Tarh-e No.

Zeraati, Naser. 2004. *Behrouz Vossoughi (Yek Zendeginameh)*. San Francisco: Aran Press.

Zeydabadi-Nejad, Saeed. 2009. *The Politics of Iranian Cinema: Film and Society in the Islamic Republic*. London: Routledge.

Ministry of Culture and Islamic
Guidance (MCIG), *(cont.)*
General Department of Cinematic
and Audiovisual Affairs, 127; General
Department of Development and
Audiovisual Collaboration, 128; General Department of Production and
Support, 128; General Department
of Research and Film Relations, 128;
General Department of Supervision
and Evaluation, 129, 151; Islamicate
cinema and, 128; IYPCS and, 137;
Khatami and, 186; liberalization and,
169–70; Ma'adikhah and, 31; mobile
film units, 156; Mohajerani and, 182;
movie house construction and, 183;
music industry and, 186–87; Najafi
and, 45, 84, 124, 179; national cinema
development by, 144; periodicals, 143;
policies, 128; production licenses,
129, 151–52, 168; rating system and,
153; as reporting to Iranian president,
129; as sponsor of films, 70, 76;
Supervisory Council, 169; Torabi and,
78, 110, 111; VVIR and, 45, 129, 136–37,
172, 176
Ministry of Reconstruction Crusade
(MRC), 133–36
Mirbaqeri, Davud, 125, 182
Mir Ehsan, Ahmad, 163
Mir-Karimi, Reza, 186
Mirlohi, Hashemi, 81
Mirlohi, Reza, 81, 165
Misaqiyeh, Badi'eh, 33
Misaqiyeh, Danesh, 33
Misaqiyeh, Mehdi, 33–34
Mission (Safai television movie), 45
Mr. Hieroglyphic (Erfan film), 29
Mobarekeh Steel Company (Shirdel film),
65, 66
Moddares, Hasan, 111–12
Modernity: vs. anti-modernity, 133;
cinema and, 7–8, 126, 127, 138, 172,
175, 184; Constitutional Revolution

and, 116–17; as contagion, 5;
corruption and, 32, 175; identity and,
8, 13; individuality and, 12, 109, 153,
188; Islamicate cinema and, 127;
Islamicate values and, 10–11, 13–14;
mediawork and, 6; nationalism and,
174; Westernization and, 10, 13–14,
133
Modern Times (film), 24
Mofid (periodical), 143
Mohajerani, Ataollah, 170, 182
Mohammad the Messenger (Akad film),
24
Mohammadzadeh, Hasan, 174
Mohammed (Prophet), 13
Moini, Majid, 53
Moini Shirazi, Hojjatoleslam, 45
Monaco Cinema, 22
Mona with the Children (music video),
105
Monotheism, 8
Monster Within, The (Sinai film), *132*, 133
Montand, Yves, 56
Moqaddasian, Mohammad Reza, 58
Morris, Joe Alex, Jr., 60
Mortazavi, Ali, 38
Mosaddeq, Mohammad, 19, 20, 72,
110–11, 112
Moshiri, Manuchehr, 48, 50–54, 57, 60,
135–36
Mostazafan Foundation (New York), 209
n. 24
Movie houses: burning of, 1–4, 15–22,
75, 118; decline of, 156–58, 183; grades
of, 153; increase in, 155–56; martial
law and, 21. *See also* specific movie
houses
Mowlavi, Ahmad, 70
Mozhdehbakhsh, Zahra, 110
MRC. *See* Ministry of Reconstruction
Crusade
Mujahid (Shervan film), 78
Musavi, Mir Hosain, 122, 153
Musavi Tabrizi, Hojjatoleslam , 3, 18

Hamid Naficy is a professor of radio-television-film and the Hamad Bin Khalifa Al-Thani Professor in Communication at Northwestern University. He is the author of *An Accented Cinema: Exilic and Diasporic Filmmaking* (2001), *The Making of Exile Cultures: Iranian Television in Los Angeles* (1993), and *Film-e Mostanad* (*Documentary Film*, 2 volumes, 1979).

The Library of Congress has catalogued the first volume in this series as follows:

Library of Congress Cataloging-in-Publication Data
Naficy, Hamid.
A social history of Iranian cinema / Hamid Naficy.
p. cm.
Includes bibliographical references and index.
ISBN 978-0-8223-4754-5 (cloth : alk. paper)
ISBN 978-0-8223-4775-0 (pbk. : alk. paper)
1. Motion pictures—Iran—History.
2. Motion pictures—Social aspects—Iran. I. Title.
PN1993.5.I846N34 2011
791.430955—dc22   2011010869

Volume 3: The Islamicate Period, 1978–1984
ISBN 978-0-8223-4865-8 (cloth : alk. paper)
ISBN 978-0-8223-4877-1 (pbk. : alk. paper)